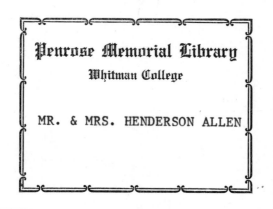

GUNNAR MYRDAL
ASIAN
DRAMA

An Inquiry Into the
Poverty of Nations

An Abridgment by Seth S. King of
The Twentieth Century Fund Study

 PANTHEON BOOKS

A Division of Random House

NEW YORK

HC
412
.M9
1972

FOREWORD

Even before Gunnar Myrdal's monumental *Asian Drama* was published in 1968 the Twentieth Century Fund decided to produce a condensed version of it. There was precedent for such a step in the Fund's own experience. The Fund had often found that significant original research needed ample space to present the findings in the form required for scholars and specialists. To achieve its ultimate effectiveness, however, a work also has to be presented to the general public in a shorter, more readable form. Thus Jean Gottmann's important *Megalopolis*, a book of 810 pages, was followed by a popularized version of 128 larger pages titled *The Challenge of Megalopolis*. Some other Fund studies also have been produced in abridged versions.

In the case of *Asian Drama* another factor came strongly into play. The cost of a three-volume work would be a serious obstacle to its most effective use in the underdeveloped countries of Asia and other regions which it was most designed to help. For these reasons the Trustees of the Twentieth Century Fund decided to sponsor a one-volume edition to include the heart of Professor Myrdal's searching analysis and recommendations.

Obviously the condensation of a study almost 2,300 pages in length and a decade in the making was a challenging and formidable task. Seth S. King, a conscientious and experienced writer, proved a happy choice to undertake the assignment. He not only possessed personal knowledge of South Asia but had great admiration for Gunnar Myrdal's thorough grasp of the area. He at-

v

tempted to capture the essence of *Asian Drama* instead of introducing either fresh or personal material. Recognizing the unique contribution made by Professor Myrdal in assessing the many factors—population, politics, psychology, social traditions—that have a bearing on development, he sought to duplicate, in condensed form, a study in the round. He also appreciated that despite accelerating change the underlying concepts and the relationships among them that Professor Myrdal had set forth remained valid and timely. And he had one other advantage—the benefit of Professor Myrdal's guidance.

Yet the condensation could not be achieved without rigorous selectivity, which meant the omission of much important detail and some changes in emphasis. Mr. King was primarily responsible for choosing what material to leave out and how best to treat the substance that remained. His version of *Asian Drama* is an independent rather than a collaborative work and stands on its own. But it is faithful to Gunnar Myrdal's belief that economic development cannot be comprehended unless it is studied in a broad political and social framework.

While a condensation cannot reproduce the full scope of the original, I feel that Mr. King has succeeded in preserving many of *Asian Drama*'s special insights. It captures the bold unorthodoxy of the parent work and its realistic appraisal of the conditions that thwart development. It can be read with profit by anyone interested in the future of economic development. But I hope that readers of Mr. King's abridgment will be moved to consult Professor Myrdal's full-length study.

So far as events and developments in South Asia and the world are recorded and commented on in *Asian Drama,* the study ended January 1, 1966. The present volume makes no attempt to update the content. Even if the fundamental facts and relations between facts stand unchanged, there have been some new developments of importance—for instance, the "green revolution" in agriculture. A later work of Gunnar Myrdal, *The Challenge of World Poverty: A World Anti-Poverty Program in Outline* (Pantheon Books, New York, 1970), takes these later developments into account.

The Fund is grateful to Professor Myrdal for the time he devoted to reading and commenting on Mr. King's work. It is most appreciative of Mr. King's discrimination and faithfulness and hard work. I trust that the result will contribute to a wider understanding of the causes of the poverty of nations.

> *M. J. Rossant, Director*
> *The Twentieth Century Fund*
> *May, 1971*

CONTENTS

Contents

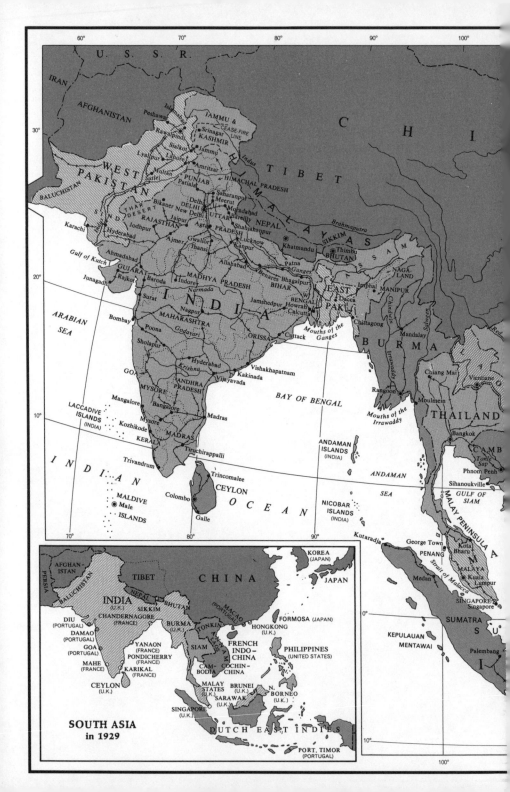

SOUTH ASIA in 1929

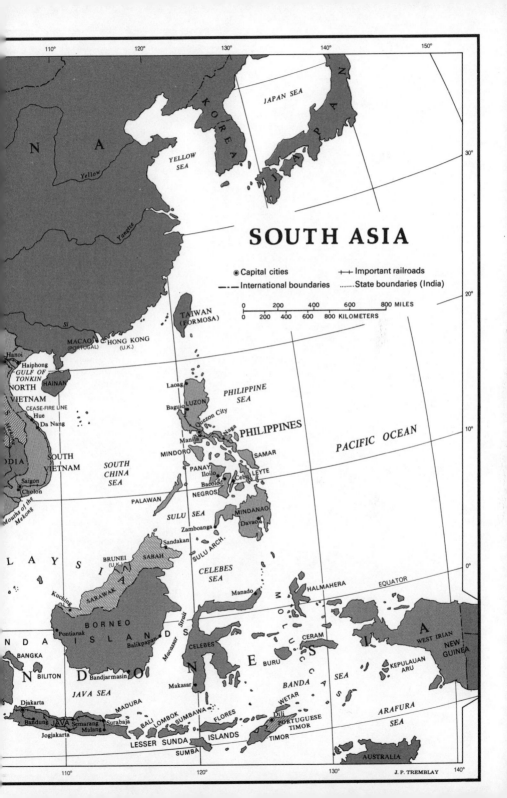

Part One

INTRODUCTION

Chapter 1

THE BEAM
IN OUR EYES

In the years since the end of the Second World War the dimensions of the world have been shrinking. When it is possible to reach virtually any section of our globe in less than twenty-four hours, there is little left that is remote. In hand with this contraction in the world's figurative size has come a new interest and, to some extent, a new concern over the fate of the world's people. This concern has turned, in particular, toward the gap, which grows wider with each generation, between the world's rich and the world's poor. A new wave of research and study has washed over the underdeveloped countries of the world.

A great many of our resources in the social sciences are now employed in these studies. The tide is rising and we economists are riding the crest of the wave. Before the war the most intensive work in the underdeveloped countries of the world was done by cultural anthropologists, sent out from the centers of learning in the rich Western countries. They described for us, usually in static terms, the structure of institutions and attitudes by which people

3

in those countries lived, worked, and survived. Changes were usually analyzed in terms of "disturbances." Now the lead has been taken by economists, who study the dynamic problems of underdevelopment, development, and planning for development.

This tremendous re-direction of our work has not been an autonomous and spontaneous development of social science, but a result of vast political changes. There has been the rapid liquidation of the colonial power structure, accompanied by the craving for development in the under-developed countries themselves, or, rather, among those who think and act on their behalf. Finally, international tensions, culminating in the cold war, have made the fate of the underdeveloped countries a matter of foreign policy concern in the developed countries.

So far as the Western countries, their scholars, and their scholarly institutions are concerned, it is clear that this third cause has been foremost in arousing interest in the problems of the underdeveloped countries. In the under-developed countries themselves it is fairly well under-stood by native intellectuals—and has occasionally given rise to cynical comments—that the readiness to give aid to them and, more fundamentally, the interest in their condi-tions and problems on the part of both the West and the Soviet Union are largely due to the world tensions that lend international significance to the internal affairs of the underdeveloped nations.

It should be remembered that the economic and social conditions of the South Asian countries today are not very different from those existing before the disintegration of the colonial power system. The only major change has been the recent rapid acceleration in the rate of popula-tion increase. But the outburst of scientific interest in their economic problems preceded this acceleration, and, even more, our full awareness of it. On the whole, the masses in South Asia in pre-war times were as poor and their lives as miserable as they are now.

Their poverty and misery did not, however, induce economists to take any great interest in their situation, let alone concentrate attention on the problems of how to engender development through economic planning and coordinated large-scale state intervention. Practical action along such lines was not then within the realm of political feasibility. Still less was there a feeling of urgency about such action.

This lack of interest among social scientists, particularly economists, was clearly a reflection of the existing world political situation. More specifically, this lack of interest reflected the character of the colonial regimes and their effect on us as well as on the subject peoples. These regimes were not such as to call forth large-scale research on economic underdevelopment by giving political importance to these problems. For social scientists it is a sobering and useful exercise in self-understanding to attempt to see clearly how the direction of our scientific exertions, particularly in economics, is conditioned by the society in which we live, and most directly by the political climate. The major recastings of economic thought that we connect with the names of Adam Smith, Malthus, Ricardo, List, Marx, John Stuart Mill, Jevons and Walras, Wicksell and Keynes were all responses to changing political conditions and opportunities.

To obtain a more sophisticated picture of research in the social sciences, we must first acknowledge that the changed world political situation is responsible for our shift of emphasis to the problems of the underdeveloped countries. Once we admit the importance of this influence, we must ask whether it does not affect the manner in which research is conducted as well as the field of research chosen. Although this shift of *field* represents a rational adjustment of our work to the needs of our society, we must suspect that the effect on the *approach* used in our research efforts may be to introduce irrational biases.

The world political situation since the Second World War has been characterized by the almost complete liquidation of the colonial power system. The colonies have been replaced by independent states in which influential groups are pressing, with varying success, for state planning to bring about economic development that would lift their countries out of stagnation and poverty. Concomitant with these two major changes has been another set of changes: the rise to power of the Soviet Union; the staggering gain in size of territories and populations under Communist governments, especially the emergence of Communist China; and the ensuing cold war. To both sides in the world conflict the political allegiance—or at least the neutrality—of the underdeveloped countries has become a stake in the struggle for security and power. Nor is this concern restricted to the foreign policy of the underdeveloped countries. Their attempts at national consolidation and economic development have also become aspects of the cold war in the sense that the effectiveness, the speed, and, even more, the direction of their reforms have become politically important to the contending power blocs.

Impelled by the immense interests at stake, it is natural that the national authorities, the institutions sponsoring and financing research, and, indeed, public opinion in the West all press for studies of the problems of the underdeveloped countries. This clamor for research is entirely justified, as these problems are of increasing political importance to the Western countries themselves. But the studies are also expected to reach opportune conclusions and to appear in a form that is regarded as advantageous, or at least not disadvantageous, to official and popular national interests. This same concern with national interest is also being seen in the underdeveloped countries themselves. Their institutions and their educated classes are becoming more and more touchy about most questions dealing with social study.

The implication is that studies of the problems of underdeveloped countries are now too often undertaken with a view to the fortuitous and narrow political or strategic interests of one country or one bloc, instead of with a view to the universal and timeless values that are our legacy from the Enlightenment. All sorts of studies are now justified by their contribution to the "security" of the United States or Western countries.

A major source of bias in much economic research on poor countries is the endeavor to treat their internal problems from the point of view of the Western political and military interest in saving them from Communism. Taking an outside view does not in itself constitute a fault in the methodology of scientists. What is important is that this approach must be clearly accounted for by a set of explicit value premises. Instead, this approach usually goes hand in hand with a retreat from scientific standards, which permits the entrance of uncontrolled biases—and this, of course, gives substance to the suspicion and irritation in underdeveloped countries. Western political and military interest in saving the underdeveloped countries from Communism also invites inhibitions, for instance, about observing and analyzing the shortcomings of political regimes in underdeveloped countries, unless, let it be noted, these governments are unfriendly toward the West. An indication of such tortuous reasoning, which lends itself to opportunistic arrangement of the facts, is the use even in scholarly writings of labels like "the free world" or "the free Asian countries" to denote, not that people are free in the ordinary sense of the word, but the purely negative fact that a country's foreign policy is not aligned to that of the Communist bloc.

The cold war certainly has considerable bearing on events in the underdeveloped countries of South Asia. The alignments they make, or their neutrality, can even affect the pattern of their development efforts. An underdeveloped country that, for whatever reason, comes under Communist rule, will likely apply Soviet methods of planning for economic development. Similarly, a country's dependence on the Western bloc for credits and aid may well influence its attitudes and internal policies. But to recognize these causal relations is not to say that the Western interest in winning the underdeveloped countries as allies or at least keeping them neutral is an appropriate value premise for the study of their development problems, least of all when it is not explicitly accounted for.

- The political influences on Western social research do not usually encourage unkind treatment of underdeveloped countries—as long as they are not hopelessly lost to the enemy. On the contrary, what national communities more or less overtly demand from their social scientists are essays in practical diplomacy pleading certain directions of external and internal policy and attempting to give a more solid and scholarly foundation to such pleas.

This tendency to think and act in a diplomatic manner when dealing with the problems of the underdeveloped countries of South Asia has, in the new era of independence, become a counterpart to the "white man's burden" in colonial times. No one with any critical sense can be unaware of this trend. I can myself testify that British and American and other Western scholars have confessed, when speaking "among ourselves," to the necessity of "bending over backward" when discussing conditions in the underdeveloped countries. Scholars, as well as politicians, often apologize in public appearances for making even slightly derogatory remarks. A Russian scholar addressing a South Asian audience is equally tactful now that the policy of the Soviet Union is friendly toward the "bourgeois-nationalist" regimes in the region.

I am here not arguing against diplomacy, except in scientific research. A scientist should have no other loyalty than to the truth as he perceives it. But apparently to many it is easier to speak boldly in a wealthy country like the United States than to do so in the underdeveloped countries. It should be understood that diplomacy of this kind is tantamount to condescension, while to speak frankly is to treat the nationals of these countries as equals. If South Asians realized this, they should be offended by such diplomacy.

An indication of how our thinking has become biased in this direction is the escape into terminology that is thought to be more diplomatic than the ordinary usage, such as when one or another euphemism is preferred to the term "underdeveloped countries." The now widely used phrase "developing countries" is one such diplomatic euphemism. With few exceptions the countries in question are not developing very fast—if at all—while most of the rich Western countries are continuously developing at a rapid rate. Thus the term does not serve to distinguish the very poor countries on whose behalf the demand for development is raised. Also, by using a term that presupposes that these very poor countries *are* developing, an important question is begged. To ascertain whether development is under way, and to throw light on whether a country has real possibilities for further development, must be among the purposes of study. Definite answers to these questions should not, to say the least, be assumed *a priori* by means of a loaded definition of a country's present situation.

Another primary source of bias is a more mechanical one, caused by the rapidity with which we have undertaken massive research in a previously uncultivated field. As research must of necessity start from a theory, a set of analytical preconceptions, it was tempting to use the tools that had been forged in the West, without careful consideration of their suitability for South Asia. But, as we will discuss at length in many parts of this book, this must be regarded as a biased approach.

Economic theorists, more than other social scientists, have long been disposed to arrive at general propositions and then postulate them as valid for every time, place, and culture. We have inherited from classical economics, and thereafter further developed, a treasury of theories that are regularly posited with more general claims than they warrant. As long as their use is restricted to our part of the world this pretense of generality may do little harm. But when they are used in the study of underdeveloped countries in South Asia, where they do *not* fit, the consequences are serious. When we economists, working within our tenacious but variegated and flexible tradition of preconceptions that admittedly are not too badly fitted to our own conditions, suddenly turn to countries with radically different conditions, the risk of fundamental error is exceedingly great.

This risk is heightened by the dearth of empirical data on social realities in the underdeveloped countries. The problem is compounded yet again by another consequence of the approach which has become the conventional one in the post-war era. When new data are assembled—as, for example, when the underutilization of the labor force in the South Asian countries is analyzed according to Western concepts of unemployment, disguised unemployment, and underemployment—the conceptual categories used are inappropriate to the conditions existing. The resulting mountains of figures have either no meaning or a meaning other than that imputed to them.

Our main point is this: in the Western world, an analysis in "economic" terms—markets and prices, employment and unemployment, consumption and savings, investment and output—that abstracts from modes and levels of living and from attitudes, institutions, and culture, may make sense and lead to valid inferences; but a similar procedure plainly does not do so in underdeveloped countries. There one cannot make such abstractions; a realistic analysis must deal with the problems in terms that are attitudinal and institutional and that take into account the consequences for development of very low levels of living and culture.

The Western approach to South Asian development has another, more subtle appeal. It abstracts from most of the conditions that are not only peculiar to South Asian countries but responsible for their underdevelopment and for the special difficulties they meet in developing. These conditions and difficulties are all of a type that South Asians and their foreign well-wishers must desire to forget. They were the features of the social structure that were prominent in the thoughts of the European colonial masters, both in their stereotypes and in their more sophisticated reasonings. Exaggerated emphasis on these impediments to development served their need for rationalization. It explained away their responsibility for the backwardness of colonial peoples and their failure to try to improve matters. Both the ideologies of the liberation movements and the post-colonial ideologies were deeply stamped by protest against that way of thinking. And so the pendulum of biases swung from one extreme to the other. The intellectuals in these countries want to rationalize in the contrary sense, and it serves their needs to make the abstractions implied by Western economists.

Optimism, and therefore approaches that make optimism seem more realistic, is also a natural urge for intellectuals in South Asia. That all planning in the region tends to err on the side of optimism is rather palpably clear. The leaning toward diplomatic forbearance in the Western countries fits equally well with biases toward unwarranted optimism among their economists. In Western countries, especially America, optimism is even prized, as a foundation for enterprise and courage; it is almost a part of the inherited cultural pattern—what George F. Kennan once called "the great American capacity for enthusiasm and self-hypnosis." In the contest for souls, it is felt to be to the interest of the West that the underdeveloped countries outside the Communist sphere have development and be made to believe in it.

But quite aside from the cold war and the opportunistic tendencies to bias emerging from it, we of the West are by tradition disposed to be friendly to peoples in distress, once we begin to take an interest in their condition. And it is our earnest hope, apart from all selfish interests, that they will succeed in their development efforts. That we wish them to develop into national communities as similar to our own as possible is a natural ethnocentric impulse that would make itself felt in the calmest world situation.

Nevertheless, we must not let these understandable and genuine feelings influence our perception of the facts. It is the ethos of scientific inquiry that truth and blunt truth-speaking are wholesome and that illusions, including those inspired by charity and good will, are always damaging. Illusions handicap the pursuit of knowledge and they must obstruct efforts to make planning for development fully effective and successful. For this reason, the present book is intended to be undiplomatic. In our study we want to step outside the drama while we are working. We recognize no legitimate demand on the student to spare anybody's feelings. Facts should be stated coldly: understatements, as well as overstatements, represent biases.

One more point should be mentioned before we leave this attempt to characterize briefly the forces tending to create biases in research on development problems in South Asia. As these biases engender an over-optimistic view of development prospects, they sometimes provide encouragement; but mainly they are apt to create undue complacency. In any case, a more realistic view makes it clear that *development requires increased efforts: speedier and more effective reforms in South Asia and greater concern in the West.*

. . . .

Our criticism of the post-war approach in studying the conditions and problems of the underdeveloped countries in South Asia should not be understood as a denial of the right to start out with a theoretical preconception about how things are or, indeed, of the necessity of doing so. Questions are necessarily prior to answers, and no answers are conceivable that are not answers to questions.

In strict logic a non-theoretical approach in scientific work is thus impossible; and every theory contains the seed of an *a priori* thought. When this theory is stated explicitly we can scrutinize its inner consistency. Theory must not only be subjected to immanent criticism for logical consistency but must constantly be measured against reality and adjusted accordingly.

The two processes go together. As we increase the volume of observational data to which we are led by our analytical preconceptions, our original theories are re-fitted in order to make sense of the data and explain them. This is the crux of all science: it always begins *a priori* but must constantly strive to find an empirical basis for knowledge and thus to become more adequate to the reality under study. This is also the reason why we can never achieve perfection, but merely an approximate fitting of theory to facts. But there are differences in how close we can come to the facts. In the underdeveloped countries of South Asia, most of the crucial data are deficient in scope and reliability.

Theory is thus no more than a correlated set of questions to the social reality under study. What must be emphasized is that *all knowledge, and all ignorance, tends to be opportunistic,* and becomes the more so the less it is checked and reconditioned by solid research directed to the empirical facts. In the longer time perspective I see no reason for pessimism about the study of the underdeveloped countries in South Asia. Inherent in all honest research is a self-correcting, purifying force that in the end will affirm itself.

. . .

As we are far from satisfied with the conventional approach to the development problems in South Asia, it is incumbent upon us to sketch an alternative theory that can serve as an analytical framework for the conduct of this study.

In reality, there are no exclusively "economic" problems; there are simply problems, so that distinctions between "economic" and "non-economic" factors are, at best, artificial. The very act of clarifying what we should mean by "economic" problems or "economic" factors implies an analysis that includes all the "non-economic" determinants as well. The only worthwhile demarcation— and the only one that is fully tenable logically—is between relevant and less relevant factors, and that line of demarcation will vary with the characteristics of the environment under study.

We shall use as a starting point the incontrovertible fact that the basic social and economic structure of the countries of South Asia is radically different from that existing in advanced Western or Communist countries. Conditions in the developed countries today are such that, broadly speaking, the social matrix is permissive of economic development or, when not, becomes readily readjusted so as not to place much in the way of obstacles in its path. This is why an analysis in "economic" terms, abstracting from that social matrix, can produce valid and useful results. But that judgment cannot be accurately applied to South Asian conditions. Not only is the social and institutional structure different from the one that has evolved in developed countries, but, more important, the problem of development in South Asia is one calling for induced changes in that social and institutional structure, as it hinders economic development and as it does not change spontaneously, or, to any very large extent, in response to policies restricted to the "economic" sphere.

The essential first step toward an understanding of the

development problem of the South Asian countries is to try to discover how they actually function and what mechanisms regulate their performances. Failure to root analysis firmly in these realities invites both distortions in research and faults in planning. So our approach is broadly "institutional" and we plead for greatly intensified research efforts along these lines. To be really fruitful, this new approach must be more than an accounting of those things that have so often been left out of conventional economic analysis. As the very theories and concepts utilized in such analysis guide it away from those "non-economic" factors, what is needed is an entirely different framework of theories and concepts that is more realistic for those societies.

Our goal is also the more ambitious one of replacing conventional theories and concepts by other, new ones better fitted to the reality of these countries. And we need not only to establish the mechanisms that can explain the unique properties of these economies but also to build an analytical structure fitted to the dynamic problems of development and planning for development.

Economists are generous in stating general reservations about the importance of the "non-economic" factors, without, however, letting this change their approach. It is also worth noting that often attempts in the region to formulate development plans include programs for action extending over the entire field of social relations. This inclusiveness in the general layout of planning stands, however, in sharp contrast to the tendency to lay the main stress on the "economic" factors, conceived in terms of the Western concepts of markets and prices, employment, savings, investment, and output.

To engender and accelerate development, induced changes in *all* social conditions and relations must be assumed to be instrumental or even to play a strategic role in the cumulative causation of a development process. While these convictions have determined the approach to the problems dealt with in this study, we cannot pretend to have come far toward formulating a completely general framework of analysis. *Essentially this remains a study of major economic problems in South Asia, though one that maintains a constant awareness of the broader setting of these issues.*

We have consciously directed our inquiry toward analysis, toward the clarification of problems. We have tried to steep ourselves in the empirical details thoroughly enough to prevent our going astray when seeking answers to relevant questions about broad interrelationships and trends. But many of the essential facts are elusive and unrecorded, and on many points the empirical evidence is contradictory. We have often drawn inferences that are only indicative or suggestive and that, at times, have been based on our own impressions from looking at things and talking to people. The conclusions reached and the supportive reasoning are thus highly conjectural, as we shall often have occasion to remind the reader. It remains a worthwhile scientific task to state clearly what is not known but *should* be known in order to understand what is happening. Indeed, one of the main purposes of this book is to indicate gaps in knowledge and to spell out at some length a system of rational hypotheses for further research; and this can be done only by conjectural reasoning.

In this book we argue that there is a need not merely for qualifications and reservations, but for a fundamental change in approach. If we are correct, there is room for more interdisciplinary research, and we should welcome efforts by sociologists and others to improve our system of theories and concepts. Many will challenge them; it is healthy that they should. For an essential ingredient to progress toward an understanding of the complexities of the development process is the dialogue in which generalizations are advanced, challenged, and then modified and corrected. In this fashion, the sources of differing inter-

pretations and conclusions can be isolated and inspected. This function of generalizations should be borne in mind by readers of this book. The text is not splashed with question marks but, for convenience, is largely written in declarative form. This should not obscure the role and function of the generalizations contained in it.

This is the point when at last we have to raise the question of objectivity in research as a problem of logic.

In principle, it would seem easy to lay down the rules for objective research on the South Asian countries. The student should have no ulterior motives. He should confine himself to the search for truth and be as free as possible from both the pressures of tradition and of society around him and his own desires. He should in his research have no intention of influencing the political attitudes of his readers, either inside or outside the countries whose conditions he is studying. These are laudable principles well worth expressing, but they do not solve the methodological problem of how to avoid biases.

The problem of objectivity in research cannot be solved simply by attempting to eradicate valuations. On the contrary, every study of a social problem, however limited in scope, is and must be determined by valuations. A "disinterested" social science has never existed and never will exist. Efforts to run away from the valuations are misdirected and foredoomed to be fruitless and damaging. The valuations are with us, even when they are driven underground, and they guide our work.

We have argued here for making the value premises explicit that research may be "objective" (in the only sense that term can be used). But we also need to specify them for a broader purpose: clarity and conclusiveness in scientific reasoning. Here we touch on the main problem of the philosophy of knowledge. There is this relation between that problem and the problem of the sociology of knowledge, which has been the focus of interest in this chapter: that the elucidation of our general views and the definition of our specific value premises are more obviously imperative, and at the same time are made easier, once we realize that we must not naively expect our ideas, even in scientific research, to be unconditioned by anything other than our urge to find the truth.

The title of the book, *Asian Drama*, was chosen in order to express the conception of events in South Asia held by the author at the beginning of his work and fortified in the course of study. Behind all the complexities and dissimilarities we sense a rather clear-cut set of conflicts and a common theme as in a drama. The action in this drama is speeding toward a climax. Tension is mounting economically, socially, and politically.

To some degree all of us are participants in this drama. It is as if the stage, set for South Asia, were enlarged and drew onto itself the entire world, so that no one could be merely a spectator. But the leading figures in this drama are the people of South Asia themselves, and above all their educated class. The participation of outsiders through research, provision of financial aid, and other means is a sideshow of rather small importance to the final outcome.

This main drama has its unity in a set of inner conflicts operating on people's minds: between their high-pitched aspirations and the bitter experience of a harsh reality; between the desire for change and improvement and mental reservations and inhibitions about accepting the consequences and paying the price. Such conflicts are a part of human life in all times and places. But in the countries under study they have an exceptional, mounting intensity and assume a unique form.

In South Asia one cannot escape the feeling that what one is observing is precisely this unfolding of a drama in the classic sense. It involves hundreds of millions of people. But through its complexities and dissimilarities, as through a classical drama, runs an essentially simple theme.

In the classic conception of drama—as in the theoretical phase of a scientific study—the will of the actors was confined in the shackles of determinism. The outcome at the final curtain was predetermined by the opening up of the drama in the first act, accounting for all the conditions and causes of later developments. The protagonist carried his ultimate fate in his soul, while he was groping for his destiny.

But in life, while the drama is still unfolding the will is instead assumed to be free, within limits, to choose between alternative courses of action. History, then, is not taken to be predetermined. Rather, it is within the power of man to shape it. And the drama thus conceived is not necessarily tragedy.

Chapter 2

THE REGION

In what follows in this book we have framed our analysis within the general outline of the region we call "South Asia." Actually, the regional approach has no intrinsic justification. There are no mystical qualities in geographical proximity that make neighboring nations a "unit" in any real sense, culturally, politically, or economically. In the specific case of the South Asian countries many circumstances have combined to make their present-day mutual relations feeble. Economic planning and, indeed, all economic policies in the countries we are studying have a rather narrow nationalist horizon, and in recent years the trend has been toward a reduction in the scale of their economic inter-relationships.

This study, embracing the whole region in its frame of reference, is partly justified by its attempt to draw analytical comparisons among the countries of South Asia. These countries display enough similarities in basic conditions to make such comparisons relevant, and enough differences to make comparisons rewarding for an analysis of the main causal relations.

We have attempted to present the main facts for all South Asia in connection with each problem discussed.

But the paucity of reliable materials has reduced our ability to make comprehensive comparisons between the countries in many cases. Thus discussion must often center on one or a few countries, or even districts of a country, that display features of particular interest or where the available material is more satisfactory. As our main concern is analytical rather than merely descriptive, we have not felt obligated to produce exhaustive factual details or to spread the discussion uniformly among the several countries of South Asia. India, because of its huge population and its political importance in both South Asia and the world, looms much larger in the study than do the other countries. Also, it has, from the colonial times, continuously had literature and debates that are richer than in the other countries. To say that this book is mainly about India with numerous and systematic attempts at comparisons with other countries in South Asia would not be far from the mark.

India's neighbors, Pakistan, Ceylon, and to some extent Burma, have also been given rather close attention. Because of a dearth of material, Afghanistan and Nepal—and Sikkim and Bhutan—have not been considered. In Southeast Asia, Indonesia is a big country of great importance, and we have tried to keep its problems within the focus of our study, though we have been unable to treat them as thoroughly as we could have wished. For Thailand, Malaya (not the newly-formed Federation of Malaysia), and the Philippines, available material has been richer. The problems of Singapore are so unusual that it has been left outside the main focus for the most part. We reluctantly abandoned the original intention of encompassing the countries that emerged after the collapse of the French Indo-Chinese colonial empire—North and South Vietnam, Laos, and Cambodia—as some of them are primitive and all are in flux. Occasionally we have touched on the last three of these when information of interest was available.

Thus in this study "South Asia," or "the region," takes in Pakistan, India, Ceylon, Burma, Malaya, Thailand, Indonesia, and the Philippines, and sometimes South Vietnam, Cambodia, and Laos as well. The subregion "Southeast Asia" excludes India, Pakistan, and Ceylon. The expressions "the Western countries" or "the Western world" refer in this study to the highly developed countries in Northwestern and West Central Europe (but not Eastern and South Europe), to the United States, and to those British Dominions populated by people of European stock (Canada, Australia, and New Zealand); the latter are sometimes referred to as "the white dominions." South Africa is an anomaly and is not included in the classification.

Comparisons with the outside world have generally been restricted to Western Europe. This procedure is to an extent rational because in most of South Asia domination, until recently, by Western European nations has had profound commercial, social, and cultural influences.

The countries with which we are concerned have proximity in space. All are located within the tropical, or subtropical, zone, though there are significant differences in climate among and even within the countries. In each, the populations are "colored" or, as this expression has gone out of fashion in South Asia, "non-white." Although this fact is now usually played down, both in these countries and abroad, it gives an important undertone to most of their thinking about themselves and about their relations with the rest of the world. It is notable that their protests against colonialism regularly include the word "racialism."

But perhaps the strongest thread that binds these countries is the historical experience they have shared and its subsequent effects on their view of political problems and processes. All save one, Thailand, are ex-colonies. The periods of colonial rule, though of varying length, were of such duration and intensity as to leave a definite imprint on almost every aspect of their existence. Even Thailand lived in the shadow of colonialism and its destiny, too, was molded by colonial intervention.

The recent liberation of these countries has been of tremendous importance to their entire national life. This liberation came as a result of a world development in which the people of South Asia played a secondary role. But in all these countries it is true that independence was in the end brought about by members of the small, articulate elite groups within the educated class—"educated" in the special sense the term has in South Asia—comprising only a small percentage of the total population. These elite groups now have the responsibility of consolidating the new nation-states. Among them, however, there were and are differing degrees of cohesion and internal unity behind the drive for consolidation.

With the termination of colonial rule the realization that people can shape their own destiny, and have the responsibility to do so, has brought all relationships within society into challenge. This fluid state has often been characterized as a "revolution of rising expectations." That the change in attitude has thus far mainly affected the educated class and scarcely touched the lower strata does not make it less important in countries where that class is dominant. These aspirations are bound to rise over time, and to spread to an ever larger part of the population. In a political sense, the aspirations now paramount have been formulated in terms of the modern democratic welfare state of the rich Western countries. In fact, they have their roots in the era of the Enlightenment that inspired the American and French revolutions. One of the ironies of history is that these ideas and ideals were brought to the countries of South Asia mainly by colonialism, which thereby unwillingly, and unwittingly, destroyed its own foundation.

Initially all these countries declared their intentions to

build their constitutional and civic structure on the lines of parliamentary democracy, based on free elections and adult suffrage for men and women, and on an extensive list of civil liberties. But in none of the South Asian countries has the experiment with ultra-modern political democracy been anything like a complete success; many of them have come under authoritarian rule of one shade or another, and this movement may still be in the ascendancy.

There is a similarity in the basic economic conditions of the South Asian countries. All are very poor and, in general, the largest are the poorest. Social and economic inequalities are extreme, and are usually most pronounced in the poorest countries. All have endured a long period of stagnation in regard to the larger part of their economies, and in most of South Asia levels of living for the masses of people are either lower or not substantially higher today than they were before the Second World War.

All of the new nations in South Asia are now pledged to the promotion of economic development through the planned and coordinated efforts of governments. Only a few, however, have come far in this direction. The obstacles to rapid economic expansion are formidable and their significance must not be minimized. In the main they are rooted in the inefficiency, rigidity, and inequality of the established institutions and attitudes, and in the economic and social power relations embodied in this framework of institutions and attitudes. Again there are differences in degree among the several countries, but the point is that there is a fundamental difference in kind that distinguishes the economic environment of South Asia from that of advanced Western nations.

A main purpose of this book is to offer an intensive analysis of the reasons for this dramatic contrast between development in South Asia and development in Western and East European countries. All the new governments of South Asia are committed to the idea of overcoming the mass poverty of their peoples through state policies co-ordinated by state planning. The existence among the politically articulate in these countries of an urge to achieve economic development by means of modernization of their economies and their societies is the main determinant of the viewpoint and approach adopted throughout the present study.

We must therefore begin our analysis by considering the nature of the states that are required to play so central a role in the economic development of South Asia. How did these states come into being? How were they affected by the legacy of colonial rule, and what kinds of social forces have since determined their character and their actions?

In strict chronological sequence the Philippines, in 1946, was the first to achieve full political independence. But this event was not a sudden or unexpected occurrence; it had been scheduled by the United States more than ten years previously.

The first major breach in the walls of colonial domination came with the peaceful ending of British rule in India in 1947 and the creation of the Union of India and the Republic of Pakistan as successor states. Political independence for Burma and Ceylon followed in 1948. Since the Dutch and French attempted to reimpose their rule over their territories by force, Indonesia did not achieve full independence until 1949, and the constituent parts of the French Indo-Chinese Union were not independent until 1954. The Federation of Malaya did not become an independent state until 1957, owing to the relatively slow development of national political consciousness and British military intervention to put down a Communist rebellion. Singapore remained under full British rule until 1959, when it was granted self-government. Four years later it was merged with Malaya and two remaining British colonies in Borneo, Sarawak and Sabah, to form

Malaysia. Singapore again became an entity when it was pushed out of Malaysia in 1965. Thailand had managed to maintain its formal independence as a buffer state between the frontiers of British and French imperialism, although it had been forced to make several territorial concessions to these two powers and its economy had become dominated by foreign interests.

Just as naval supremacy had made possible the European conquest of Asia, so superior Japanese naval strength ultimately undermined the military basis of European imperialism in South Asia. The handwriting had been on the wall ever since the Japanese victory over Russia in 1905. It is no coincidence that after that event the forces of nationalism took on a more militant form in various parts of the region. The Second World War is correctly designated as the catalytic agency that started the dissolution of the colonial empires in South Asia. But such a momentous political transformation would not have occurred unless the situation had already been ripe for radical change.

In the first place, the imperial powers themselves had created an educated class to provide administrative and professional services in the colonies. This class was not the product of economic development but of legal, administrative, and educational structures built up in order to rule and advance the colonies according to the interests and ideals of the metropolitan countries. Particularly in the period between the two world wars, many members of this elite were permitted to qualify as administrators of relatively high rank, and the colonial governments began to share their power by setting up consultative assemblies with appointed and/or elected members. As this elite grew, they came to press for more posts for their own kind and for more responsibility at higher levels. The most important observation in the present context that can be made about this development, which proceeded with different speed in the several countries, is that it introduced a trend that was antithetical to colonial rule. The educational experiences of the elite had exposed them to Western ideals of justice, liberty, and equality of opportunity. In the Western countries themselves these ideals could not be reconciled with colonialism any more than with the harsh political, social, and economic inequalities remaining at home.

In retrospect it is difficult to avoid the conclusion that the dissolution of colonial rule in South Asia was inevitable. But in the colonies, the arrival of independence was a traumatic experience and one that justifies the common description of it as a political revolution. All of the new states had to face the fact that independence did not automatically bring about a condition of national consolidation. Instead, each new state faced the immediate task of asserting its authority over its territorial inheritance.

The physical outlines of the South Asian nations today are almost entirely the result of colonial arrangements, which in turn resulted from rivalries among the West European countries. The main structure of South Asia was not founded on any historical or even ethnic necessities. If Britain had not restored Holland's East Indian possessions after the Napoleonic Wars, the territories on both sides of the Malacca Straits would have been ruled by a single colonial power, and we might now have a large Malayan state in Southeast Asia, encompassing not only the hundred million people in what is now Indonesia but also the ten million recently brought together in the Malaysian Federation. Had Britain decided to promote a closer relationship among its territories in South Asia, Ceylon and Burma might have been cast in the same mold as India.

But these arrangements did not occur and the outlines of nations in South Asia are a continuation, in general, of the status quo that existed as each became independent. Furthermore, all of them have had compelling reasons for clinging to this *status quo*. Once the transfer of sover-

eignty had been effected, each new state had to establish
its authority over the whole of its territory and it became
a matter of national pride or prestige to avoid divisions in
what had been previously administered as a single unit.
This nationalist appeal was not sufficient to prevent serious internal splits and rebellions. Nor has the sanctity of
the territorial legacy of colonial rule always been accepted on both sides of every national boundary line. But
the first and almost instinctive reaction of every new
government was to hold fast to the territory bequeathed
to it. What the former colonial power had ruled, the new
state also must rule.

A major exception to this, of course, is the case of
Pakistan and India. It is not a clear-cut exception, however, for, apart from Kashmir, the main line of division
between India and Pakistan, and even the principles on
which it was drawn, were worked out and accepted under
British guardianship. The separation of Singapore from
Malaya may seem to be another violation of our general
proposition regarding the continuation of political entities
in South Asia. But the government of Singapore had never
been integrated with the Malay states so far as British
rule was concerned. Nor is the division of Vietnam an
exception; like East and West Germany or North and
South Korea, it represents a temporary position in the
cold war and one that neither protagonist regards as satisfactory. An exception can be made, however, for the more
recent inclusion of Sarawak and Sabah in Malaysia; these
two territories became free of colonial rule only through
incorporation.

In most cases, colonial domination resulted in the creation of larger political entities than those which existed in
pre-colonial times. It also brought a measure of internal
consolidation in these new entities. In India and in Pakistan as well, it is now generally recognized that not only
the unification of British India but also the measure of
political integration that made possible the creation of

two independent states was the result of the last hundred years and more of British rule. Similar induced changes operated in other colonial regions in South Asia and there, too, they fostered political unity. It can unreservedly be stated that the conception of the Indonesian archipelago as a nation-state is the result of Holland's hegemony in the area and its attempts to tie the islands together politically, administratively, and, to an extent, economically. Despite the perilous road the territory has travelled since the Dutch were driven away in the Second World War, a political climate has been evolving wherein an appeal to Indonesian national unity strikes a chord. Much the same process took place in the Philippines and in the states of continental Southeast Asia, though the latter remained smaller and less unified internally.

Chapter 3

VALUE PREMISES
AND VALUATIONS

There is a constant need in a social study such as ours to make quite clear and explicit the value premises that have shaped our initial concepts and formed the framework for our research, as well as helped us avoid hidden valuations that lead to biases. This is vital for the sake of relevance, effectiveness, and objectivity. All social study, even on the theoretical level where facts and causal relations are ascertained, is policy-directed in the sense that it assumes that a particular direction of social change is desirable.

In the present study we have attempted to look at problems in the countries of South Asia as they appear from the point of view of the interests and ideals, norms and goals that are relevant and significant in these countries themselves. The interests of foreign countries are left out of consideration entirely, so far as the value premises are concerned.

The task of specifying the relevant and significant value premises anchored on the valuations the people them-

selves hold is an immensely difficult and challenging one
—far more so than are similar exercises in Western countries. One reason is ignorance of how people in different
occupations, social and economic strata, and locations
really feel, the intensity and tenacity of their feelings, and
the extent to which they can be influenced by policy
measures aimed at changing them. There are great
lacunae in our knowledge of such matters in Western
countries; what is ascertained about the public's valuations is often only vague and uncertain. But the difference
between what we know about these valuations in a Western country and in any one of the South Asian countries
is, of course, very considerable.

A second cause of difficulty is the fluid, uncertain, and,
from an egalitarian point of view, skewed character of the
processes by which public policies are decided in South
Asia. Apart from the educated class, "citizen" participation is low throughout the region. By itself this might
seem to make it easier to determine relevant and significant valuations by concentrating on the small groups who
hold the power. But every government in the region, even
the military juntas, must consider the desires of the
people and what they will tolerate. The masses may be
passive about policy decisions, but within this passivity
there is often resistance to the carrying out of these
policies. Every regime must reckon with the possibility
that its people will be roused to resistance against the
policies it is trying to impose upon them. Non-participa-
tion by the people thus constitutes a vast problem con-
taining much uncertainty.

But there is a third severe obstacle to laying bare the
actual valuations of the people: their immense heterogeneity. In the course of the Great Awakening that followed the post-war ending of colonialism and the
beginnning of independent nationhood, aspirations, interests, and ideals have been exploding in discrete sections of
societies that are culturally and economically ill-prepared

to assimilate them systematically. One effect of the inverted and telescoped historical sequence of social and economic development in the region is that people in the various layers of society live very different kinds of lives and consequently have very different outlooks toward the world. Indeed, most individuals harbor within themselves sharply conflicting valuations.

In Western countries such differences also exist. But through a long process of national consolidation, or of what in India is called "emotional integration," these differences have diminished. The modern democratic welfare states developed in the West during the past half century have a high degree of "created harmony" of interests and ideals. It has thus become possible to study problems in the Western countries on the basis of a fairly explicit national creed that determines people's long-range strivings, if not their daily conduct of life. This is true even when the problem concerns such departures from the creed as discrimination in America against Negroes and, particularly in earlier times, against Jews and immigrant groups. The situation in the South Asian countries is, of course, utterly dissimilar. In none of them is the degree of national consolidation and "emotional integration" comparable to that in the Western countries, either now or when they were on the eve of their industrial revolutions.

The heterogeneity of actual valuations in South Asian countries and the magnitude of our ignorance about them and about the actual power relations make it the more essential to insist on clearly stated value premises. Most important is that those value premises that have actually determined the approach in a study be made explicit and permitted to fulfill their function. Whatever these value premises are, and however they were reached, their elucidation is what methodological clarity demands in the first place. It should be clear from the foregoing that considerable doubt remains whether the value premises chosen in this study *are* relevant and significant. Of this doubt the reader, as well as the author, should remain conscious.

Among all the dissimilar and conflicting valuations that exist in the countries of the region, we have deliberately selected the new ones directed toward "modernization." These valuations, which for brevity we label "the modernization ideals," were impressed on the region in the Great Awakening following independence, though the educated and articulate class of people in South Asia had been gradually conditioned to them by influences from the Western world during colonial times and, more recently, by influences from the Soviet Union. They have become the "official creed," almost a national religion, and are one of the powerful strands of the "new nationalism." They now appear as the declared main goals in the development plans with which all the countries of the region are equipped and in the introductions to reports by public commissions considering questions of major reform. In choosing these ideals as the value premises, we are, in a sense, taking these nations at their word.

There are differences among the countries in the region and among the groups in a single country. The modernization ideals are expressed more clearly in India, Pakistan, Ceylon, and the Philippines than in Indonesia and Burma. In particular, emphasis on the several elements of the creed varies. In terms of the conventional Western axis of conservatism-radicalism, Pakistan, Malaya, Thailand, and the Philippines give a more conservative slant to the modernization ideals, while the official creeds of India, Ceylon, Burma, and Indonesia tend to be more radical. There are also movements along this axis in time. On the whole, Ceylon has moved toward the left. Burma, which for a time tended toward the right, has recently moved toward the left, while Indonesia has turned back toward the right. India is still moving toward the left in public declarations, though hardly in practical politics.

Viewed in the light of prevailing conditions, however, the creed is radical throughout the region, for even modest realization of the ideals would drastically change their economic, social, and political conditions. In fact, this official creed of the South Asian countries is composed mainly of the ideals long cherished in the Western world as the heritage of the Enlightenment and more recently realized to a large extent in the "created harmony" of the welfare state.

In South Asia the ideals are still more than usually vague and at times internally inconsistent. These logical deficiencies are part of the reality that must be faced; they cannot be disposed of by conceptual tricks that tidy the argument. They indicate that the valuation viewpoint is not really a point but rather a limited space within which the key concepts are often blurred at the edges. Further, the modernization ideals are mainly the ideology of the educated and politically articulate part of the population—particularly the intellectual elite. The judgments that follow refer to the opinions of these groups. But the inclinations of the broader strata of the population greatly influence the prospects of initiating and implementing policies that conform to the modernization ideals. At least the masses can resist unpopular policies and create obstacles. And we should also be aware that the modernization ideals have to compete with conflicting traditional valuations, established through the centuries and often sanctioned by religion. Even politically alert and active members of the educated class are often of two minds and engage in awkward and frustrating mental compromises. Although such conflicts are characteristic of ideologies of this nature everywhere, in South Asia they are magnified by the vast distance between ideals and reality.

Naturally, the choice of this set of value premises

would be more fully justified if our study were to indicate that their realization represented with some certainty the trend of the future. This finding did not emerge. But one of the convictions we hold is that, particularly in view of the accelerating population increase, rather rapid strides toward the realization of the modernization ideals must be made in order to avoid increasing misery and social upheaval. These ideals all have a rationale. We should also bear in mind that, in one sense, these countries have all passed the point of no return, for the modernization ideals are already in effect in South Asia, at least to the extent of preventing these countries from reverting to their traditional undisturbed status. This is what gives our set of value premises, or rather a study of the countries in the region undertaken from that angle, practical importance.

The writer must in honesty add that the distinct aura of Enlightenment surrounding these ideals in South Asia is congenial to him and to his collaborators, who are conservative in their moral allegiance and are personally deeply attached to those inherited radical ideals. Undoubtedly this attitude made it easier to work with, and stick to, this set of value premises. Nevertheless, these premises were not selected on a personal ground, but rather for their revelance and significance in South Asia.

In abstract form, the modernization ideals making up the official creeds in the region have been given expression to an extraordinary degree. We stress that the role they now play in South Asian countries represents a significant difference in "initial conditions" as compared with the Western countries in their early stages of development.

Many of the modernization ideals in South Asian countries overlap. But there is a framework within which they are set. We can thus set forth below the outlines of these basic, guiding ideals of our study:

A. *Rationality*. It is regularly assumed in public debate that policies should be founded on rational considerations. It is also taken for granted and often stressed that such a course represents a break with tradition. Superstitious beliefs and illogical reasoning should be eradicated. This valuation is occasionally expressed explicitly, as in the statement that the nation is now entering the "scientific era." An important element in this valuation is the need to apply modern technology in order to increase productivity, but it has been given much broader interpretation embracing all economic and social relations. History, tradition, and indigenous attitudes and institutions are taken into account, in principle, only on the rational grounds that their preservation is practical for the attainment of specific objectives to do so. No one publicly defends views while acknowledging them to be irrational.

B. *Development and Planning for Development*. The desire for these flows directly from the quest for rationality and represents in the economic and social field the all-embracing and comprehensive expression of the modernization ideals. Development means improvement of the host of undesirable conditions in the social system that have perpetuated a state of underdevelopment. Planning is the search for a rationally coordinated system of policy measures that can bring about development.

C. *Rise of Productivity*. Higher output per head of the population or of the labor force is a commonly shared goal of development planning. It is generally assumed to be achieved primarily by improved techniques and increased capital investment in all branches of production and by an improvement in what we shall call the modes of production. These are in turn dependent on raised levels of living, improved attitudes and institutions, national consolidation, and, in fact, on the realization of all the other value premises listed below.

D. *Rise of Levels of Living*. It is not surprising that this valuation is so commonly accepted in view of the extremely low levels of living in South Asia, especially in the bigger and poorer countries. Indeed, a main reason for desiring a rise in output per head is that it could raise levels of living. It is commonly believed, however, that substantial improvements in levels of living must be postponed for some time in order to permit capital accumulation and even higher productivity and levels of living in the future. This need would assume a partial conflict, at least in the short run, between higher consumption and higher production. But there is also a positive relationship between these conditions to which we shall often call attention—that improved levels of living are a pre-condition for higher labor input and efficiency and, generally, for changes in abilities and attitudes that are favorable to rising productivity. This interdependence between productivity and levels of living is much stronger in the countries of South Asia than in Western countries, though the relationship is mostly obscured by application of the conventional post-war approach in the economic analysis of South Asian development problems that we criticized in the first chapter.

E. *Social and Economic Equalization.* In all the countries of South Asia the ideal that social and economic stratification should be changed in order to promote equality in status, opportunities, wealth, incomes, and levels of living is commonly accepted in public discussion of the goals for planning and for policies generally. Occasionally, non-realization of the equalization ideal has been excused, in a vague way, by references to the priority of raising output; this explanation could imply a conflict between the ideals under *C* and *E*. But the opposite can be and sometimes is argued: in the conditions prevailing in South Asia, greater equality is a pre-condition for speeding up production and development. Our study has led us to believe that this latter proposition is correct.

F. *Improved Institutions and Attitudes.* In general, it is held that social and economic institutions and attitudes should be changed, in order to: increase labor efficiency, effective competition, mobility, and enterprise; permit greater equality of opportunities; make possible higher productivity and well-being; and generally promote development. It is even quite common in all the countries of the region to discuss these desired changes as a social, as well as an economic, "revolution" and to proclaim that such a revolution is necessary for development.

The institutions envisioned in the modernization ideals would imply a united and integrated national community within which there is solidarity and "free competition" in a much wider sense than the term generally implies in economic analysis. In such a national community the social and cultural divisions would be swept away. There would be formed a nation with marked social and economic equality and mobility, where people were able to move from one area to another as well as from one economic level to another. The desire for such "modernization" of institutions is most clearly expressed in India, where, ironically, the barriers to free competition in the wider sense are strongest and most pervasive.

The modern welfare state in the rich Western countries is, of course, much closer to the realization of this ideal, as are, at lower but rising levels of living, the Communist countries in Europe. From the perspective of national consolidation, all South Asian countries are much more amorphous and splintered. The ideal system is viewed as a unified and integrated nation-state, branching out into smaller communities bound together by loyalties to the nation-state. In reality, however, the social and political framework is traversed by lines of interests and allegiances to other types of communities that do not fit into the ideal order but are inimical to it.

Attitudes, in turn, are understood to be supported by and at the same time to uphold established institutions. In regard to attitudes, the general ideal of a social revolution is commonly referred to as the creation of the "new man" or the "modern man," the "citizen of the new state," the "man in the era of science," the "industrial man," and so on. What is implied is illustrated below, though the list should not be regarded as complete, nor should the individual items be viewed as independent of one another:

(1) efficiency;

(2) diligence;

(3) orderliness;

(4) punctuality;

(5) frugality;

(6) scrupulous honesty (which pays in the long run and is a condition for raising efficiency in all social and economic relations);

(7) rationality in decisions on actions (liberation from reliance on static customs, from group allegiances and favoritism, from superstitious beliefs and prejudices, approaching the rationally calculating "economic man" of Western liberal ideology);

(8) preparedness for change (for experimentation along new lines, and for moving around spatially, economically, socially);

(9) alertness to opportunities as they arise in a changing world;

(10) energetic enterprise;

(11) integrity and self-reliance;

(12) cooperativeness (not limiting but redirecting egoistic striving in a socially beneficial channel; acceptance of responsibility for the welfare of the community and the nation);

(13) willingness to take the long view (and to forego short-term profiteering; subordination of speculation to investment and of commerce and finance to production, etc.).

The desirability of changing attitudes, though accepted at a very general level, is usually played down in public debate. Least of all does discussion take the form of demands for specific policy measures aimed directly at changing attitudes. Attitudinal changes are glossed over even in the formulation of educational policies.

Together the modes and levels of living, the attitudes, and the institutions form a complex social system that is difficult to change, particularly as all these countries are reluctant to apply compulsion. This escape from thinking or doing much about institutions and attitudes is made easier by the application in economic analysis and planning of what we shall call the conventional post-war approach, which takes into account solely the "economic" factors.

G. *National Consolidation.* Ideally, national consolidation means a national system of government, courts, and administration that is effective, cohesive, and internally united in purpose and action, with unchallenged authority over all regions and groups within the boundaries of the state.

Throughout South Asia the idea of national consolidation, even in a narrower sense, is still being contested. In every country there are groups of people who want to disassociate themselves from the existing national entity; they demand autonomy or at least more independence than is compatible with a reasonable degree of national consolidation. Aside from such movements there are also divisions of culture, religion, caste, and economic interests that work against national consolidation.

H. *National Independence.* This ideal is firmly adhered to and, of all the ideals, is given the most explicit expression. National independence, like a reasonable degree of national consolidation, holds a key position among the modernization ideals. In one sense, even the rebellions constitute no exception to the general urge for national independence. South Asian rebel groups are not shifting their allegiance to a foreign country, but are fighting for an autonomous existence.

I. *Political Democracy.* All the countries of South Asia began their independent existence by declaring their ambition to become democratic nation-states; they declared that they had constitutions with representative assemblies founded on free elections and universal suffrage. They also attempted to establish legal guarantees for civil liberties and to give these a very inclusive interpretation. Some of these initial attempts were modified to include certain alternative ideals such as "guided democracy" in Indonesia. But enough was retained of the ideals of democracy and civil liberties to support a common assumption that the national regime should be not only in accord with the interests of the people, but willingly accepted by the great majority, and that it should permit general freedom of thought and action, even if it engages in some suppression of public opposition.

Yet it may be doubted whether the ideal of political democracy—with power based on free elections and with freedom of assembly, press, and other civil liberties—should be given weight in formulating the modernization ideals. Value premises represent merely an angle from which actual conditions are viewed and need not be "realistic" in that sense; many of those stated above are not. But experience has shown that, unlike the other value premises, this ideal is not essential to a system comprising all the other modernization ideals. These can be attained by an authoritarian regime bent on their realization. On the other hand, the substitution of an authoritarian regime for a more democratic one gives no assurance that policies will be directed toward the realization of those ideals, or that, if so directed, they will be more effective. The writer may be permitted the observation that few things in the outcome of this study have been more disturbing to him, in view of his own personal valuations, than the conclusion that political democracy is not a necessary element in the modernization ideals.

J. *Democracy at the Grass Roots.* Somewhat independent of the political forms and the power basis of a national government is the degree to which responsibility for their own affairs should be delegated to local and sectional communities and accepted by the people in those smaller communities. This ideal of local and sectional self-government and cooperation has much in common with the ideal of changed institutions and attitudes. South Asian governments nowadays must strive for economic development, and successful development presupposes a rather high degree of popular acceptance of the development goals. All effective governments, whether democratically based or authoritarian, must enforce some measure of social discipline through compulsion; but even an authoritarian regime cannot record major achievements unless it can somehow mobilize acceptance, participation, and cooperation among the people.

Thus it should not be surprising that this ideal, referred to in South Asia as "decentralization" or "democratic planning," which is directed toward the creation of conditions for popular cooperation and joint responsibility within the nation, is—on the general level—a more widely accepted valuation than any of the modernization ideals other than the quest for independence.

K. *Social Discipline versus "Democratic Planning."* These countries are all "soft states," both in that policies decided on are often not enforced, if they are enacted at all, and in that the authorities, even when framing policies, are reluctant to place obligations on people. By "democratic planning" is meant that policies should be decided on by some sort of democratic political procedures (under *I* above) and that they should, as far as possible, be implemented with the cooperation and shared responsibility of local and sectional communities (under *J* above). More specifically, it is implied that policies should not require compulsion, and this is often held to be a fundamental difference from the practice of the Communist countries. The abstention from compulsion has thus been permitted to masquerade as part of the modernization ideals.

This interpretation of the ideal of democratic planning is not among the value premises of this study. On the contrary, the success of planning for development requires a readiness to place obligations on people in *all* social strata to a much greater extent than is now done in any of the South Asian countries. We cannot claim that this ideal of a more disciplined nation is shared by a large number of people, even among the intellectual elite in South Asia. It is another example of how our study has forced us to choose a value premise that is not widely accepted, in order that the system of value premises may be coherent and in accord with the primary quests for rationality and planning for development.

If this value premise does not conflict in principle with the ideal of democracy, it often does so in practice. Conflict arises when the modernization ideals do not have enough force to induce people, including the intellectual elite, to voluntarily undertake diligent efforts toward their realization and to cast aside conflicting valuations. This very serious problem should not be concealed, because under present South Asian conditions development cannot be achieved without much more social discipline than the prevailing interpretation of democracy in the region permits.

L. *Derived Value Premises.* We have noted that the modernization ideals cannot be entirely independent and *a priori;* they are partly dependent on the outcome of the study for which they serve as value premises. In one sense all of the modernization ideals are contained in, and derived from, the ideal of rationality and planning. It follows that as we take up concrete problems many value premises that are more specific will emerge and have to be stated. We have therefore adopted a number of derived value premises—for instance, that non-discretionary controls are preferable to discretionary administrative ones, and that popular education and the spread of literacy should have a leading role in education and reform. We have also accepted the value premise that everything within practical limits should be done to improve health conditions and prevent premature death. This latter value premise is not derived; it stands as a moral imperative.

Outside the sphere of the modernization ideals are all the other relevant and significant valuations that should be accounted for in order to put our chosen value premises into perspective. Not all of these other valuations conflict with the modernization ideals: some actually give support to them; some are neutral; and some are ambivalent and can be used either for or against attempts to realize these ideals.

Insofar as these other valuations clash with the modernization ideals, from the point of view of their effect on planning for development they act as *inhibitions* when held by members of government and by those who participate in shaping and carrying out government policies. When present only among the majority of the people who are not active participants in policy formation and execution, these conflicting valuations act as *obstacles*. As such, they occupy in principle the same position in the analysis as do other obstacles—for example, climatic difficulties or a downturn in the demand for a country's export commodities.

These other valuations, held by the mass of people and in large part also by the intellectual elite, are mainly "traditional": they are part of an inherited culture long identified with a stagnating society. In all the South Asian countries the modernization ideals are so firmly fixed among the articulate elite that rationality and planning for development are the recognized precepts for policy-making, however unsuccessful the planning efforts are in practice. Even those traditionalists who oppose these ideals have not managed to produce a reactionary "plan" of their own, for this would necessitate organizing their valuations on the principles of rationality.

For the young nations of South Asia some valuations that further the post-war ideals produce inhibitions but are both rational and necessary. The value of an indigenous language is an example of this. Furtherance of the modernization ideals requires the extended use of indigenous languages. No real emotional integration of the new nations, and therefore no secure national consolidation, is possible as long as the members of the tiny upper class in charge of administration communicate in a European language and the masses speak only their native tongue. On rational grounds, increased use of the indigenous language must be part of the planning in all South Asian countries. But in many of them there is not one indigenous language that is used by the masses or that the masses are willing to accept as the official language. In some South Asian countries the users of one regional language or dialect fear a loss of economic opportunity if another regional language or dialect is made official. This is further complicated by the use of different scripts in which a regional language is written.

In Malaya and the Philippines, in Ceylon and India steps have been taken toward an official indigenous language and script. But in Malaya and the Philippines this has been accomplished against some resistance, and in Ceylon and India it has on occasion resulted in disruption and bloodshed. Yet it is a valuation premise that must be pursued with official courage. In India, for example, as long as debates in the Union Parliament are conducted in English, national politics must remain a class monopoly estranged from the people.

There are other specific traditional valuations that are widely held and articulated systematically enough to be easily observable. They often conflict with the post-war ideals and thus represent inhibitions and obstacles to planning for development. From a practical point of view the most important of these valuations is the Hindu taboo on killing animals, epitomized in the ban on cow slaughter. The cattle stock in India has recently been increasing, and there is a real danger that the number of unserviceable and unproductive cattle will increase even faster with control of local famines and improved treatment of cattle. Yet the religious taboo that places the life of cattle on a par with that of human beings finds expression in legislation throughout the country.

The simple fact is, of course, that it is impossible to plan a rational policy for husbandry in India if cattle cannot be selectively killed to the extent and at the age that is most advantageous economically. It is self-contradictory to ask for both rational husbandry and a ban on cow slaughter, and this ban represents a very serious complex of inhibitions and obstacles to planning.

The conflict between articulated specific traditional valuations and the post-war ideals can be expressed in terms of the costs to the latter through lost opportunities. In the case of the ban on cow slaughter in India, these costs are very high, though never calculated.

Yet with some few exceptions, of which cow slaughter and the language question are the most important practically, the post-war modernization ideals have reigned supreme in public discussion and overt public policy-making in South Asia.

Insofar as there are considerable and systematic differences in conditions among the several South Asian countries, there is undoubtedly something to the concept of a "national character." And as the differences in conditions are much more pronounced between these countries as a whole and the Western world, there is room also for the concept of the "Asian"—or "South Asian"—mind. But these terms are not suitable for scientific use. They have been contaminated by being made to serve—in South Asia as in the Western world—nationalistic, aggressive, or apologetic ideologies. For convenience we shall refer to these values as "Asian values"; in criticizing them we have in mind South Asian, and particularly Indian, conditions.

It is often held that people in Asia are more spiritual and less materialistic than Westerners. They are other-worldly, it is said, selfless, and disposed to disregard wealth and material comfort. They sustain poverty with equanimity and even see virtues in it. They have a special respect for learning and a capacity for contemplation and meditation. Their attitude toward the environment tends to be timeless, formless, and therefore carefree and even fatalistic.

Stereotypes like these abound in the literature, and allegations of common traits are injected into almost all public pronouncements about Asian countries and their problems and policies. But the most cursory examination reveals that the alleged cultural and personality traits bear little resemblance to reality—as little as their counterparts in the Western world. For instance, the charity and tolerance often attributed to the Indians is in direct contradiction to the extreme intolerance bred by rigid social stratification and the callousness toward those in a lower social stratum that is found among the most cultivated Indians and soon adopted by Westerners who live in India for any length of time.

The widely accepted idea that Asians are bent on settling disputes peacefully and by mutual agreement, without resort to legal procedures, is refuted by the popularity of litigation in all South Asian countries once there is access to the courts. Against the claim that people in Asia are particularly spiritual and non-materialistic must be placed the common observation of a propensity for narrow materialism in all social strata—which is not surprising, considering the general poverty and the strains of social inequality. Outward austerity, even on the part of those who could afford luxury, was propagated and observed by Gandhi, and was certainly in agreement with his personal ideals. Clearly, however, the continued observance of simple, folksy dress, for instance, which has become almost a uniform for popular leaders, is more a symbolic rite and a political device than a sign of a basic attitude.

If these remarks—based on personal observation and on comments of journalists and others who do not pretend to write as professional social scientists—seem deprecating and unfriendly, that impression is unwarranted. They seem so only in juxtaposition to the completely unrealistic views commonly expounded as a defensive cover.

To do more than scratch the surface we must examine all the mental inclinations that determine the behavior of the peoples in South Asia. For that wider category we shall use the commonly accepted term "attitudes," meaning the totality of the beliefs and valuations that cause behavior to be what it is. These are the attitudes behind all inarticulateness and all protective and rationalizing precautions, attitudes that have been molded by a long spiritual and material history and that are causally related to levels of living and to the entire framework of institutions.

Religion is, of course, crucial, but not the interpretation of old scriptures and the lofty philosophies and theologies developed over centuries of speculation. It is, indeed, amazing how much Western, as well as South Asian, writers think they are saying about the peoples of the region when they refer loosely to the impact of Hinduism, Buddhism, or Islam, which they think of as general concepts and often as intellectualized and abstruse. Religion should be studied for what it really is among the people: a ritualized and stratified complex of highly emotional beliefs and valuations that give the sanction of sacredness, taboo, and immutability to inherited institutional arrangements, modes of living, and attitudes. Understood in this realistic and comprehensive sense, religion usually acts as a tremendous force for social inertia. The writer knows of no instance in present-day South Asia where religion has induced social change. Least of all does it foster realization of the modernization ideals. From a planning point of view, this inertia related to religion, like other obstacles, must be overcome by policies for inducing changes, formulated in a plan for development. But the religiously sanctioned beliefs and valuations not only act as obstacles among the people to getting the plan accepted but also as inhibitions in the planners themselves insofar as they share them, or are afraid to counteract them.

Among the masses, these traditional beliefs that with their related valuations have religious sanction are normally irrational, for they are superstitious and imply a mystical rather than a logical way of thinking. Religious conceptions as irrational as these have not been commonly held in the West for centuries. To a considerably lesser extent, irrational beliefs sanctioned by religion are also present among the educated class. Even Islam and Buddhism, which at the rarefied "higher" level are so rational and free from iconism and magic, have, in the forms in which they actually influence life and social relations, become demonological and permeated by taboos, magic, and mysticism. In particular, social and economic stratification is accorded the sanction of religion. The attitudes, institutions, and modes of living and working that make up this stratification do constitute very real inhibitions and obstacles to planning. The strength of this stratification is evidenced by the unwillingness of the underprivileged and exploited lower strata to challenge them. Instead, they mostly accept them as a fate ordained by the gods and the whole paraphernalia of supernatural forces. It is this feeling, for instance, that restrains the untouchables in India from pressing into the temples and using the wells of the higher castes.

It should be noted that from the point of view of the

modernization ideals, what is needed is merely the eradication of the ballast of irrational beliefs and related valuations. No religion on the "higher" level need be in conflict
with the modernization ideals. But as religion is part and
parcel of the whole complex of people's beliefs and valuations, it needs to be reformed in order to break down
inhibitions and obstacles to development.

It is remarkable that today practically no one in South
Asia is attacking religion. Nor are there nowadays any
substantial attempts to reform religion in South Asia.
Even the Communists do not take a stand against religion
in any of the South Asian countries. What is insisted on in
India and constantly preached by those intellectual
leaders who support the modernization ideal is that religion should be relegated to private life; it should not
influence those in public life. The general tendency to
avoid any interference with the religious establishments
has some pragmatic basis. Important legislative reforms—
for instance, legislation in regard to marriage, inheritance,
and other family matters—are being carried out, and
support for them is found in the "higher" forms of religion
now prevalent among the intellectual elite, while silence
is preserved about the fact that popular religion is different. The hope is that through these and other reforms,
and through education, religious reformation will take
place without a frontal attack. There are, however, the
urgent problems of whether "communalism" can be eradicated; whether the reform legislation will be observed in
practice; whether, more generally, people will change in
the way development requires; and whether all these
changes will happen rapidly enough, without a deliberate
reformation of popular religion.

By characterizing popular religion as a force of inertia
and irrationality that sanctifies the whole system of life
and work, attitudes and institutions, we are, in fact, stressing an important aspect of underdevelopment: the resistance of that system to planned, induced changes along

the lines of the modernization ideals. This wider definition of popular religion by the social scientist is defensible on the ground that any narrower definition is arbitrary and does violence to reality.

Among the educated and the intellectuals the irrationality inherent in traditional thinking undoubtedly contributes to the relative lack of interest in facts and in straight reasoning from those facts that has been commonly observed as a regional characteristic. But a more important general problem is whether peculiarly South Asian attitudes and institutions are caused by South Asian poverty and low levels of living. For instance, the survival-mindedness of the people, their unresponsiveness to opportunities for betterment, and their scorn of manual labor, especially work for an employer, may result from long ages of hopeless poverty. The inegalitarian social stratification, in particular, may partly be a result of stagnation in poverty. It should be an hypothesis for further study that people in this region are not inherently different from people elsewhere, but that they live under conditions very different from those in the developed world, and that this has left a mark upon their bodies and their minds. Religion has, then, become the emotional container of this whole way of life and work and by its sanction has contributed to rendering it rigid and resistant to change.

Since gaining independence during the past two decades, the forces and factors pressing for dynamic social change in South Asia have grown steadily. A common assertion in much of the literature is that what we are seeing is a "revolution of rising expectations." Even if for the time being this meant a widening gap between aspirations and realizations, it would not be a bad thing from the point of view of the modernization ideals, and is apparently not so considered by those in the intellectual elite who are pushing planning for development.

But the concept of "rising expectations" is rather loose and borders on meaninglessness unless it is quantified. The word "revolution" implies that the changes in attitudes are great and proceeding fast. In the present context, only one preliminary remark need be added. Without doubt, the idea of the rising expectations as a revolutionary movement among the masses is in large part a false rationalization. It reflects the Western observer's and the indigenous intellectual's feeling of how he would react if he had to live in the dire poverty of the masses, and his bad conscience when confronted by this extreme inequality. Among other things, the radical tone of most South Asian political proclamations is difficult to understand unless it is assumed that in them speak the members of a privileged class, who wish to identify themselves with their nation and, despite the great social distance, are aware of the misery of the broader strata. It represents how they themselves would react if they had to live under similar circumstances. But the actual feelings of the masses must be ascertained by studying the attitudes of these people with a minimum of sentimentality and preconceived ideas. This is not done to any large extent. We need only note here that in none of the South Asian countries has a political regime been unseated by means of a popular revolt.

Yet through our study we have grown more and more convinced that *often it is not more difficult, but easier, to cause a big change rapidly than a small change gradually.* And this problem is related to another one: what policy measures are felt to be available for carrying out reforms. On the general level, the public debate in the countries of South Asia is filled with pronouncements that a social and economic revolution is needed. A study of their actual conditions can hardly avoid strengthening this view. But in practice the policies resorted to are piecemeal and gradualist, often in the extreme, and all these countries remain "soft states."

When faced with the realities of the "soft state," students from developed countries are, moreover, apt to play down their observations for reasons of diplomacy. For economists in particular, this tendency is abetted by the conventional post-war approach, which implies an abstraction from those types of social facts that represent resistance to change: modes of living, attitudes, and institutions. The South Asian countries are regarded as unable to master a policy of more rapidly induced change—except by relying on totalitarian and monolithic methods. "Democratic planning," with reliance on persuasion, is thus rationalized to defend the avoidance of radical reforms through changing the institutions.

And so the South Asian planners remain in their paradoxical position: on a general and non-committal level they freely and almost passionately proclaim the need for radical social and economic change, whereas in planning their policies they tread most warily in order not to disrupt the traditional social order. And when they do legislate radical institutional reforms—for instance, in taxation or in regard to property rights in the villages—they permit the laws to contain loopholes of all sorts and even let them remain unenforced.

In South Asia the traditional values that have held on in the face of change have had their emotional base in religion. The competing modernization ideals have had their base in nationalism, and some of these ideals need nationalistic emotions in order to be grasped. People must have a conception of the nation as a whole and attach positive valuations to this ideal before they can feel that national independence and national consolidation are goals worth striving for and that all the other modernization ideals can only be realized in the setting of an independent and consolidated nation-state. Part of the emotional appeal of the modernization ideals stems from the expectation that as they begin to be realized the nation-state will become stronger, more united, and better consolidated. Nationalism, therefore, is commonly seen as a force for good by all those in the intellectual elite who are bent on planning policies aimed at development. To them, fostering nationalism will provide the means of breaking down inhibitions and obstacles.

But the movement toward nationalism, which in Europe spanned centuries and proceeded step by step, is violently telescoped in South Asia and then becomes confused and chaotic as events and situations tumble over each other with no orderliness of historical precedence. The states in South Asia were created anew, partly as an effect of rising nationalism. And they were immediately given a ready-made democratic ideology, if not much democratic reality. The practical problems in South Asia are: how to consolidate and strengthen the newly created states brought into existence by the collapse of the colonial power system under the onslaught of nationalism; how, at the same time, to make governments in these new, not very advanced, states stable and effective; and how to do all of this in the turmoil of nationalism with some degree of democracy from the beginning and attempts at what we have called democracy at the grass roots. What in Europe could unfold gradually and proceed as a grand symphony with one movement following the other in thematic sequence is by destiny syncopated in South Asia into almost a cacophony.

There certainly is a melody of progressive and rational ideas in the new nationalism in South Asia, soaring above the tumult of noises. This is the nationalism that appeals to unity and condemns all internal, spatial, religious, and social particularisms. It stands for rationalism against superstitious beliefs, and expresses the will to modernize society and to achieve economic development. But this is not the sole component of South Asian nationalism, and in many countries and at many junctures not even the dominant one. For it is also a brand of nationalism when particular groups held together by religion, language, or ethnic origin fight each other.

In all the South Asian countries there are leaders and groups in the intellectual elite who are aware of the need to harness the nationalist emotions in a productive system of channels. How far such efforts will be successful is uncertain, but they are an essential phase of the drama that is unfolding in these countries and will determine its outcome.

Part Two

ECONOMIC
REALITIES

Chapter 4

DIFFERENCES IN
INITIAL CONDITIONS

In any analysis of underdevelopment, development, and planning for development in South Asia, comparisons between this region and the highly developed Western countries are valid and relevant. Present conditions in South Asia can be compared either with present conditions in Western countries, or with conditions in the Western countries on the eve of their rapid economic development, particularly their industrialization. It is this latter comparison that we are chiefly concerned with in this chapter. We shall attempt to spell out the main differences in "initial conditions" for economic development between the South Asian countries and the Western countries, a comparison considered relevant to the problem of formulating economic policy in South Asia. The countries of this region recognize that they are underdeveloped and that they should develop. Their plans are all built on a desire for modernization, especially industrialization, and it is natural to believe that they could learn a great deal from the experience of the developed countries.

These differences in initial conditions are extremely significant, and they regularly work to the disadvantage of South Asia. In many instances these differences are so great as to prohibit a pattern of growth anything like that experienced by the Western countries. It is important to note the newness of the development problems confronting the countries of South Asia today because of the tendency to overlook their uniqueness, a tendency inherent in the biases common in research and also prevalent in planning and, generally, in public discussion.

In the conventional post-war approach to the economic problems of the South Asian countries the comparisons, either with the West as it currently is or as it was at the time of its industrial revolution, are related to each other by the assumption that the present differences represent a time lag in development. This concept of a time lag implies that in the history of the West there was a period —somewhat differently located on the time axis for different countries—when conditions were essentially "comparable" to those that now exist in South Asia—again with individual variations among the countries. This also implies that it is possible to postulate a fairly uniform development for countries, which in turn implies that the entire set of conditions relevant for development moves together with a degree of internal harmony. Finally, the time lag concept implies that the present world environment, if not identical to what it was in the Western countries in the period of comparison, is at least not so much less favorable as to block or seriously hamper South Asian development.

But there is a logical weakness in this theory when we try to decide at what period the Western nations were underdeveloped in the same sense as South Asia today, and after which they began to develop. One thing is certain: at the beginning of what we recognize as the industrial revolutions (for we see them as a series rather than a single event) of the Western countries, they had behind them many years—in some cases centuries—of social, political, and also incipient economic development. In a number of ways the Western countries were at that time already much more favorably situated for further development than South Asia is today. In many respects, therefore, the period of comparison should be fixed centuries before the industrial revolutions in the West. In other respects there are conditions in South Asia today that are comparable to those in the West at any time in recent history. Efforts to define the time of "take-off" in the Western countries assume a basic similarity among these countries in initial conditions and in the process of development—an assumption that is open to question. To use this Western concept of a "take-off" and attempt to locate on an assumed general development axis the "stage" at which any South Asian country now is, is to do violence to the facts.

Thus we intentionally leave the period of comparison in the history of the Western countries vague. (Of course, in some instances, such as climate, population, and natural resources, the differences between South Asia and the Western world are constant in time.)

South Asia, as a region, is poorly endowed with resources. Only India is known to have enough coal and iron ore to support heavy industry. With the exception of Indonesia, there does not seem to be much oil in the region. Land resources are often poor, either because they were that way to begin with or because they have been damaged by overcrowding and climate. There are exceptions, however. Ceylon has excellent, though limited, land for producing tea, cocoanuts, and rubber. Malaya and Indonesia also have excellent and less limited lands for growing rubber. There are large forested areas in Malaya, Thailand, Burma, Ceylon, and the Philippines not yet fully utilized.

The climate in South Asia might be treated as a natural resource endowment. But since it also affects the productivity of labor, it is more accurately treated as a separate condition. Although we have little knowledge of its precise implications for development, climate constitutes another major difference between South Asia and the Western world. It is a fact that all successful industrialization in modern times, including that of Japan, the Soviet Union, and even China, has taken place in the temperate zones. The South Asian countries are situated in the tropical or subtropical zones, as, indeed, are most of the underdeveloped countries of the world.

Even if little research has been carried out about the importance of climatic conditions for development, it is clear that, generally speaking, the extremes of heat and humidity in most South Asian countries contribute to a deterioration of soil and many kinds of material goods; bear a partial responsibility for the low productivity of certain crops, forests, and animals; and not only cause discomfort to workers but also impair their health and decrease the participation in, and duration and efficiency of, work. It is possible in some small ways to alter the climate; more important, the effects of climate on productivity can be changed in many ways, and both production and consumption can be better adapted to the climate. But this requires expenditure, often of the investment type.

In pre-industrial times population growth in the West was comparatively slow. By contrast, population growth in South Asia has been increasing over a very long period, and is increasing even faster today. As a result, the heavily populated areas now start out with a considerably higher man/land ratio than did the European countries. To this must be added the effects of the population explosion. Present population density and the prospect of very rapid population increase constitute a very important difference between South Asia and the West in initial situation.

It is commonly recognized that expansion of markets for their exports played a crucial role in the early development of the Western countries. Since the end of the First World War, the South Asian countries have seen the demand for their exports shrink relative to the development of world trade. Nor is the future outlook for their export earnings very bright. The whole climate for development through trade has also changed fundamentally since the nineteenth century, an era of unequalled freedom in international trade. The Western countries, having the field virtually to themselves, exploited the resources and peoples in the huge backward areas of the world and kept them politically and economically dependent. Now that these large areas are trying to emerge, they cannot simply repeat the development process of the developed countries.

To the Western countries who were late-comers, capital was easily available at low rates of interest. But the old competitive international capital market has almost disappeared. A new element in the situation has been the flow of capital in the form of grants and loans from foreign countries and international agencies. But since the present tendency is to give this aid in the form of loans the payment of interest and principal places increasing burdens on the payment balances of the South Asian countries for the future.

By approaching the problem of capital investments imaginatively, it is not difficult to envision policies that could offset the disadvantageous commercial and financial conditions under which South Asia now labors. The South Asian countries could be given more trade preferences to stimulate their exports. The Western countries could reduce domestic production in fields where the South Asian countries have the best chance of becoming competitive. They could make available to the South Asian countries more grants or loans with low or no interest rates. While these steps are not to be expected within the foreseeable future, the ability to offset some of the most serious disadvantages of the South Asian countries in trade and in capital movements clearly exists. Until then, the closely interrelated developments in trade and in capital movements must be regarded as another difference in initial conditions that is very much to the disadvantage of the South Asian countries.

Heroic efforts have been made to compare levels of income per head in South Asian countries today with those in the Western countries in pre-industrial times. But logically viewed, an over-all index figure must be regarded as unreal. Our very broad impression is that on the Indian subcontinent the masses live in worse poverty than did those in the Western European countries at any time during the several centuries before the industrial revolution. In Malaya, on the other hand, the average economic level may be higher than in the Western European countries at the time their industrial revolution began. The other South Asian countries fall somewhere in between.

But what significance do income levels have for development prospects? When references are made in the literature to income differences in time and space, it is usually assumed that the level of income has a direct bearing on a country's ability to support the savings needed for those investments considered to be crucial for development. But savings do not play the exclusive role in development assumed for them in most economic writings on South Asia. Attitudes and institutions are more important than are levels of income *per se*. What is saved out of income depends very much on the effectiveness of government policy. In fact, low incomes probably hamper development more by keeping down consumption than by limiting savings, because inferior living conditions reduce labor efficiency. Strangely, this point is overlooked in most comments concerning the effect of low income levels in South Asia.

The emphasis on the low levels of income in South Asia, the strained comparison with Western income levels at an earlier period, and the conventional post-war approach to income, savings, and investment in South Asia, all represent attempts to apply an over-simplified and narrow formula to an intricate complex of social, economic, and even political conditions, all of which impede development.

But even if we reject the savings-centered approach and remain skeptical of the inter-regional comparison involved, it is true that the great poverty in South Asia, particularly in those countries with the bulk of its population, is in itself a major barrier to development. Moreover, the foreseeable increases in population will lead to further lowering of the levels of living unless resolute development policies are pursued, and this trend implies another difference in initial conditions, detrimental to all the South Asian countries. And, although we have little information on which to judge whether economic inequality today is greater than in the Western countries of pre-industrial times, it is probable that on the Indian subcontinent social inequality is more pervasive and more detrimental to free competition, in the wider sense of the term, than anywhere in the Western world in recent centuries. On the whole, we believe that attitudes and institutions, particularly political institutions, in the South Asian countries are less favorable than were those in the now developed Western countries at the start of their industrial revolutions, or even in the centuries before. Obviously, South Asia is attempting to close a yawning gap in attitudes and institutions. In this as in other respects, those Western countries that in their day were also late-comers to industrialization were in a more advantageous position.

All of the differences in initial conditions accounted for so far make the problem of economic development more difficult for the nations of South Asia than it once was for the Western nations. There is one difference that could counterbalance this: technology has advanced far since the nineteenth century. The South Asian countries need not go through a slow, painful process of experimentation. As Edward S. Mason says in his *Economic Planning in Underdeveloped Areas*, "a highly productive technology . . . is available for the borrowing." Increased availability of technical knowledge greatly aided the late developers in the West. But it does not necessarily follow that advanced technology is similarly helpful to the latecomer nowadays. It is often the case that the increased output from advanced technology will be much more than the limited domestic markets can absorb. This becomes more important when one considers the absence of regional cooperation and the generally unpromising outlook for manufactured exports.

A further problem involving modern technology is its requirement of large initial investments. Since present-day technology is mainly a product of economies that have a scarcity of labor and a relative abundance of capital, it tends to be labor-saving and capital-intensive. Much of it may therefore be beyond the means of the very poor, capital-starved economies of the region. Even if this challenge can be overcome, modern technology entails more investment in transport and power than was necessary in earlier periods in the West.

The shortage of skills in South Asia is a fundamental hindrance to progress and another main difficulty in advancing to a higher technological level. There can be little doubt that the educational level of management, technical personnel, and workers now considered minimal for successful operation of a modern industrial establishment is substantially higher than it was in the early period of Western industrialization.

While industrialization is unquestionably of crucial importance for long-range development, the more immediate problem in the South Asian countries is agriculture, and here the application of modern technology is even more difficult for South Asia. In Western agriculture, technology has been aimed at raising yields while the labor force in agriculture has been declining. This pattern simply does not fit South Asian conditions.

It may be true that South Asian entrepreneurs and states have vastly superior technology available to them than was available in the pre–industrial revolution period in the West. But what is important is that the West is rapidly moving toward much higher levels of technological and scientific achievement. Only to a very minor extent does this help South Asia. Most economic writings have concealed the obvious fact that this advance in the West has had, and is having, a detrimental impact on the development prospects of South Asia. Advancing technology in the West has already caused deterioration in the trading position of the South Asian countries. It has raised agricultural productivity and, as a result, lowered the use of raw materials from South Asia for industrial production. It has allowed the substitution of synthetics, such as synthetic rubber, for South Asian products. And gains in Western medical science have lowered mortality rates in South Asia, contributing to the population explosion in this region. The advance of Western science and technology has also raised the educational levels needed by management and technical personnel to a higher point than was needed in the early period of Western industrialization. These specific effects of scientific and technological advance are, of course, recorded, but the general conclusion is not drawn.

Restriction of scientific and technological advance is, of course, out of the question. But its unfortunate impact on South Asia could be counteracted by aiming more of its research toward solving the problems of this region. This could be another type of aid by the developed countries: aid on a greater scale than anything previously done or now contemplated in the way of technical assistance. This research effort would have to be large and in the right direction. Otherwise, the dynamics of technological progress will work to ever greater disadvantage of the under-developed countries, increasing their difficulties and decreasing their development potential.

The true significance of the foregoing observations can only be grasped when we realize that technological advance, now proceeding so rapidly in the developed countries, can be expected to proceed ever faster in the future. Change was not rapid in the beginning of Western development prior to industrialization, and it is difficult to overestimate the importance of gradualness in the early development of the Western countries. All the major "revolutions" of the West—religious, intellectual, geographic, and even political (the emergence of consolidated nation-states)—occurred long before the industrial revolution. They proceeded slowly, and Western Europe had several centuries in which to become accustomed to, and prepared for, change. So the ideas of change, adaptability, and mobility were gradually accepted as a way of life, until Westerners became accustomed to the kind of "permanent industrial revolution" in which they live today.

It is generally recognized that progress in science and technology was a result of, and at the same time a driving force in, this gradual development. The underdeveloped countries cannot possibly realize their aspirations in the same way, except in very limited, insignificant fields. Modern science and technology to them are forces emanating almost entirely from outside.

For South Asia the need is for telescoping, not gradual, changes. These must take place faster than they ever did in the early development of the Western countries—even faster than they are now taking place in those countries. But the long stagnation in the underdeveloped countries has solidified institutions and attitudes and hardened resistance to change in all strata of the population. It is evident that modernism will not come about by a process of "natural" evolution, and this constitutes the case for radical state policies. The aim of planning is to engender development by state intervention, in spite of the greater difficulties we have noted throughout this chapter. And the emergence of the ideology of state planning for development thus itself constitutes a difference in initial conditions.

Chapter 5

POPULATION AND DEVELOPMENT OF RESOURCES

The basic geographic features of South Asia have been shaped, as have those of the rest of the world, by climate, soil, and population growth. Added to these is the impact of Western colonial domination. The forces that have evolved from all these factors are economic realities that must be taken as the basis when planning for development.

Contrary to the prevalent assumption, the ratio of man to land in South Asia is not strikingly high compared with other parts of the world. The number of inhabitants per unit of cultivated land is comparable to the European average. It is half that of China and, of course, much lower than that of Japan. What really distinguishes South Asia is the very low output per unit of farm land and per unit of work on that land. South Asia as a whole produces probably only about half as much per acre of cultivated land as China or Europe, and only about one-fifth as much as Japan. South Asia's output per acre may be roughly equal to that of the United States and the Soviet Union. But those countries, with more than three times as much agricultural land per head of total population, cultivate this land very extensively with a much smaller proportion of their total labor forces.

The basic fact accounting for South Asia's low level of economic development is that its agricultural output, whether measured per acre or per worker, is very low. Other countries whose output per acre is equally low have the advantages of a greater amount of land per inhabitant and an even greater area per unit of labor devoted to agriculture. In the light of these figures, South Asia appears to have the worst of both worlds.

Broadly speaking, there are two distinct types of farming practiced throughout most of the world. The more sparsely populated countries, such as North America, Australia, and the Soviet Union, utilize their soil extensively, and the type of crops they grow and the space in which they grow them produces a very low output per unit of land. In the more densely populated lands with high man/land ratios, such as parts of Europe, China, and Japan, intensive land utilization, with high yields per hectare, is practiced. South Asia fits into neither of these main groups. It forms a third and very unfortunate category: namely, that of extensive land use combined with a high man/land ratio. This naturally results in disastrously low levels of nutrition and real income. Not only is agricultural output low per person, but almost three-fourths of the total labor force is tied up in the production of a meager diet in which cereals usually account for more than two-thirds of the total caloric intake. In South Asia only about one out of every four male workers is available for activities other than the direct production of food. In the United States nine out of ten, and in Europe two out of three, males can devote themselves to non-agricultural occupations.

Over-all comparisons such as these indicate the dimensions of the basic economic problems of the region. More particularly, they suggest that the growth of more food per acre of land is an essential condition for raising levels of living and supporting industrialization. It is beside the point to talk of expanding the economy by draining off surplus manpower from agriculture and turning it into industry. Even by the most optimistic reckoning, only a small portion of the natural increase in population can be absorbed by industry in the decades immediately ahead. The so-called surplus manpower must, in fact, remain in agriculture, and the foundation for economic advance must be laid by intensifying agricultural production.

South Asia's population is extremely dense in some areas, but just as thinly spread in others. In some of the dense areas the concentrations of people are as great as those in highly industrialized regions of Western Europe. Half the population of India lives on less than a quarter of the total available land, and one-third is concentrated on less than 6 percent of the land. At the other extreme, vast areas continue to be almost uninhabited.

These contrasts throughout the region are closely related to the type of agriculture practiced. Wet paddy cultivation (growing rice under water) and the cultivation of plantation crops (such as rubber, tea, or cocoanuts) usually mean high population density. Sedentary dry land farming (wheat and other cereals) and shifting cultivation (moving from area to area for planting) mark the sparsely settled areas. The most thickly populated of the dense wet paddy areas are the Irrawaddy Delta in Burma, the lower range of the Me Nam in Central Thailand, the Red River valley in North Vietnam, and the Mekong Delta in South Vietnam. The greatest concentrations of plantations are in Ceylon, along the west coast of Malaya, on Java and Sumatra, and in the Philippines. Great areas of West Pakistan and North and Central Asia are limited to dry land farming, although in Southeast Asia only Central Burma and Northeast Thailand are limited to this type. Shifting cultivation is mostly in the form of slash and burn, where small forest areas are cut down and burned and a crop planted. When it is harvested, the peasants move on to another section of forest. This highly destructive type of farming occurs in many parts of the region, especially on the fringes of the great jungles in Southeast Asia.

On a purely territorial basis, the Indian subcontinent is seen to be more than twice as densely populated as Southeast Asia. But if the population, or that portion of the population that is dependent on agriculture for its livelihood, is related to the cultivated area, the picture is reversed and Southeast Asia would appear to have the higher density and might thus be expected to be saddled with a more serious problem of population pressure. However, wet paddy lands and plantations are more prevalent here, and agricultural output per acre is much higher. In fact, the volume of agricultural output in Southeast Asia per acre is higher by more than one-fourth than that in the Indian subcontinent, with the exception of East India and East Pakistan, with their wet paddy areas. This offsets the effect, to a degree, of the very dense concentrations of population. Actually, agriculture output per head of population does not differ from country to country as much as might be expected. The densely populated regions are also those where land resources have been more intensively utilized.

The areas of dry land farming and shifting cultivation offer more long-term scope for increasing productivity through irrigation or forest clearing. But this would require organized migrations and large-scale land projects. With the pattern of population density adjusted to facil-

ities and techniques in each area, there appears to be little
opportunity for a spontaneous, unorganized flow of people
from high- to low-pressure areas. However, this is not to
say that the agricultural resources of the region are very
fully utilized. The outer islands of Indonesia and Sumatra
have hardly begun to be opened up. In Burma, Thailand,
and Malaya, as well as in Laos, there are vast stretches of
cultivable land that are unused. It is true that the reserves
of usable land in India and Pakistan are small by Asian
standards, but in view of the low output per acre at
present, a considerable intensification of agriculture
should be possible, assuming crucial reforms in institutions and attitudes.

It is commonly assumed that far too many South Asians
are engaged in agriculture for the amount of land available. It is then assumed that the main requirement for
development must be to reduce agrarian density by
"skimming off" excess manpower in the villages. But it
should be apparent that there are important qualifications
to the common view that South Asia is severely "overpopulated" and that this density of people results in
"unemployment" or "underemployment," which are the
main causes of poverty in the region. It is true that the
number of persons engaged in farming per unit of cultivated land is considerably higher in South Asia than in
Europe. There are not much more than 4.9 acres (two
hectares) per agricultural family in South Asia, compared
with some 12.3 (five hectares) in Europe. But to bring
this comparison into proper perspective, allowance must
be made for the huge differences in farming techniques.
In most of South Asia, human labor and bullocks are still
the sole sources of power. Countries like Pakistan and
India are still at an intermediate stage—that of the
bullock—in regard to agricultural techniques. Japan, with
advanced techniques and seeds, has almost three times as
high an agrarian population density as South Asia in
terms of males per acre, but it has over five times higher

output per acre and roughly double the output per active male.

The very low average agricultural yield per acre in the larger parts of South Asia contradicts the impression that throughout the region rural poverty is mainly the result of too much labor being devoted to too little land. The implication, instead, is that *even without radical changes in technology, it should be possible to extract very much larger yields from the available land by raising the input and efficiency of the labor force.* In some parts of South Asia the climate may be partly responsible for low yields. But the effects of the climate are not a function of high population density; these effects would not be less severe if the man/land ratio were lower.

There are many other factors keeping labor productivity down in most sections of South Asian agriculture. The very low living levels decrease the efficiency of labor on the land. A vicious circle makes poverty and low labor productivity self-generating, and behind this is a social system of land ownership and utilization that inhibits productivity. Considering these broad causal interrelations, it is impossible to regard the poverty among the peoples in the region as merely, or even mainly, an effect of population density.

At least the causation is not a direct and simple one. But indirectly the long upward climb of population has undoubtedly strengthened other factors that keep down labor productivity. This has been an effect, not of population density as such, but of population growth. The effects of this population growth on the social system have been important. Within the villages it has undoubtedly not only caused fragmentation of holdings but thereby also fortified the class structure, making it more rigid and less egalitarian by increasing the relative number of the landless and poor and thus making it more inimical to the success of efforts to raise productivity in agriculture.

The upward trend in population has meant that more food has been needed to maintain even the traditionally low levels of nutrition. More labor has had to be put in by a growing labor force to produce this additional food. By a process of gradual adjustment, this additional labor force has been given work, to some degree, in food production, and the whole social situation has been subtly arranged to absorb the continual increase in the labor force. In part this adjustment has consisted in extending the area under cultivation or raising its productivity by irrigation, or changing over to other methods or crops. But the impulses for change in indigenous agriculture have been weak. In particular, the abundant supply of labor has inhibited whatever impulses there may have been for changes in production methods that would increase the efficiency of agricultural labor. The labor force has been utilized, but not as intensively or effectively as it might have been, and average yields have remained low. That considerably higher yields could be obtained through increased intensity and efficiency of work is proved by the example of Japan and many areas of South Asia itself. The fact that these examples show there is scope for a greater input of work in agriculture gives a more favorable cast to prospects that otherwise would appear desperate, not only in India, Pakistan, and Java, but also in some other parts of the region.

Despite these major population expansions, most people in the larger part of South Asia have continued to work within an agrarian structure whose paramount objective is to produce the basic necessities of subsistence. The economic history of these countries has been dominated largely by the people's struggle to match the population increase with a corresponding increase in the production of basic foods in the villages where they were born. On the Indian subcontinent, in particular, there has been a remarkable lack of internal mobility in spite of the trends toward urbanization and toward marrying outside the local community.

When food production has been increased by expanding cultivated areas, the blessing has often been mixed. This expansion has often caused damage to the soil, particularly in areas of shifting cultivation. Deforestation and overgrazing, combined with the Indian taboos against cow slaughter, have made it harder to keep production level with population increases. While irrigation has helped increase yields in some areas, it has pulled water tables down, increased salinity in the soil, and even caused waterlogging in other areas.

Given all this, it remains to be explained how food output per head could have been maintained as well as it was, particularly in British India, despite the enormous increases in population. Ironically, one factor may have been the steady shift from individual ownership of land to tenancy and sharecropping. These practices, in themselves, are inimical to progress and impose an artificially low ceiling on productivity, but when first introduced they forced the new sharecroppers, who were required to give part of their yields to their landlords, to produce more to maintain their families' portions. However, any increase in aggregate food output attributable to this institutional pressure cannot have been sizable.

Another dynamic factor—the spread of commercialization—has influenced the long-term adjustments that have occurred in indigenous agriculture. The aggregative impact of monetized production on the indigenous agriculture has been felt much more in Southeast Asia than on the Indian subcontinent. The most dramatic developments occurred in the 1870's in the deltas of Burma, Thailand, and South Vietnam, and much of the growth of commercial farming in these regions took place with no help or support from the government or Western enterprise. This response to the new opportunities for commercial farming is worth stressing, as it demonstrates that South Asian peasants under favorable circumstances can display as much alertness and market consciousness as peasants anywhere else. These responses, however, have been mainly confined to those situations in which peasant proprietorship has been dominant. Where sharecropping and leasing arrangements have prevailed, the assimilation of innovations has been slower, if it occurred at all. Yet, ironically, this move to commercialization has often meant that these farmers exposed themselves to excessive indebtedness in expanding their cash crops and thus lost their land. The result has been an erosion of peasant ownership and an increase in sharecropping.

One of the main factors affecting agricultural production and the deployment of agrarian populations was the coming of huge plantations. This expansion occurred in the second half of the nineteenth century and was one of the greatest legacies of colonialism. The growth of plantations in South Asia, rather than in other tropical lands in Africa and South America, was due, in part, to the relative ease with which labor could be obtained. Soil and climate were less important factors. It should also be noted that all the major plantation areas are situated along the trade routes between Europe, South Asia, and the Far East.

Plantation agriculture is essentially different from traditional, indigenous farming. Plantation crops, such as rubber, tea, cocoanuts, tobacco, coffee, sugar cane, and spices, are "cash crops," grown to be sold, not eaten. In the beginning, most of the large plantations were developed by colonials whose primary aim was to export the products. The operation of a plantation is close to that of a manufacturing industry. It demands a labor force, and this in turn increased the maximum population an area could support. This need for a labor force produced, in South Asia, another very significant effect. In Ceylon and in Malaya, particularly, the local peasants were not enthusiastic about plantation work. As a result, the plantation owners imported labor, mostly from the densely populated wet paddy areas of East and South India and South China. This alleviated, somewhat, the population pressures in those areas. But it created much of the present-day ethnic difficulties of the Tamils in Ceylon and the Chinese in Malaya.

One side effect of the coming of plantations was the stimulation of local interest in cash crops—either crops similar to those grown on the plantations or ones that would fit in with the processing of plantation products. Further, the new demands for food for plantation workers stimulated rice production in the delta areas, which had enough to export then, as they do now. The South Asian peasants themselves took the lead in seizing these new opportunities. They displayed, under these circumstances, as much alertness and market consciousness as peasants anywhere else. This did not increase their willingness to adopt new techniques, but it did increase the degree to which money, and the earning of money, played a part in the economy. But it also too often increased the indebtedness of monetized peasants and, as a result, drew the swarms of moneylenders and middlemen that have too many of South Asia's peasants in their grip today.

There is a degree of comparison between the spread of the plantations in South Asia and the beginning phases of industrialization in Western Europe. However, the side effects of accumulated capital were frustrated in South Asia. Instead of the profits serving as a source of capital, they were too often sent to Europe with the exports. The spread of cash crops increased the amount of money in peasant hands, but it did not increase the demand for capital equipment, since there was little change in farming techniques. The plantations increased the demand for labor. But this was for unskilled workers, and too often the skilled ones were brought in from the outside. This is what is meant when it is said that the plantations spurred the industrialization of the Western countries but not of South Asia. The plantations were, in effect, extensions of the metropolitan countries. Similar development took place in the mines and timber enterprises. With the plantations, they became enclaves of prosperity amidst a stagnant economy.

Manufacturing industries did not develop. In the precolonial era many sections of South Asia had not been inferior to the countries of Western Europe in manufacturing of a pre-industrial character. At first contact the West was in many cases at a distinct disadvantage. Thus many parts of South Asia were not significantly behind Western Europe economically, possibly even as late as the eighteenth century, but about this time the fortunes of South Asia and Western Europe began to diverge. Western Europe had its industrial revolution while the South Asian economies stagnated. Many factors were responsible. A principal one among them was the rigid social stratification in South Asia and the absence of the rationalism that in Europe paved the way for an industrial revolution. No corresponding set of institutions and attitudes was evolving in South Asia. That is why it may be doubted whether there would have been an industrial development in the South Asian countries had there been no colonial domination.

Certainly, though, the colonial regimes in South Asia were generally inimical to the development of manufacturing industry in the colonies. The home countries themselves protected their own budding industry against competition, especially from their colonies. At the same time, they needed these colonies as markets and as a source of raw materials. The result was a lopsided economy precisely suited to the stimulation of manufacturing in the metropolitan country. When these policies were later

modified and deliberate restrictions progressively abandoned after the First World War, the change came too
late to engender vigorous responses.

Despite colonial policies, some manufacturing had
developed rather early in India in cotton textiles and jute,
and later in steel. In the 1920's Britain began to show
some concern for the lack of industrialization in her colonies and instituted some protection for the local manu-
facturers. The Second World War further stimulated the
textile and steel industries in India. Today, following
independence, foreign control in India has generally been
replaced by Indian ownership.

Whereas in Western Europe the rapid growth of manufacturing industry brought a steady decline in the population dependent on agriculture, inhibition of industrialization in the colonies had an adverse effect on agriculture.
The dominance of colonial manufacturing tended to stifle
small-scale cottage industries. Many of the artisans and
craftsmen had to turn to the land to live. Thus, although
the plantations represented modern capital enterprise and
technology, the South Asian countries remained rural and
predominantly agricultural.

The coming of the plantations and the corresponding
growth in commercial farming among South Asian
peasants produced another pattern that remains today,
along with the ethnic distributions in South Asia. The
plantation countries—Ceylon, Malaya, and parts of Indonesia—became rice importers and the less densely populated wet paddy deltas of Burma, Thailand, and South
Vietnam (before the Vietnam war interrupted it) began
to export rice to them. The utilization of land in this
manner had another significant effect: it gave rise to
important migratory movements across territorial boundaries. The poverty in the regions of subsistence farming
in India and South China provided the push, and the pull
came from the growth of plantations and commercial food

production. The migratory movements that resulted explain the present politico-demographic patterns in Southeast Asia and Ceylon.

The countries of South Asia have thus entered the present with three major types of cleavage in their societies, two of which are partly the legacy of colonialism. First there is a sharp difference in the level and character of civilization between the dominant ethnic groups and the smaller tribal peoples of hills and mountains. This division is ancient and generally unrelated to European domination. It poses problems especially in India, Burma, South Vietnam, and to a lesser extent in the Philippines and the outer islands of Indonesia. Second, there is the contrast between modern, market-oriented and profit-seeking enterprise and the traditional subsistence economy. This is most apparent in the plantation countries. Finally, there is the division of ethnic groups, which is closely tied to the second cleavage. The most important examples are the presence of the Indian Tamils in Ceylon and of the Chinese and Indians in Malaya. In fact, the Malays and the Chinese are almost numerically equal in Malaya, and the result has been the holding of economic power by the ethnic Chinese and of political power by the Malays.

Southeast Asian societies have thus become rather extreme examples of plural societies, where it is said that the various groups mix but do not combine. The achievement of independence exacerbated the problem of pluralism. It brought to the fore a number of minority problems and has thus thrown into relief what has aptly been called the "demographic immaturity" of these countries, where, as C. A. Fisher has said, "no lasting adjustment has yet been reached between land and state."

There is also another sense in which South Asia is demographically "immature." This is in urbanization. Not only has South Asia experienced in recent decades a rapid rate of urban growth without significant industrialization, but this growth has been accompanied by relative stagnation of agricultural production. It has not, therefore, been either a response to rapidly rising productivity in agriculture or a growth of labor opportunities in industry. This is contrary to Western experience. In the West one of the traditional accompaniments of industrialization has been a rise in the relative importance of urban centers, not only with regard to population but also in terms of output. A steadily increasing number of jobs has become available in the cities while an equal rise in agricultural productivity has created an excess labor supply in the rural areas that could fill these urban jobs. In all countries of South Asia as well, most cities are growing correspondingly faster than the growth of the entire population, but this movement cityward is unrelated to any vigorous increase in urban employment opportunities. The cities, in fact, are beset by serious unemployment and underemployment problems of their own. And in view of the squalor, overcrowding, inadequate housing, and sanitation in urban centers, the movement toward the cities cannot in general be motivated by any increase in their net attractiveness.

Therefore the principal cause of South Asian urbanization must be an increase, relative to urban areas, in rural poverty and insecurity which creates a push toward the cities. Urbanization is, then, a reaction *against* the lack of vigorous economic growth. Indeed, much of it is due to factors inhibiting economic development, such as civil wars, instability, and crop failures, as well as to excessive rates of population growth. Instead of symbolizing growth, as it did in the West, urbanization in South Asia is an aspect of continued poverty.

Chapter 6

NATIONAL OUTPUT AND STRUCTURE OF ECONOMY

What a country produces and how much its people earn for their efforts play central roles in the discussion of underdevelopment and development in South Asia. We have argued that the levels of these factors are at best only rough indicators of the levels of development. This qualification is heightened by the lack of statistics from so much of South Asia or the poor quality of those statistics now available. Throughout this chapter we will repeatedly stress the extreme frailty of the statistical material available. We deem this an important scientific task, since in the analysis of the development problems of these countries, unreliable figures are commonly used with a naive credulity that greatly impairs the value of the conclusions drawn.

It must also be remembered that in determining levels of national income in South Asia it is often misleading simply to relate the national income directly to the net geographical output. To begin with, not only is national income per head a very crude indicator of the degree of development or underdevelopment, but there are certain logical difficulties involved in the way such an aggregate is defined and the data are compiled. In the Philippines or Malaysia, for example, a substantial part of the total earnings is siphoned off in remittances to parent companies and profits to foreigners. However, in the days since independence, there have been curbs on such remittances and dividends. Some of the larger foreign holdings in other parts of South Asia have been nationalized. Taxes on alien-owned property have been increased. Native residents have been filling higher administrative posts and entering what used to be European economic preserves, so there has been some narrowing of the discrepancy between output and income. While all the figures on these indicators should be accepted with great caution, they can be useful if they are looked on as measures of output or of "potential income" for the average South Asian. In the latter regard they should become more realistic as native personnel increasingly take over ownership and control of the country's assets.

There is another problem with accounting of South Asian economies. This is the actual valuation of output. Large sections of the economy are non-monetized and without much link with any markets. It is difficult to put a value on this bartered output, and where this is done it implies that tastes and preferences in the monetized and bartered market are identical and that the prices would be similar if the bartered goods were sold for money.

Our judgment is that the data for India and the Philippines are perhaps the best in the region and those of Indonesia and South Vietnam the poorest. The rest fall somewhere in between. Yet even the material for India leaves very much to be desired, and if the Philippine data have received less criticism than the Indian, doubtless this is because they have not been examined so closely. It is extremely important to stress the frailty of the data, because to the extent that planning in South Asia relies on the data available, it is likely to be misguided, in some cases very seriously. Whether as a tool for planning or as an indicator of results, the statistics are unreliable and inadequate. Yet we have hazarded discussing these figures for several reasons.

In the first place, figures on national income play an important role in economic planning in the region. Indeed, changes in national income are frequently viewed as the main indicator of success or failure of development plans. Secondly, such comments as we have already made lay bare the overwhelming importance of clarifying the concepts and perhaps changing the entire focus of the discussion of development in South Asia. The uncritical application of Western concepts to a completely alien environment cannot, except by accident, materially assist in resolving the pressing problems of South Asia. Finally, there is, of course, a possibility that evidence presented here may have some rough relationship to reality. Thus it may not be too unreasonable to present these figures on the hypothesis that it is better to paint with a wide brush, of unknown thickness, than to leave the canvas blank.

Broadly speaking, the comparison of income per person indicates a wide disparity between the poorest country in the region—Pakistan, with an estimated income per head of only 220 rupees per year—and the most opulent— Malaya, with an average income of 780 rupees per person. If we eliminate Malaya, which stands out as exceptional, the spread narrows. Although the differences shown are not absolute, the following ranking may not be unreasonable: Pakistan and India emerge as the poorest countries; the Philippines, Thailand, Ceylon, and Malaya—in ascending order—appear relatively much better off; and Indonesia, Burma, and South Vietnam lie somewhere between.

The rates of change in individual incomes could perhaps be more meaningful. It should be noted that the concept of aggregate real output used differs from country to country. For this data to be comparable, this implies that the relationships between gross national product, gross domestic product, national income, and similar aggregates at either market prices or factor cost of some particular year, are stable for each country. This may or may not be true, since the sketchiness of the available data for most countries does not permit a close check of this point. Nonetheless, it does not seem unreasonable to assume a relatively high degree of stability of these relationships over time; at least there should not be so much instability as to render the comparisons meaningless.

These data would seem to suggest that Burma has exhibited by far the fastest rate of growth. But this conclusion must be qualified by noting that by 1960 the level of output per head was still probably about 15 percent below that prevailing in 1939. And there is a strong probability that stagnation or even decline has occurred in the recent decade. Indonesia showed what appears to be rapid growth during most of the 1950's, but national accounts are extremely unreliable. As things looked at the beginning of 1966, there seemed to be little prospect of rapid growth in Indonesia.

The general picture for South Asian countries whose data seem somewhat more reliable appears to be roughly as follows: Pakistan, Thailand, and Ceylon were relatively stagnant in terms of output per person. However, there are indications that in recent years Pakistan has emerged from the stagnation of the previous decade. Malaya recorded a slight gain of less than 7 percent in real gross domestic product per person in the seven years between 1955 and 1962, but a higher rate in more recent years. The Philippines showed a steady and fairly rapid growth of income per person during the 1950's, but in later years this index showed a tendency to decline. In India it is believed that by 1948–49, income per person was almost 16 percent below the 1931–32 level. Except for the Philippines and Burma, the countries of South Asia had a very slow and erratic rise in output per person during the 1950's. During the first half of the 1960's, this indicator has declined or become negative except in Thailand, Malaya, and, to an extent, in Pakistan. Furthermore, recent levels of income per person may mostly be below whatever peak they reached in pre-war times.

When trying to get a broad picture of the structure of the economy in the South Asian countries, the natural course would be to break up the aggregate figure for national income into its component parts and relate the income originating in each main sector to the number of persons employed in, or earning their livelihood from, that sector. Unfortunately, the statistics on occupational distribution are especially unreliable. Indonesia and Burma have had no complete census for several decades, and the census data on occupational distribution for India, Pakistan, Ceylon, and the Philippines are known to be particularly weak. Nor can the figures for the other countries of the region be considered superior since many of them are listed as "estimates," "provisional," and so on. Thus we stress only the simple distinction between the agricultural and non-agricultural category. Even the simple two- or three-sector split-up of the national income aggregates leads to rather anomalous results which give even more emphasis to the doubts about the aggregate figures for national income or product.

Again, the definitions of "agricultural" and "non-agricultural" vary from country to country and the statistics coupled with these definitions are questionable. But it generally appears that over half the national income in South Asia originates from agriculture and some two-thirds to three-quarters of the people gain their livelihood from this source. In trying to determine the more important element of trends in agricultural production, we are again handicapped by inadequate and misleading statistics. But it appears that agricultural output per person remained relatively stagnant in the region as a whole during the 1950's and early 1960's. This must account in large measure for the failure of national income per person to show any signs of vigorous expansion.

In the structure of South Asian economies the non-agricultural category is, of course, a mixed bag. It includes such occupational groups as services, construction, manufacturing, mining, and commerce. Putting aside for the moment manufacturing industries and crafts, the general impression is that retail trade, domestic service, and government positions occupy an excessively large proportion of the population, particularly in view of the low productivity attached to such activities.

The proliferation of retail outlets and petty traders and the growing number of middlemen can easily be seen. Free-lance traders abound throughout the region, engaging in a sort of *ad hoc* trading. In 1947, more than half of the persons active in "commerce" in Malaya were hawkers and peddlers working for themselves. The large numbers engaged in such trading activities do not perform a very efficient or sophisticated function, nor is the turnover of retail trade very high. Indeed, this is clearly underutilization of labor, parallel to that in agriculture. The plethora of petty traders and peddlers is not so much a response to rising demand for their services as a reaction against the prevailing low productivity and cheapness of labor. This reaction, when coupled with a disinclination to work for an employer, induces a "push" into "own account" employment, stimulated by the meager capital and minimal skills required. A similar situation exists in traditional crafts, where markets have been dwindling because of imports and, in more recent years, expanding local industrialization. However, here there is a tendency to remain in the area of traditional crafts while performing less work. The growth of petty trading has been a response to a trend toward urbanization that is neither related to nor caused by rising employment opportunities in the industrial sector. Both reactions perpetuate the low levels of labor input and labor efficiency.

Conditions are not fundamentally different in the realm of government jobs. Public expenditures for government activity have risen in response to the needs of development efforts and newly won independence, but the number of people employed in the civil service has risen much more significantly. Only part of it is called for by an extension of essential governmental activities. It cannot be denied that key personnel of high quality are too few in number and probably overworked as well, but much of the rise in employment occurs at the lower levels of the civil service hierarchy. Inefficient use of manpower in government is certainly not unknown in the West, but it appears to be far more extensive in South Asia. Duplication of functions, splitting of departments into new ones with parallel tasks, noting and passing of files through many hands, all tend to expand employment in the public sector at the expense of efficiency. It may seem that efficient use of manpower is less essential when the labor force is large and underutilized; however, such a growth in bureaucracy causes delays in important development projects and is essentially inflationary, since incomes are paid for no corresponding increase in output. What is more, the aim of development plans is to raise output per person, and any type of boondoggling, either public or private, is detrimental.

In South Asia, one explanation for this increasing waste in the public sector is the pressure exerted by the so-called "educated" unemployed in the towns. They seek clerical positions, and they attach very high prestige to civil service posts. The inability of the soft state to resist such pressures doubtless accounts for the rise in the number of lower civil servants out of proportion to real needs.

It is worth noting that 1960 census estimates available for Malaya, Ceylon, Pakistan, and the Philippines all indicate a rise in the proportion of the labor force working in "services and commerce," as we noted above. The number in "services" alone exceeded that in manufacturing for these countries and also for Thailand and India. This indicates the comparatively minor role that industry presently plays in the economies of the region. The data are statistically unreliable, but they confirm in a vague way what is generally known: the widely held view that the number of persons in tertiary occupations increases as a country becomes richer is not applicable to the under-developed countries in South Asia. Even though few countries in the region appear to have made much economic progress, especially compared with the pre-war situation, most of them have a very high percentage of their non-agricultural population in tertiary employment, and this percentage is increasing. There is a continuing growth of population in the face of relative stagnation in agriculture and an inability of the as yet tiny industrial sector to absorb much of this increase. There is a push into petty trading, services, and the like. And this provides yet another example of a particular trend that accompanies economic growth in the West but in South Asia is more symptomatic of failure to achieve rapid growth. Thus, as we saw in the trend toward urbanization, quite contradictory forces can produce processes in South Asia that are analogous to those experienced in the West. And as we have stressed, the applicability of Western developmental processes in South Asia should be regarded as questionable.

We believe that plantations in South Asia should be considered as industrialized agriculture. They play the dominant role in export programs in Ceylon and Malaya and to a smaller degree in Indonesia. Most of the exports in South Asia are agriculture products, and exports constitute a significant percentage of national income. We should not be surprised, therefore, to find that the ratio of exports to national income is highest for Ceylon and Malaya, with the largest acreage in plantations, and lowest for Pakistan and India. From this it could easily be concluded that present levels of income per person could be directly affected by the predominance of an agricultural sector organized along plantation lines with a heavy export orientation.

This suggests that two main avenues of growth are open to the poorer countries: to rationalize agricultural techniques and to reduce the relative significance of traditional agriculture. Both imply some sort of industrialization, which all countries in South Asia are now emphasizing. However, concentration on one or a few export crops, although this appears to account for higher levels of income per person, creates a precarious situation. Not only does it subject the entire economy to the substantial instability of fluctuating markets; in addition, the prospects of such concentration do not appear conducive to rapid or sustainable growth. Putting all the eggs in one basket is a dangerous way to live and an improbable basis for steady development. Apart from these questions, only Malaya and Indonesia have the space to extend plantation acreage, particularly in rubber. Ceylon has less room, but much can be done to raise yields on existing acreage through replanting and fertilizers. For the other countries, the prime focus must be on ordinary agriculture. Here the analogy to past Western experience is much closer except for two ominous facts: first, a significant rise in agricultural productivity has not taken place prior to industrialization; second, whatever "agricultural revolution" is induced must be achieved despite a population growth rate that is two or three times greater than those of Western economies in their early periods of development. The population growth casts a long shadow, because, even at best, industrial development can grow only very slowly.

Since the South Asian countries look to industrialization outside the agricultural sector, it is important to study the present structure and trends in manufacturing.

Any nation attempting to industrialize without adequate natural resources will have to import substantial amounts of raw materials. The relative burden of such imports depends largely on the levels of wages and labor productivity. If these levels are high—implying a highly disciplined and efficient labor force and large capital investment—the costs of these imports will obviously be less of a hindrance to economic growth. These costs will take up a smaller share of the total production costs and the imports they buy will be more effectively used. There have been nations that industrialized without any appreciable natural resources, including Denmark, Switzerland, and Japan. Their success seems largely attributable to their high degree of labor discipline and efficiency.

However, where capital is scarce and labor is plentiful and cheap, it is difficult to raise productivity simply by capital investment. A combination of capital scarcity with low levels of labor skills, work discipline, and efficiency results in low productivity and wages in South Asian economies. This in turn makes the relative burden of importing raw materials more severe. It is the combination of these adverse features that makes the South Asian resource endowment more significant than it would otherwise be.

In general, nature has not been particularly generous to South Asia. Only India possesses iron ore, coal, or power resources in quantities adequate for a high degree of industrialization. Some countries in the region are endowed with one or a few major metals, and exports of these ores provide an important source of foreign exchange earnings. Yet only India has a favorable combination of resources for industrial development. On the other hand, few of the countries have really been pushing against the limitations of their natural resources. Where these are being exploited, it is often only for export of the raw material, rather than to supply an expanding domestic industry. In part, this reflects the lack of a favorable resource combination. But it must be stressed that the very meager extent of industrialization in South Asia is less a result of few resources than of other limitations and inhibitions.

Despite the problem of classifying the types of manufacturing in South Asia, it is apparent that in India, Pakistan, and the Philippines, a much higher share of the manufacturing is in consumer goods than in the United States and the Western countries generally. By 1960 India had three new steel plants, and there has since been a sharp increase in mechanical industries, but they still constitute a very small sector, and India's industrial structure has not changed very much despite its earlier start. Another outstanding feature is the predominance of textiles in India and Pakistan and the amount of food processing in the Philippines. This reflects the lack of diversity generally found in underdeveloped countries. In India, for example, five major industries—basic iron and steel, cement, paper, cotton textiles, and sugar—accounted for 60 percent of the employment of all twenty-nine industries included in the 1951 census and generated about 60 percent of the total value added. In the other countries virtually all of what little manufacturing there is concentrates on handicrafts and the processing of raw materials. Heavy industry, producing consumer durable goods, is conspicuously absent, except in India.

But of greater importance for future industrialization than the specific types of products is the nature of the so-called "industrial" establishments within particular branches of manufacturing. There are three main types: cottage industry, small in scale and frequently confined to a single dwelling unit, as the name implies; small-scale industry, using modern techniques, which produces radio sets, bicycle parts, electric motors, furniture, soap, and so on; and large-scale industry, using large capital investments and raw materials. In India there is an overwhelming preponderance of cottage industry. Almost 70 percent of the workers questioned in a 1955 survey reported that they were employed in this type of manufacturing. Over two-thirds of Indian manufacturing employment occurs in enterprises with fewer than five workers. It may be assumed that most such establishments lack mechanical power, in view of the rural location of so many cottage industries and the general lack of rural electrification in India. This disproportionate concentration on cottage and small-scale industry results in a major economic disadvantage, since so much of what is produced is consumed locally, with little of it going for export and the foreign currency earnings most South Asian nations need so badly.

The Indian pattern is fairly typical of the region as a whole. South Asian industry is dominated by rural enterprises using little capital and employing few workers, whose output is very low per worker. Not only does this keep down the over-all level of industrial productivity, but it tends to perpetuate the low living levels of rural areas. The familiar pattern of cumulative causation appears once more: output per man in cottage industry is limited by the constricted village market, which in turn is limited by low agricultural and, to a lesser extent, industrial productivity. Thus both the ability and the incentive of cottage enterprises to increase efficiency are blunted by existing circumstances. Again we arrive at the question of how to break out of the trap of low-level productivity on the village level.

Were it not for the enormous numbers of people involved in cottage industry, an obvious solution would be to stake everything on accelerating the growth of factories. But large-scale, and even small-scale, modernized enterprises are generally labor-saving, with high capital investment. Neither feature is particularly attuned to economies characterized by large-scale underutilization of the labor force and capital scarcity. A rapid destruction of cottage industry would not only eliminate a source of supplementary rural income but would also accentuate the push toward urbanization and further aggravate congestion in the urban areas, where those moving in so often turn to peddling and low-level commerce to survive. While trying to industrialize, the South Asian countries have more than sentimental reasons for protecting rural cottage industry, particularly in the field of consumer goods. Such a policy can perhaps be only a holding operation during a period of transition, but that period may have to be long.

Chapter 7

LEVELS OF LIVING

AND INEQUALITY

By levels of living we mean the amount of goods and services regularly consumed by the average person in the various countries of the region. The high degree of inequality that exists implies that the masses of people in the lower income strata have levels of living much below those indicated by the average figures.

Levels of living are, in themselves, important. Indeed, it is a major goal of planning for development in the region to raise the abysmally low levels of living for the mass of the people. In circular causation a rise in levels of living is likely to improve almost all other conditions, in particular the effort put into work and the efficiency of labor, and thus productivity. Equally, attitudes and institutions are affected by rises in these levels.

To begin with, it is important to note that a rise in the levels of living has a much greater instrumental value in the South Asian than in the advanced countries, where the levels are already so high that a change in them has little or no effect on productivity. In the West, therefore, individual and group income can be clearly divided into two parts: that spent for consumption and that saved and invested. The level of living in these countries can be measured by subtracting these savings from total income, and the savings then correspond to tangible assets accumulated through the non-consumption of some part of the current output. But in the underdeveloped countries of South Asia, levels of living are so low as seriously to impair health, vigor, and attitudes toward work. Consequently, increases in most types of consumption represent *at the same time* "investment," as they have direct effect on productivity. This is one more reason for the inapplicability, for South Asia, of the conventional post-war approach and of economic models which stress the relationships among output, employment, savings, and investment.

Under closer scrutiny it becomes apparent that the published statistics on "savings," meaning non-consumed incomes, are so utterly frail that they are not useable. Under these circumstances it is more honest to resort to the income levels, referred to in the previous chapter, without attempting to subtract "savings," which anyhow usually do not amount to more than a few percentage points, if that much, for the masses of the people. When following this course it has to be remembered that besides "savings" going into investments that are internally financed, much of the national incomes are going into unproductive expenditures, in particular for military purposes. These types of expenditures have in most South Asian countries shown sharp increases, prompted in part by India's border conflict with China, the tension and fighting between India and Pakistan over Kashmir, Indonesia's "confrontation" of Malaysia, and the war in Vietnam. Given a relatively static level of national output, the accelerated defense activities reduce the amounts left over for food, clothing, shelter, and other household needs.

· · ·

The whole idea of expressing an average level of living by one single figure, when levels of living vary so greatly within the countries and between the countries, is an extravagant one. This, of course, is particularly true when comparisons are made between one of the countries in the region and a rich, developed country. To say, for instance, that the level of living in the United States is 15, 20, or 30 times as high as in a particular South Asian country is meaningless. More meaningful would be comparisons in terms of the goods and services actually consumed. For making such comparisons, however, there are not many reliable statistical sources.

In choosing those items that seem to cover the most pertinent aspects of levels of living in South Asia, we list the following: food and nutrition; clothing; housing, including sanitation; health and educational facilities; information media; energy consumption; and transportation. For each of these components, there is some imperfect, summary statistical evidence available. But in making comparisons with the Western developed countries, and even between South Asian countries, there are hazards.

There are vast differences in quality, especially compared with the West. South Asian foodstuffs frequently have a low nutritional value, those sold in the market are often adulterated, and they are, at least for the bulk of the population, available in far less variety than in the West. Thus the differences in amount of consumption understate by a substantial degree the actual discrepancy between South Asia and the West. Moreover, and perhaps more important, the averages fail to reveal the enormous inequality in the consumption of various items by different income, social, or ethnic groups in South Asia, between urban and rural areas, and even between various regions in a country itself. Many of the items for which data are available are consumed, in large part, by a tiny upper-class minority, usually concentrated in the urban centers.

It is true that differentials between income groups, social classes, and rural and urban areas exist in developed countries as well, but the degree of inequality is far less than in South Asia. Few regions of the United States, for example, do not have electricity; most rural homes have radios, television sets, telephones, and mechanical conveniences.

In South Asia, almost two-thirds or more of total private consumption expenditures are for food, whereas in the developed economies the proportion is normally well below two-fifths. Thus a very pertinent indicator of levels of living is provided by food consumption, as measured by the total calories consumed by each person daily. This calorie intake, estimated in 1958, ranged from Pakistan's 2,030 calories to Malaya's 2,290. These figures compare with 3,100 in the United States and 3,290 in Britain. The variance within South Asia follows fairly closely the variance in income per person, with Pakistan at the bottom and Malaya at the top. There are deviations from this in rice-exporting Burma and Thailand, where food consumption is better than their general economic situation, while the opposite is true for Ceylon, which relies heavily on imported foodstuffs. Even these estimates may be questioned, because they are based on population sizes, which are often underrated. Thus the narrow differences in food supply among the South Asian countries may not be real at all, and there may be substantial differences both in levels of consumption and in the order of rank.

But one thing is clear: while calorie intake in the advanced countries significantly exceeds requirements, in South Asia it falls short of minimum needs by at least 10 percent and probably by much more, except possibly in Malaya. Moreover, because of the serious inequalities in what is consumed, a substantial proportion of the population receives even less than these low averages.

There has been some improvement in calorie intake in the Philippines and in India. Comparisons with pre-war

times, although inconclusive, suggest that by 1958 the
calorie supply slightly surpassed the 1934–38 level in the
Philippines and the Indian subcontinent but was about
the same or a little lower elsewhere.

Another facet of the South Asian food situation—the
monotony of the diet—is clearly shown by the available
evidence. Cereals constitute more than 70 percent of the
Pakistani calorie intake and about two-thirds of the Indian and Philippine, compared with less than one-quarter
in the United States. In the Far East as a whole, it has
been estimated that staple cereals and starch roots com-
prise about three-quarters of the average diet. This heavy
reliance on one or a few crops not only fails to provide the
needed balance of protective elements against disease, but
leaves the consumer precariously vulnerable to crop failures caused by adverse weather or plant disease. The low
consumption of meat throughout South Asia leads to
anemia due to iron deficiency.

The monotony of the diet is not caused by poverty
alone, although poverty is the main reason why people
embrace one staple food, like rice or wheat. Ignorance of
the nutritional value of various foods and tastes that disregard nutritional considerations, together with poor
methods of food preparation, also play a part. Thus the
deficiency of vitamin A, which may affect vision and
which is caused by a paucity of green leafy vegetables, is
not always most common in the lowest income group.
Deficiency of vitamin B, and consequent susceptibility to
beriberi, has been on the increase since the Second World
War, because people have turned more and more to
polished rice, which tastes better than home-husked rice
and is easier to handle. Another factor aggravating the
food situation is the inadequacy of storage and transportation facilities. Although no statistical data are available, it is known that large quantities of cereals and other
foodstuffs are spoiled by heat and humidity or are de-
voured by birds, rats, or insects.

In summary, it is probably safe to say that the average South Asian simply does not get enough to eat. Even where food intake is above starvation level, its nutritional content is generally insufficient to provide minimal safeguards to health. Above all, there has been no substantial improvement in diets since the 1930's.

The monotony observed in the South Asian diet carries over into clothing. Moreover, the poorer classes do not consume anywhere near the national average in textiles. Large numbers of South Asians have only one set of clothing, which is seldom washed except in bathing. The same clothes are worn day and night, since pyjamas and even underwear are luxuries a great many people can ill afford. While most of the South Asian climate is warm enough to require very little clothing, there are many millions whose raiment is well below minimum standards of health. It should also be remembered that large sections of northern India and Pakistan have cold seasons with low night temperatures, as do the mountain regions elsewhere in South Asia. Those people fortunate enough to possess blankets here must often use them to protect their cattle against the cold. Figures of textile consumption per person tell nothing about everyday realities such as these.

For the most part, housing conditions in South Asia are as poor as the food and clothing. The majority of the people live in poorly built, overcrowded, unsanitary, and scantily furnished homes lacking nearly all the amenities. Indeed, next to insufficient food, poor housing is the most obvious component of the low levels of living. There are also important geographical differences in the quality of housing. The situation is less desperate in those rural areas where lumber is available, as it is in much of Southeast Asia and, to a lesser extent, in the hilly regions of India and Ceylon. In central India and West Pakistan, where the climate is arid, more than two-thirds of the

houses are built of mud, which is easily eroded and far
from rainproof. But if housing in the rural areas is generally inadequate, there is little variation in the extent of
squalor in the slum areas of large cities. The situation has
worsened in the last decade of rapid urban growth. Today
the bulk of the urban population lives in dwellings far
more crowded and inadequately ventilated, and usually
with poorer sanitation facilities, than those in rural areas.
It has been conservatively estimated that from one-
quarter to one-half of all city dwellers live in slums or
makeshift arrangements. Large numbers do not even possess these miserable shelters, and must sleep under
monuments and bridges or on the open streets. Even some
industrial workers suffer from unhealthy housing conditions. In the hovels set up for migrant laborers, who are
obliged to leave their families behind in the villages, there
may be forty to fifty men living, with one or two women,
in a room licensed for less than a quarter of that number.

Directly related to the housing problem is the problem
of sanitation. Again the deficiencies are tremendous and
improvement slow. This is particularly obvious in the case
of water and sewerage facilities. In rural areas, the shal-
low wells are usually open and may be merely holes dug
in the ground. Very little is done to clean them and other
water sources, or to use disinfectants. On the contrary,
each villager helps spread disease from house to house as
he draws water in his bucket. Waterways that serve
household purposes also serve for transport and carrying
away wastes. As most villages and even many urban areas
lack sewerage, refuse is thrown into lanes and backyards,
where flies breed unhampered, and is washed into water
sources by the rains.

The greatest problem of all is perhaps the disposal of
human waste. In the rural districts throughout South
Asia, it is common practice to defecate in the fields and
bushes near human habitation. In consequence, people
walking barefoot are daily exposed to hookworm. The

wind-blown fecal dust makes eyes sore. When it rains the parasites that thrive in human waste are washed into streams and wells. Where there are latrines, they are usually poorly constructed and unclean. In many cities, especially in the slums, sanitary provisions are hardly better and may be worse. According to a recent estimate, roughly 6 percent of the total population of India has a protected water supply, while only 3 percent has a sewerage system. In the absence of safe water supply and proper sewage disposal, it is no wonder that South Asia abounds in diseases spread by inadequate sanitation. And in the face of this constant threat of disease, there are crippling shortages of doctors and auxiliary health personnel and hospital facilities. Those that are available usually tend to serve only the wealthy in the cities.

South Asia's supplies of fuel and electricity are, in general, far below minimal standards in the developed countries of the West. There is little rural electrification anywhere in South Asia. Except for a few weak oil lamps, most of the villages are completely dark after sunset. Even if the literacy rate were far higher and newspapers and books were available in rural communities, the inadequate lighting would preclude much reading. This, of course, stands in the way of raising standards of literacy and increasing the availability of printed matter. The familiar mechanism of circular causation with cumulative effects is once again apparent.

In general, transportation is also insufficient throughout the area. Small-scale inland and coastal shipping and movement by bicycle, draft animal, and small boat are the important forms of transport in South Asia. Indeed, in India, where roads are very poor, bullock carts may still be carrying more freight than railways. Road transport has grown relative to rail transport. Only in a few areas, such as Malaya, has the building of roads kept pace with this increase in motor traffic. Yet a continued rise in goods and passenger facilities is indispensable for economic progress, not only to widen the market but to break down regional isolation as well. One difficulty, of course, is the heavy concentration of transport facilities in the urbanized areas. Until the vast rural areas are brought within the network of improved transportation and distribution, regional inequalities will widen and the backwash effects will help perpetuate rural poverty. Industry will continue to be of an enclave character even though under control of indigenous personnel.

The plight of the masses in the underdeveloped economies of South Asia would be serious enough if income were evenly distributed. That way, each inhabitant or income recipient in each country would receive an amount equal to the extremely low national average. Instead, the high degree of inequality that exists means that the vast majority in each nation are forced to eke out an existence on annual incomes well below the already inadequate national average.

The proportion of income received by the very lowest and the very highest income groupings is larger in the underdeveloped countries than in the developed. In the developed countries high income taxes, progressively larger on higher incomes, tend to equalize the average income. At the lower end of the scale in the developed countries, the social welfare services available also tend to equalize. But in South Asia tax collections are notoriously lax and the social policies, such as they are, rather tend to benefit the not-so-poor income strata. But even if the given degree of over-all inequality were comparable to that of the developed countries, it would be worse for South Asia, because a given degree of inequality wreaks considerably more hardship on the less developed economies and is much more serious than appears on the surface.

Furthermore, in contrast to the developed countries, a South Asian's social and economic position tends to be static. Inequality of income at a particular point of time is more permanent in South Asia. In a Western setting, not only does the average level of income tend to rise rather rapidly, but individuals have more opportunity to improve their relative income positions. The opportunities for advance afforded to individuals in the lowest income group in the West are far greater than in the corresponding group in South Asia, even if both obtain the same share of total income. A high turnover or circulation of individuals in different income classes typifies the West, but not South Asia. Further, in South Asia the extent of inequality within occupations or sectors appears to be much greater than in the developed countries. Problems of finding comparable occupational classifications and other statistical deficiencies preclude much valid empirical documentation of this assertion. On *a priori* grounds, however, a higher degree of occupational and regional inequality is to be expected where mobility is restricted. Large wage and salary differentials of a non-equalizing kind can obviously persist longer when possibilities for economic and social movement are few. Since economic and social rigidity is far greater in South Asia than in the Western countries, it follows that inequalities within particular segments of the South Asian economies are more substantial and persistent than in the West.

In South Asia, low average income, income inequality, and social stratification are causally interrelated. But social stratification is itself an aspect of inequality. The degree of income inequality among the poorer classes in South Asia cannot be very great, since their average income is so close to the bare subsistence level. Thus it may well be that the upper strata in a poor village in India do not have a significantly higher income than sharecropping tenants or landless peasants. Yet there is an important difference between these groups: the former often receive incomes without working while the latter do not. A distribution of income by social strata would therefore indicate a high degree of equality when in fact the social structure is harshly inegalitarian.

Hence, far more pronounced inequalities would appear if distribution statistics could be made to reflect the broader facts of social stratification. Particularly in the South Asian rural setting, inequality is in fact mainly a question of land ownership—with which are associated leisure, enjoyment of status, and authority. There is a close connection between these economic and social factors. Inequality in social status often lessens desire for productivity. Leisure becomes highly prized when there is little more to be gained by working. The fact that everyone in a village may be almost equally poor does not imply that everyone is equal; on the contrary, they are all so poor because they are so unequal. Even in those cases where income inequality is less than in the West—mainly among the poorer classes—the fact of far greater social inequality not only offsets this but ensures the perpetuation of rigidity and lack of opportunity.

The effects of inequality have been heightened by the evidence that in some South Asian countries where there has been some increase in the tempo of development, it has been the tiny upper and middle classes whose income has increased more rapidly than that of the poor. Here again comparisons between South Asia today and the developing West of yesterday are irrelevant. It is generally believed that in the early stages of industrialization in Western Europe the distribution of income became more unequal and only later, with the diffusion of side effects and the increase in social legislation, was this reversed. But the opposite is true in South Asia. As with urbanization and the relative growth of subsidiary industries, the apparent increase in inequality has not been accompanied by rapid growth.

There also appears to be a growing inequality in South

Asia between various regions in the individual countries and between urban and rural workers. For example, monthly consumption expenditures per person in India are estimated as about one-third higher in the towns than in villages, and in cities more than twice those in rural areas. In Thailand, a rice exporting country, a Bangkok survey indicated that the urban diet was far superior to the rural. There is also a great discrepancy in income between the professionals and the workers in the cities. Where in Western countries the ratio between the income of professionals and industrial workers may be three or four to one, it is fifteen or twenty to one in Asia.

Finally, in South Asia there is often a particular form of inequality governed by ethnic lines. In Ceylon, for example, there is wide disparity between the average incomes of Ceylon Tamils and Tamils who have immigrated from India. This is largely explained by the large number of traders with high incomes among the Ceylon Tamils. In Malaya, where the ethnic Chinese and Indians specialize in plantation work or generally occupy the top rungs in the professions and commerce, there is an inevitable income gap between them and the Malays, who are largely rural paddy growers and workers on small holdings, or are low-paid drivers, messengers, and clerks. But again, among the ethnic Chinese in Malaya, Singapore, and Thailand there is a vast difference between top income and that of the coolie laborers.

The story is similar in other countries of the region, although in India and Pakistan caste and religion are more important than purely racial distinctions. There are also the extreme instances of inequality found in all the former European colonies because of the concentration of Westerners in the higher paying business posts, even though several development plans have attempted to restrict these alien groups, including "Oriental aliens."

The foregoing specific manifestations of inequality are all closely interrelated. The entire structure of inequality is bolstered by the caste system, the color line, ethnic discrimination, nepotism, and the general set of social and religious taboos. The vicious circle of cumulative inter-relation and causation is thus perpetuated. Present institutional arrangements impede the rise of social, regional, and occupational mobility and perpetuate the persistence of segmentation in social and economic life. This is a major obstacle to economic growth.

Chapter 8

FOREIGN TRADE AND CAPITAL FLOWS

In Western Europe, increases in exports once paved the way for importing capital goods that perpetuated and stimulated development. In South Asia, investment in plantations and mines helped expand these initial activities. That is why, today, income levels in Ceylon and Malaya exceed those in India and Pakistan. In Western Europe, North America, and Australasia, industrial development took place initially through a buoyant and expanding volume of international trade. In South Asia the rising demand for the region's raw materials was filled by enterprises mostly initiated and run by foreigners from the West European countries, who sent their profits home, bought their manufactured goods from abroad, and seldom assimilated with the local population. While export opportunities expanded for South Asia right up to World War I, they failed to trigger rapid over-all growth in the region's economies. Since independence, as we have noted, efforts have been made to gain more local benefits from these foreign-dominated enterprises. The beneficial effects on the region's economy should have thus been greater since independence than before. However, the international situation has changed. There is no longer any significant stimulus to be derived from expanding export markets. In fact, demand for most of South Asia's traditional exports is expected to rise hardly at all. Nature has not only been stingy with resources for South Asia, but now the world demand for those the region does have is stagnant.

What is more, while export expansion and diversification are made difficult enough by all of the internal barriers implicit in the very notion of underdevelopment, the problems are aggravated by the restrictive import policies of the industrial countries. The developed countries of the West all too frequently impose tariffs, quotas, and other restrictions upon the products of allegedly "cheap" foreign labor. Nor have the Communist countries yet adopted trade policies that would assure substantial outlets for manufactured products from South Asia.

If development is to occur in the South Asian countries, it will not come as a response to foreign demand for the products in which the region has traditionally had a comparative advantage. Not only does this fact mean that economic growth is a more difficult task than it was when the developed countries confronted this problem, but it also implies that there will be much more autarky and much less "automatic" response to external forces in the growth process itself. Development must mostly be internally based and deliberately prodded and nurtured, since the spontaneous growth-inducing stimulus of a relatively free and expanding international trade is no longer present.

Factual material on foreign trade and the flow of capital in and out of South Asia is comparatively superior to other economic data and thus the conclusions drawn from it are less qualified. The countries with the highest income per person, Ceylon and Malaya, have the highest ratio of foreign trade, while India and Pakistan, the poorest countries, have the lowest. Exports and imports, as a proportion of national income, are less than 10 percent for India and Pakistan, while for Ceylon and Malaya they are over 30 percent. With its plantations and mines, Malaya exports more than Pakistan, whose population is nearly twelve times as large.

As indicative as the general foreign trade ratios may be, the significant aspect of the foreign sector is the composition of exports and imports, and more especially the lack of variety among them. In five of the South Asian countries one commodity makes up more than 50 percent of the export total; these countries are Burma (rice), Pakistan (jute), South Vietnam and Malaya (rubber), and Ceylon (tea). Only three countries have more than one major export. The Philippines sells sugar and cocoanuts; Indonesia, rubber and petroleum; and Thailand, rice and rubber. And only India has significant exports of manufactured goods. Further, with the exception of rice, there is very little internal demand for any of these commodities, and virtually all of what is produced is exported. This makes the South Asian countries uniquely dependent on external markets—over which they have little influence, at least on the demand side. In the absence of any internal markets, their economies are more sensitive to changes in external demand, since there is nothing to cushion the shock of a decline in foreign buying. The instability of export earnings, even for those countries that export little, creates recurrent crises in balance of payments that not only divert attention from other facets of development, but also impede the importing of vital developmental products.

Some types of imports are clearly essential for development. In these we include that portion of food imports that could not be further reduced without adversely affecting nutritional levels. India, Pakistan, and Indonesia were until recently at a point where there was little scope for reducing food imports as a means of increasing imports of capital goods. These three countries, then, are particularly vulnerable either to a rise in import prices or to a decline in export earnings. The other countries in the region are not concentrating their imports on essentials to the same extent. A reduction in their imports would probably have a much less serious effect on development as long as the reduction could be confined to non-essentials.

This must not be taken to imply that to have a large proportion of non-essential imports is desirable. It may be regarded as a sign of general affluence in a developed country, but not in an underdeveloped one. But if a nation is poor and has geared its developmental planning in such a way that essential imports constitute a very large proportion of total imports, as is the case with India and Pakistan, any substantial cutback in imports will seriously disrupt planned development. Therefore, although India and Pakistan have the lowest ratios of imports and exports to national income in the region, the composition of their imports gives the foreign sector a strategic significance out of proportion to its size. Countries like Malaya and Ceylon, with foreign earnings from their exports, can afford to buy abroad not only large quantities of manufactured consumer goods, but also much of their food.

More recently each South Asian country's import list has been affected by the relative intensity of its development efforts. The poorer countries have been forced to reduce drastically their non-essential imports, especially of consumer goods. They have been further pressed by the rising expenditures for defense materials, which require outlays of precious hard currency. India and Pakistan have gone farthest in this direction and little scope appears to be left for significant changes in their import picture. As a result of these factors, India and Pakistan in particular have been forced into policies of import substitution, of making do with locally manufactured goods and materials or doing without, and their scope for policy in general has been severely restricted.

Another striking aspect of South Asian foreign trade is its orientation toward far distant countries. Between 50 and 60 percent of exports from India, Pakistan, and Ceylon are sent to Western Europe and North America. More than two-thirds of South Vietnam's exports and over 70 percent of Philippine exports go to these same areas. Only the big rice exporters, Burma and Thailand, and to a lesser extent Indonesia, send significant shares of their exports to other South Asian countries. The import situation is quite as striking. Malaya, Singapore, Ceylon, and Thailand receive between 30 and 45 percent of their imports from North America and Western Europe. The other countries in the region receive more than half of their imports from these sources.

Now that colonialism has ended in South Asia, those in charge of the economic destiny of the region view the present economic structure not as something static but as a base for a new departure. Regardless of the diligence with which they pursue the goal of development, however, their efforts may be thwarted by factors over which they have no control. All the countries of the region are excessively dependent on external conditions, and the trends in foreign trade over the past several decades and the prospects inherent in these trends are such as to have a seriously adverse influence on the growth prospects of every country. Since the late 1920's, world trade as a whole in processed goods has increased more than world trade in primary commodities. Because South Asia depends so much on these commodities, the whole trend of world trade has been against the region. Moreover, it is significant and ominous that the increase in international trade in these primary commodities since the late 1920's for the world as a whole has exceeded that for the South Asian countries. If we exclude petroleum, the volume of exports from South Asia at the end of the 1950's appears to have remained about the same as in 1927–29. If rubber is also excluded, the volume has declined by about 25 percent. The demand for four of South Asia's major exportable items—rice, sugar, cotton, and jute—has lagged well behind economic growth in the West. The region has also been hurt by the increase in synthetic fibres and synthetic rubber. Added to this, again, is the pressure from rising technical efficiency, trade barriers, and surpluses, especially in the United States and Canada. Economic growth in many industries using South Asian raw materials has not been translated into an equivalent growth in demand for these materials.

Part of the explanation of this over-all export stagnation lies on the side of supply. Wartime destruction—which was particularly heavy in Burma and Indonesia—in conjunction with post-war political disturbances prevented full recovery and reduced total exports for a part of the post-war period. In addition, population increase has tended to diminish exportable surpluses in some lines. Domestic consumption in India and Pakistan, for example, has taken up much of the increased supply of jute and cotton. In contrast to the stagnant export trends, import needs and actual imports as well have risen sharply. In the vital matter of food, the rise in production has been slow and the population increase has been rapid, with the result that the exporting countries have had less food available for export and the importing countries have had to increase their purchases. South Asia, which until World War II had been a net exporter of food, has turned into a net importer, with an ever greater deficit.

In summary, for the region as a whole, the past three or four decades have witnessed a steady acceleration of import needs in the face of export potentialities that exhibit no comparable dynamism. Indeed, the sharp fluctuations in actual export earnings produced by world market trends, which in themselves are falling below chronically rising import needs, are apt to involve almost all the South Asian countries in a series of acute and worsening balance of payments crises.

South Asia's dependence on Western Europe export markets, the traditional pattern of colonial trade, was actually greater in 1961–62 than in 1948. Exports to Communist countries are now somewhat larger than before the war, though not in real terms. In general, over-all trade with the East European Communist countries has been rising at a considerable pace, whereas trade with China has been falling off. At the same time, there has been a decline in trade within the region. There has been an increasing awareness that this trend, coupled with the generally unfavorable export climate, will deter economic growth. This fact should give added importance to attempts to stimulate trade within the region. But even with the best will and effort, this is a difficult task.

The general lack of economic growth in itself inhibits such efforts. Each nation tries to pare down its imports to goods required for development purposes, such as capital equipment and heavy machinery. The effect, naturally, is discrimination against other South Asian countries where this type of equipment is also in short supply. Since it is easiest for an underdeveloped economy to achieve independence in those lines that require little in the way of scarce capital, the effect is to stimulate development of industries that are competitive with those of the other underdeveloped South Asian countries. Further, the colonial trade policies linked South Asian countries with home markets but not with each other. Thus transport and communication networks were not set up to foster intra-regional trade. There was no rapid rate of economic expansion after independence, and the countries of the region were denied the flexibility this would have brought. Its absence has been of overriding importance in impeding the growth of intra-regional trade.

Equally, political frictions and traditional antipathies have divided the region, and in some instances these have grown worse after independence. India and Pakistan have fought over Kashmir, and this struggle has been beclouded by religious antagonism and reflected elsewhere in the region. Indians, who are generally disliked by the Burmese, have now largely been driven out of Burma. Relations between India and Ceylon were strained when laws were passed adversely affecting the Indian Tamils on the plantations and, to an extent, the Ceylonese Tamils in the North. Bitterness between Thailand and Cambodia led to a wrangle over the disposition of a Buddhist temple. Petty jealousies bolstered by ethnic and religious distinctions pervade the whole of South Asia. The smaller countries of the region are also inherently suspicious of the bigger ones. All of these tensions have deep historical roots, and they have not been diminishing. On the contrary, within the framework of economic stagnation, rising nationalist sentiment, and the alignment of South Asia with the major powers in the cold war, dissention appears to be increasing.

In terms of trade—defined as the unit value of exports divided by the unit value of imports—the outlook for South Asia is mixed, but there is no clear evidence of a long-term trend toward improvement for the countries of South Asia in recent decades. Although individual countries have fared differently, the indicators point to a similar movement toward deterioration in the future, particularly if the area persists in relying so heavily on primary commodity exports. In this, the South Asian countries are placed at an added disadvantage because the developed countries are more adaptable toward changes in relative prices and can buy more heavily from a poorer country when prices are lower and cut back when the market is less favorable to the buyer. The effect of this may, however, be tempered by technological advances in the developed countries, which should help reduce the costs of imports needed by South Asian countries. Further, the increase in exports from the Communist countries to South Asia has created competitive pressures that could help in keeping import costs down.

Because their export earnings have failed to keep pace with their import needs, the South Asian countries have been confronted with an increasingly serious shortage of foreign exchange. Therefore the success of their developmental efforts will depend to an important degree on their ability to attract adequate amounts of foreign capital on reasonable terms. In the Western world there has been a gradual resumption of large-scale foreign investment, almost exclusively of the direct type. The United States, as the dominating creditor nation, has continued, however, to concentrate its investments in countries outside South Asia. But the Philippines, Malaya, Thailand, and, recently, Pakistan have secured some investments. Relatively little has gone to India and Ceylon, which at one time were able to attract foreign enterprise and investment.

With so little private capital forthcoming, the main burden of helping the South Asian countries meet their dire needs for imports over and above what their stagnating export returns could finance has fallen on foreign governments, and, until the post-Stalin era, exclusively on the Western governments and in particular the United States. In the immediate post-war period a shattered South Asia was wracked with struggles for independence and the attention of the giving nation was focussed on Europe. In the early 1950's, after the coming to power of a Communist government in China, the United States began showing more concern for the region, and this was translated into a growing volume of grants and loans. By the second half of the 1950's United States aid was accelerated as the cold war grew hotter. On a gradually increasing scale, South Asia also benefited from grants and loans from some Western European countries. And for the first time the Communist countries began to provide credits in increasing amounts. Although small in comparison with either the needs of the recipients or the capabilities of the richer countries, the current inflow of foreign aid and credit to South Asia far exceeded anything the region ever received in the past.

The main reason for the increase in aid was that South Asia had become politically important to the larger powers at the same time that internal instability and other factors had created a climate unfavorable to private foreign investment. But this pattern of capital movement renders such assistance less potentially stimulating to South Asian economic development. For one thing, the specific placement of financial assistance has not been uniquely related to economic considerations. From 1954 through 1958, for example, Laos and South Vietnam received from the United States grants and loans almost equal in total to those received by India and Pakistan. In general, however, the developmental efforts of South Vietnam and Laos scarcely warranted assistance of such magnitude; India, whose population is many times greater than that of these countries, was making considerably greater developmental efforts.

Also, much of the economic assistance given South Asia has had strings attached to it. Aside from political overtones that influence which countries receive assistance, the grants and loans themselves are often made for specific purposes. Sometimes they are given to provide showcases for the assisting country. In other instances, the recipient countries are required to spend the aid they receive in the donor countries or to have what they buy carried in that country's ships. Such restrictions prevent the most efficient utilization of foreign capital by those receiving it. Frequently this assistance has fluctuated in direct proportion to a country's political attitudes. A speech by a prime minister critical of the United States could, for example, cause a review of his country's aid prospects. Pursuit of strongly anti-American policies might, on the contrary, be rewarded with enlarged credits from the Soviet Union. A regime that threatens to collapse and fall into Communist hands can extract large amounts of U. S. funds. It is clear that the present system of bilateral aid has a strong tendency toward what, from an economic point of view, can only be construed as misallocation. It is impossible to say how much of the "economic" assistance to South Asia has been misplaced, but there is no doubt that much of it has been wasted or has even inhibited essential reforms.

All this suggests that greater reliance should be placed on loans from international agencies where the political element is less pronounced. Until a more appropriate mechanism is found for channelling external assistance on a larger scale and a long-term basis to those countries who most need it and deserve it, such assistance will remain insufficient, short run, *ad hoc,* and subject to radical shifts dictated by the political situation of the moment.

None of the economic realities we have outlined in this chapter has been favorable for most of South Asia, and the prospects for improvement in the future appear just as discouraging. But the South Asian countries must take what steps they can to fight the odds piling up against them.

They could diversify their exports by adding new primary products, by increasing saleable services, such as tourism, or by making new manufactured goods. But the resource base in South Asia does not seem adequate to generate many new supplies of materials for primary products, unless there were to be new discoveries. Services will no doubt be expanded in the next twenty years, but it is unlikely that they will be expanded enough to raise the import capacity very much. This leaves manufactured commodities as the best prospect for diversification. But with the exception of a few products, such as ceiling fans and sewing machines from India, cricket balls from Pakistan, and, of course, textiles, no South Asian country has been able to make major inroads into the markets for manufactured products in the industrialized countries.

There are both natural and artificial reasons for this state of affairs. There is the relatively poor raw material base to begin with, and this represents an important constraint when labor is inefficient, wages are low, and capital is not abundant. Even more fundamental is the difficulty of penetrating established markets, which is challenging enough for the best equipped countries. Cheap labor may well be available in South Asia. But unfortunately the inefficiency of both labor and management and the absence of specialized ancillary facilities tend to raise the cost per unit of output and thus offset the advantages of lower wage scales. Adding to the problem is the structure of import restrictions and tariffs levied by most of the large market countries.

Thus the South Asian countries find themselves in a dilemma: a rise in export earnings is essential to finance the imports they need, and manufactured products constitute the only area wherein exports might have much chance to grow. The achievement of viable and dynamic economic systems therefore rests largely on the ability of these countries to increase exports of manufactured goods. Yet branching out in this direction would encounter all the obstacles and inhibitions we have enumerated.

This means that if the rich countries want the countries of South Asia to succeed, they will have to go out of their way not only to remove artificial restrictions against South Asian manufactured goods, but also to create markets in their own countries for such products and to guarantee long-run freedom from import restrictions. This would require of the wealthier nations a greater degree of understanding in their approach to the underdeveloped countries and a greater willingness to resist powerful domestic pressures for short-run protective measures than they have hitherto shown. Politically it is far easier for the rich Western countries to provide grants and credits that enable their own commercial interests to increase their exports than it is for them to permit a volume of imports that may adversely affect some branch of domestic industry. Yet an increase in manufactured exports is potentially more stimulating to an underdeveloped economy than bilateral foreign grants and loans, which suffer from great uncertainty and other shortcomings. The slogan "Trade Not Aid" has real meaning for South Asia.

Along with diversification efforts, the South Asian countries have some small scope for trade increase by developing alternative markets. There are three major areas where this could occur: the Communist countries, the countries of South Asia itself, and the underdeveloped countries in Latin America, Africa, and West Asia.

It is possible that the Soviet Union and other European Communist countries may be pushing their own reserves of natural resources to the limit. Their industrialization efforts have brought them to the position where they could be major exporters of capital goods, and these could be directed toward the underdeveloped countries. In turn, the Communist countries could take more primary or traditional products from South Asia. Mutually beneficial trade on a considerably larger scale between the Communist countries and South Asia would therefore seem to be a distinct possibility. The Communist bloc constitutes an even greater potential market for consumer goods. Consumption expenditures have risen sharply in the Soviet Union since 1950, and while it is true that these come largely from within the bloc, there should be no reason to prevent their being bought from other countries. The

Communists appear, at present, to see both political and economic advantages in stepping up their trade with some South Asian countries, notably India. Further, they appear more flexible than the United States in their willingness to open their home markets to South Asian exports of consumer goods and products and to give long-term credits repayable in their own currencies.

Trade among the countries of South Asia provides another potential path of market expansion. Although the frictions within the area cloud the immediate prospects, the South Asian nations could work toward placing their import substitution efforts on a regional basis, enlarging the potential for one South Asian country to sell to another in an exchange of products from within the region. There could be, for example, a pooling of production in what was previously imported, coupled with specialization in certain goods by the individual countries. Over time the economic pressures will mount if exports to other parts of the world cannot be greatly expanded; hence, the desirability of closer regional economic integration or cooperation will grow. There are already some cooperative projects in the region that have somehow progressed despite the national antagonisms between the South Asian countries. The Mekong River project and the Asian Highway provide encouraging examples.

But just lowering tariffs among South Asian countries would not be enough to increase trade. In the words of United Nations economists, "the market can be expanded not by liberalizing but rather by organizing." What is needed is a coordination of the national plans. At first, beneficial results could be achieved through a series of bilateral agreements. For example, Ceylon might reserve the right to establish a large-scale tire industry to supply both itself and India in exchange for giving India the right to supply the market for machine tools. Ceylon has the rubber and India has the basis for a large machine-tool industry. Joint planning and a breaking away from the narrow nationalism of present planning are essential to achieve an acceptable distribution of the gains from cooperation and to compensate for the lack of an appropriate market mechanism. There are certainly many hurdles to be cleared before any of this could be a reality. Under these conditions it is not so surprising that little has as yet resulted from the lively discussions about regional integration in South Asia. But the strivings have so much to recommend them that they will probably not be given up. Further, the rise of trading blocs elsewhere, such as the European Common Market, may drive South Asia toward closer economic association sooner than they would otherwise unite.

The third alternative, trade with other underdeveloped countries outside South Asia, seems, at the moment, the most remote. But the same logic impelling the countries within South Asia into closer economic cooperation should apply equally well to all underdeveloped countries. A kind of "poor countries" common market for cheap goods has a certain logical basis, especially when it is remembered that by competing among themselves for more export markets in the richer countries, the poorer countries will more likely hinder than help themselves.

These nagging problems of world and regional trade are discouraging enough in themselves. The prospects for significant increases in foreign investment in South Asia are just as gloomy. Import restrictions, currency controls, and general restraints on foreign industry have made many private investors hesitate even longer about coming into South Asia. Still, there are many who will continue to be tempted by the thought that they can make money in a protected market and from many by-products of their efforts. South Asian businessmen are also aware that there can be advantages to going into partnership with foreign companies which can contribute machinery and other production necessities. The businessmen would otherwise have difficulties in acquiring foreign exchange. There is a growing recognition in South Asia that foreign participation in industrial ventures has other advantages than saving foreign exchange. In particular, it brings in valuable managerial and engineering personnel and technical know-how.

But in view of the economic and political instability in South Asia, it cannot be expected that private direct investment will be much more significant in the future than it has been in the recent past. The gap between rapidly rising import needs and stagnating export returns in South Asia has been filled, in so far as it has been filled at all, by public capital in the form of grants and credits. But the general issue of financial assistance to underdeveloped countries has reached a state of acute crisis. The donor countries, particularly the United States, are lowering their aid in real terms and decreasing its quality in several respects. The situation is made the more serious by the continued deterioration of South Asian trading positions. Added to this is the concern over what the World Bank has called the "debt explosion." The continually accumulated volume of debt owed by underdeveloped countries implies that repayments of these debts are becoming increasingly burdensome. It is already evident that there should again be a changeover from loans to grants as the best form of aid to South Asia. But grants are always harder to sell to a congress or parliament than loans. Yet there must be a growing awareness that South Asia cannot realistically be expected to repay all the credits it receives. This fact should support the efforts that are under way to make loans to the region softer, in regard both to interest rates and to the time allowed for amortizing the principal.

Under these circumstances it is understandable that import substitution has been seen as a main policy line. For although it is very difficult to reach out in the export market, there is a home market that can provide the demand basis for the growth of industry. Cutting off imports from abroad not only saves foreign exchange but builds a protective wall behind which industrialization can take place. However, a program to develop substitutes for imports by stimulating new manufacturing involves the investment in plants and machinery and often the building up of utilities and transportation, in most cases raising the need for imports of capital goods and often for continuing imports of spare parts, semimanufactured goods, and raw materials. The building up of auxiliary industries to substitute for these imports will again raise the need for importing capital goods in particular.

The more serious difficulty with the import-substitution policy is, however, that the choice of line for substitution is usually not open for rational planning. Ordinarily the first thing that happens is that a country gets into exchange difficulties; it is then often forced to introduce import controls of one type or another. For natural, and, indeed, rational reasons it tries to curtail imports of the least necessary goods, which thus automatically get the highest protection. From a development point of view, this is unplanned protection.

Finally, we should stress that the South Asian countries' efforts at import substitution, if they are not coordinated in such a way as to provide a more rational labor division within the region, are likely to damage the cause of regional integration. It is often easiest to develop substitutes for imports such as food and textiles that come from neighboring countries. But even in regard to new industries, national import substitution is likely to prevail without any regard for regional coordination. When all the countries want to have steel mills, the possibility of developing an export market within the region for the country that can produce the cheapest steel is eliminated.

There is no easy solution to any of the problems mentioned in this chapter. All avenues of policy are severely circumscribed. Each has significant and often adverse repercussions on other aspects of policy. Clearly, all of the South Asian countries face a fundamentally more difficult task in trying to achieve what is glibly referred to as a "take-off into sustained growth" than any of the now developed countries of the West faced a century or more ago.

Part Three

A THIRD WORLD
OF PLANNING

Chapter 9

SPREAD AND IMPACT
OF THE IDEOLOGY
OF PLANNING

The ideology of planning for development can be considered as a theory and tested for its consistency, realism, and practicality in terms of political action. But the spread and impact of that ideology are at the same time themselves part of reality, a set of social facts having their causes and effects, which should be studied as other social facts are.

The basic idea of economic planning is that the state shall take an active, indeed the decisive, role in the economy: by its own acts of enterprise and investment, and by its various controls—inducements and restrictions —over the private sector, the state shall initiate, spur, and steer economic development. These public policy measures shall be rationally coordinated and the coordination be made explicit in an over-all plan for a specified number of years ahead.

The whole complex ideology of planning, in all its manifestations, is thus essentially rationalist in approach and interventionist in conclusions. It is committed to the belief that development can be brought about or accelerated by government intervention. Economic conditions, in particular, need not remain as they are or evolve under the influence merely of "natural forces." Instead, it is felt that these conditions and their evolution should be under state control so that the economic system can be moved in a desired direction by means of intentionally planned and rationally coordinated state policies. The strategy for these policies would emerge as a set of policy inferences from rational analysis of the facts in a country's situation and the positing of certain development goals. All those in the South Asian region who urge state economic planning agree in principle that it should benefit the common people, concentrate on raising the levels of living of the poorest strata in the nation, and express the will of the nation as a whole.

This rationalist and interventionist idea of state economic planning has represented a sharp break with the past, as the South Asian countries—outside the foreign enclaves—were, and still are, so largely stagnant, with most of their people traditional in outlook and inclined to accept things as they are. Its appearance in this Rip Van Winkle world, among people still drowsy with the slumber of centuries, makes the challenge of state economic planning all the more dramatic.

Ideally, once the people accept the possibility of changes induced through rationally coordinated state action, most of the social and political conditions in South Asia appear undesirable and in need of reform. Changes beyond the purely "economic" ones come to be regarded as themselves desirable goals for policy. Levels of living should be improved, social and economic stratifications made less unequal and rigid, opportunities more broadly opened for everybody, and participation of the whole people intensified. State policies that aim at improvements of certain undesirable conditions usually have, in addition to their independent value, an instrumental value, as they will tend to change other conditions as well in a desirable direction; changes in these other conditions are therefore means for attaining economic development. Causation is circular: not only would improvement in all sorts of "non-economic" conditions make possible, or speed up, "economic" development, but the engendering "economic" development would at the same time tend to improve other "non-economic" conditions.

In this way planning becomes the intellectual matrix— the general mold—of the modernization ideology. And the demand for national development comes to encompass all striving for political, social, and economic reform. Economic development is thus understood to be a "human" problem. Development plans often explicitly define planning as a comprehensive attempt to reform all unsatisfactory conditions. This view is reflected also in the broad goals and ambitions of most of the plans, which go beyond "economic" policies in the narrow meaning.

Superficially, at least, the planning ideology now rules supreme in the South Asian countries. It provides the terms of reference for much of the public discussion of their social and economic issues—in the literature and press of these countries, in the pronouncements of the intellectual and political leaders, and in the discussions in their deliberative bodies. These nations, or those individuals in them who are at all articulate, are in various degrees becoming "plan-conscious." Already the appearance in these underdeveloped countries of the demand for economic development (and, still more, the assumption that it is the concern of the state to engender development through planning) is a new event in history, so far as the non-Communist world is concerned. Were there no other differences in initial conditions, this ideological commitment alone would make it inappropriate to assume that the countries in South Asia will follow a course of development similar to that of the Western world.

Only a few of the South Asian countries have made really serious attempts to bring their economic life under the discipline of state planning. Even in those that have, the scope and effectiveness of coordinated state controls are not great. But the idea of planning represents an attitude, rather commonly shared by both governments and their opposition, about how state policies ought to be viewed. Even when there is little actual planning, and still less implementation, the ideology of planning serves as a rationalization for interventionist practices. When there are advances, they are presented as successful planning. When austerity and sacrifices are called for, they are urged in the name of planning, just as the planning ideology is used to cover up the slowness of improvements in living conditions and industrial development.

The planning ideology thus tends to provide the terms of reference in every controversy over public policy. While Western countries ordinarily tend to play down the economic planning they actually have, and, particularly in the United States, try to convince themselves that theirs is a "free economy," the South Asian countries tend to play it up, and pretend that their planning amounts to much more than it does. They have accepted planning as an idea even before they are able to translate much planning into reality.

The need for economic development—though not necessarily for engendering it by means of state planning—is self-evident when one considers the abject poverty in these countries. The further idea that large-scale state intervention, through a coordinated plan, is needed to bring about this economic development follows from the realization that these countries have long remained in a state of relative stagnation, while the Western world has for many generations developed rapidly. A strong, induced impetus is seen to be needed to end that stagnation and bring about economic progress, which apparently is not coming spontaneously, or at least not rapidly enough.

This argument is strengthened by closer study of the actual conditions for development. We have found the differences between the South Asian countries today and the rich Western countries when they were at a comparable level to be fundamental, and of such a nature as to make development more difficult for the South Asian countries. Indeed, these differences make it unlikely that many of these countries will develop at all unless the new element, state planning, is vigorously applied.

There are certainly many reasons for rapid and vigorous state intervention through planning. The rapidly accelerating population increase is steadily depressing levels of living and hampering development. If populations were stationary, there would be more of a possibility for spontaneous development. Then there is scarcity of capital. The trading position is unfavorable. To this list must be added the relative lack of entrepreneurial talent and training in the private sector, the disinclination of the wealthy to risk their funds in productive investment rather than in speculation and quick profit ventures, and, finally, the tendency for any large-scale enterprises to acquire an extraordinary degree of monopoly or oligopoly. For these reasons, which vary in strength among the several South Asian countries, the state will often find cause either to make the industrial beginning itself, or else to regulate and control the entrepreneurial activities in order to obtain the most rapid development in the desired directions.

Attempts to realize in any substantial measure the ideals of social and economic equality and welfare, which are declared policy goals in all the South Asian countries, would also necessitate large-scale state intervention. In poor countries especially, such policies need to be planned and integrated with all other measures in a general plan, both to be effective and to spur rather than endanger economic development. Generally the inherited inequalities and rigidities are adverse to economic development and need to be mitigated by coordinated state policies if development is to be achieved. At every stage, planning itself can also be expected to have some educational effect. To prepare a plan, publish it widely, and have it discussed should help to induce people to think rationally in terms of means and ends. All the leaders in South Asia know that development requires fundamental changes in people's attitudes toward life and work and that the grip of traditionalism must be broken.

The argument for state planning, which we have tried to spell out from the viewpoint of the conditions, the problems, and the interests of the people in South Asian countries themselves, is strongest for India and Pakistan, the poorest and most populous nations. Ceylon has a higher average income, but the population increase is so rapid and the spontaneous forces for industrialization—outside the plantations, where possibilities of expansion are limited—are so weak, that even there the case for planning is very strong. Countries like Malaya and Thailand perhaps have the potential for more spontaneous development, somewhat similar to the historical Western type. But the rapid population increase can be expected to bring even these less poverty-stricken countries to the point at which large-scale planning becomes necessary. Malaya in particular would seem, however, to have relatively good prospects for development of the semi-spontaneous type: income levels are much higher; natural resources are still abundant in relation to the size of the population, though it is growing rapidly; export possibilities appear somewhat brighter; and the large Chinese population provides industrial enterprise to an extent that is exceptional in the region. Provided Malaya could preserve a measure of internal unity and political stability among its Malays, Chinese, and Indians, it might consequently have greater possibilities than other South Asian countries of continual economic development without a high degree of state planning, at least in the near future.

Successful economic planning requires a stable and effective government. But at the same time planning itself becomes a principal means of reaching national consolidation: first, because it will create an institutional structure to articulate government policies; secondly, because the result, when planning is successful, will be higher economic levels, greater opportunties for the people, and a symbol of national achievement.

This attempt to sketch in abstract terms the rationale of the strivings for state planning of economic development in South Asia does not, of course, explain the actual emergence and spread of the planning ideology. In reality, these nations, or their leaders, did not simply form a clear picture of their situation and draw the logical conclusion that they needed state planning to overcome their difficulties and develop as rapidly as possible. The spread of the idea of planning has a much more complicated causation.

To begin with, knowledge about the true conditions in these countries is not only incomplete, even among their leaders, but also biased in an optimistic direction. Most public officials, for example, for a long time shielded themselves from realistic awareness of the serious implications of the population trends. Even today, when there is beginning to be an acceptance of population increase as an abstract fact, its serious implications are seldom fully realized and all sorts of false ideas are entertained as protection against the truth. A similar tendency can be observed in regard to most other adverse circumstances. The inhibitions and obstacles to increased production that are posed by attitudes, institutions, and low living levels should rationally motivate much more incisive remedial practices. But they are generally kept somewhat outside the main focus of the plans; and the application of the conventional post-war approach of reasoning in terms of employment, savings, investment, and output becomes helpful for rationalizing this common bias. The errors in all estimates made in the plans thus acquire a systematic optimistic bias. Furthermore, those who think, speak, and act for the new nations—politicians, planners, administrators, professionals, industrialists, and businessmen—are only a minute upper stratum in the total population. They form a rather secluded circle and live fairly comfortably, and they must be inclined to protect themselves by a system of illusions, in whose preservation they have a vested interest.

But when all this is noted, the fact remains that the difficulties confronting the leaders of these nations are so different and in many ways so much greater than those the Western nations ever were faced with, that in the end they tend to come out with a different appreciation of their situation and with different conclusions in regard to policy. One such general conclusion, which embraces many others, is the necessity for economic planning. In this way the logical reasons for state planning enumerated above come to function as causes.

Aiding in these convictions are the inclinations and patterns of paternalism carried over from colonial and pre-colonial times. Throughout South Asia there is an extraordinary expectancy about what state functionaries can do and a feeling that it is up to them to organize things for the people. This inherited dependence on authority is a tremendous impediment to local self-government and cooperation. But it has helped make the lower layers of the population at least submissive to the planning ideology. Corresponding to this has been the readiness of officials to give direction and command. In South Asia administrators —if they are at all awake to the need for change—are thus inclined to be "planners."

Among these administrators, ideological influences from the Communist world, especially in regard to planning and state direction of private enterprise, have been strong. For the pioneer planners in South Asia, the idea of state planning for economic development had a definite radical (socialist, usually "Marxist") motivation. Actually, "Marxism" has become a most confused concept and will not be used as a technical term in this book. Marx was not a planner. But for the planning ideology as it has developed in South Asia, Marx's thoughtways had a sort of general importance, both because of their stress on the economic factors and their awareness of the social forces and the general interdependence in the entire social system. Lenin's theory of imperialism as a late phase of capitalism has had a greater and more specific influence on the doctrines implied in South Asian ideologies.

From the opposite direction, South Asian intellectuals have noted the gradual spread of planning in the coordinated public policies of the Western countries, which have all become welfare states to one degree or another. This trend has had influences that do not differ greatly from those emanating from the Communist world, at least with respect to the general idea of the desirability and usefulness of state planning.

In all, on the ideological level there has in fact been astonishingly little articulate resistance to planning as such, though of course there has been plenty against the particular policies in the plans and their implementation or lack of implementation. It may, nevertheless, be the case that preoccupation with traditional ideals, particularly those of a religious and social character, somehow decreases the eagerness to induce change intentionally, which is the essence of the planning ideology. We know little about this or about the acceptance of the planning ideology among the masses. It is fairly common in South Asia and in the West, and of course in the Communist world, to speak and write as if the masses had suddenly awakened from centuries of slumber and had begun rationally to demand rapid development to improve their miserable lives. The expression "the revolution of rising expectations" is indicative of this thinking. But this view represents a rather complete misunderstanding of conditions in a stagnant society. There is a great social and psychological gap between the intellectual and commercial elite and the masses, and this often causes the upper strata to impute attitudes to the masses that the elite might have themselves if they were forced to live the same way.

Actually, what we see in South Asia is a small intellectual elite that has imbibed the planning ideology and the modernization ideals and is trying to disseminate these concepts among the people. This raises the question of what transformation the planning ideology undergoes in these efforts to spread it. The patterns of paternalism and authoritarianism carried from the past facilitate acceptance by the masses of the planning ideology. It also must be assumed that they influence its content. The people are led to expect or demand that the government do more for them, without showing much readiness to change their own ways. This does not help the cause of development, as planning in a stagnant and poor society must aim at getting people to rationalize their attitudes and, in particular, to work harder to improve their own lot.

There is a direct corollary between the impact of the planning ideology and a country's relative degree of poverty and lack of spontaneous development. In India and Pakistan the political leaders are more conscious of the need for planning efforts. In Malaya, the Philippines, and Thailand, on the other hand, more favorable conditions have made it natural for the political leaders to place greater trust in market forces. The actual accomplishments in planning correlate even more strongly with the strength of the central government and the degree of national consolidation. These determine the amount of public interest that can be given to economic planning and the possibilities for effective action. A plan is essentially a political program that requires a sequence of clear-cut political decisions.

Despite its poverty, India has gone further toward consolidation and effective government than any other country in the region. In Pakistan, serious planning began with the ascendency in 1958 of the military regime, which, at least for a time, imposed more direction and discipline on the country. The fact that efforts to plan remained so unsuccessful in Burma and Indonesia is clearly related to the insurrections and the continuous struggle to maintain unity and effective government in these states.

The level of planning and development is also correlated with the level of rationalist thinking and the influence of intellectuals. India again leads here, followed closely by Ceylon, the Philippines, and Malaya. The lower level of public discussion of planning in Burma and Indonesia—so bound by traditional inhibitions, often clad in odd nationalist and religious slogans, and generally more emotional—cannot be explained only in terms of political difficulties. More accurately, their difficulties have been much increased by the dearth of highly educated, rationalist individuals with long experience in colonial government and administration or with professional competence, and by the excessive number of leaders with training chiefly as plotters, schemers, agitators, and fighters.

However, throughout South Asia, the planning ideology has a hold over the articulate upper stratum, gives form and direction to public discussion, and has led to the establishment of governmental planning agencies.

India and Pakistan made serious and regular attempts to check on the fulfillment of their plans. It is true that this fulfillment often fell short of the targets that had been set. It is not to be denied, however, that in India, as in no other country of the region save Pakistan in later years, planning became an important part of the national political life, a tenet of national faith. Beyond doubt, one of the most important causes of the advance in actual planning in India was this intense identification with the planning ideology. But it is equally certain that this political development in turn strengthened the hold of the planning ideology. Planning became a going concern with a momentum of its own when, in India and, later, in Pakistan, the idea of planning became firmly established in economic and political life.

When that happened, it implied a number of things. Planning, then, created new institutions and, more important, changed and molded existing ones to serve its progress. An ever larger part of the articulate upper stratum of the nation acquired vested interests in planning. With growing effectiveness, the planning ideology set the frame of reference in every controversy over public policy. The government and the officialdom around it became involved and began to operate as part of a huge planning machinery. Preparing, arguing, and implementing the plan became one of government's main functions, and increasingly all government policies were presented from the perspective of the plan.

To be effective, planning must continually reconcile competing interests and determine the order of precedence among them. Under South Asian conditions, when planning became a going concern, it consisted largely of negotiations within the central government, with the governments of the constituent states, and with the business interests. It had also to face the necessity of "democratic planning" through regional and functional organization. Both newly created collective institutions and old ones, revitalized and remolded, became extensions of an institutional infrastructure intended to become the instrument for people's participation and cooperation in planning and, particularly, the implementation of planning. Certainly the organized groups in the higher strata of the nation, especially those in commerce and industry and the individual big enterprises, were much more easily involved as participants in economic planning. The mode of participation then became negotiation, the only alternative to a wholesale nationalization of production and trade. The end result was a compromise that gave consideration to the organized private business interests. But whatever the outcome, in the process of these consultations and bargainings these interest groups became a part of the institutional system molded by planning as a going concern.

There always will be opposition to the actual policies pursued, and it will always be nurtured by interests who find themselves slighted in some respect. But more important here is whether the government meets only scattered opposition on specific issues or whether it conflicts with well-consolidated interests, bent on inhibiting its planning activity and therefore deprecatory of the planning ideology itself. Systematic opposition might well be expected from the relatively wealthy groups. In the first place, planning is most likely to impinge on their activities through a plethora of direct and discretionary administrative controls. Secondly, the planning ideology throughout South Asia is committed to the improvement of mass welfare. It is a fact, however, that almost nowhere did any of this radicalism meet with much opposition on the ideological level.

Most of the benefits from planning policies have not reached the poor, even if such was the proclaimed aim and motivation. The benefits have accrued instead to the strata above them. More generally, the policies pursued have nowhere led to greater economic equality and a lessening of concentration of economic power. This reflection of the actual power structure explains why the promise of greater equality did not elicit much opposition to planning from the upper strata: what planning there has been in South Asia has generally been to their advantage. Neither have "socialism" and, in particular, the planned enlargement of the public sector as yet gone against the interests of big business or any other group above the masses. Against this background it becomes more understandable why businessmen and other inherently conservative groups did not offer more opposition to the slogans of equalization, socialism, and the controls implied in the South Asian version of the planning ideology. The fact is that these policies either were to their immediate benefit or disturbed them little. What opposition there was served chiefly to keep the government on the alert and warn it against more radical adventures.

The above remarks about planning as a going concern, particularly in India, have here been rendered in the past tense (*imperfectum*) since under the serious economic calamities from the middle of the sixties there was a three-year interruption of planning. India is now trying to come back to the routine of five-year plans. If it succeeds, the established pattern of planning will be restored.

In the Western countries today there is a considerable amount of over-all economic planning, though a rapid acceleration of this trend has come only in recent decades. Economic planning in the Western countries has been a *consequence* of industrialization and the social, economic, and institutional changes related to the emergence of a more mature industrial society. In the underdeveloped countries of South Asia, planning is, instead, applied *before,* or at a very early stage of, industrialization. In South Asia, furthermore, planning, in principle and in approach, is thought to *precede* organized acts of control and interferences with markets. Planning cannot be left to grow pragmatically, as in the Western countries, by a "natural" process. Planning in South Asia is thus not the result of development, but is employed to foster development. It is envisaged as a *pre-condition*—indeed, is motivated by the assumption that spontaneous development cannot be expected. The underdeveloped countries in the region are thus compelled to undertake what in the light of Western history appears as a short-cut.

By the very logic of their situation, planning in the countries in South Asia, unlike that in the West, becomes *programmatic*. This follows from the fact that planning is introduced early. The logic of their situation also implies that this planning through programs should, in principle, be *comprehensive* and *complete*, not *ad hoc*, partial, and piecemeal as in the Western countries, particularly in the early stages.

In the Communist world, however, programmatic and comprehensive planning has been used for the very purpose of engendering and directing economic development from a state of underdevelopment, which is what is also sought by the countries in South Asia. It can be said with a good deal of truth that what the underdeveloped countries in South Asia are attempting is to use elements of the Communist techniques for programmatic and comprehensive state planning but to avoid some of the conditions under which these techniques have been utilized in the Communist countries.

The South Asian countries are all intent on "democratic planning." Neither where political democracy has been faltering nor even in those countries that have come under a military dictatorship are the leaders prepared to enforce a totalitarian and monolithic regime. And even if they were so disposed, they are not constituted and equipped to impose the fanatical discipline of the Communist system. Aside from these fundamental political inhibitions, there is also a difference in their economic institutions. They have not, like the Communist countries, nationalized production and made state enterprise and collectivism the rule. Nor have they organized their foreign trade and exchange relations in a pattern of state monopoly.

Their economic planning is thus of a third type, different from that of the Communist countries as well as from that of the Western world.

Chapter 10

EQUALITY
AND DEMOCRACY

The South Asian countries have accepted the ideology of planning for development, and, more fundamentally, they have treated economic development as a concern of the state and thus a political issue. This is an important fact that differentiates their situation from that of the Western countries when they stood on the threshold of industrialization. Another fact is South Asia's commitment to egalitarianism, which is an integral part of their ideology of planning. In turn, this ideology, in its various forms, played a role in the liberation movements.

In terms of a national ethos, the official sanction given to the egalitarian ideals, whatever their degree of influence on political action, implies a similarity between the South Asian countries and those of the West. However, there is a time dimension involved. When the Western countries entered an era of rapid development, the concept of the social welfare state was still embryonic. It was contained in the abstract premises of scholars and in the visions of rebels, but formed no part of the established

146

policy declarations of governments. The ruling classes regarded it as dangerous. In sum, for the pre-industrial countries of South Asia to commit themselves politically to an egalitarian doctrine is an act without historical precedent outside of the Soviet sphere.

In all the plans that spell out goals for development, the egalitarian ideology is prominent. Since the plans regularly focus on the economic aspects of development, they stress the equalization of incomes and wealth and the more widespread ownership of the means of production. Other welfare ideals are usually relegated to separate chapters, if they are included in the plans at all. Part of the rationale for greater social and economic equality is, of course, the widespread intellectualized feeling that it is an intrinsic good—in our terminology, possessed of an independent value. This implies that, within limits, rational motivations would support the quest for greater equality, even if it were attainable only at the cost of slower economic development. From a broad social viewpoint it is clear, however, that the type of inequality still prevalent in South Asia, particularly in the poorest countries, often hampers economic progress. In this case, levelling would have an instrumental, as well as an independent, value for development.

All those inequalities inherent in traditional social stratification are recognized as being obstacles to development. Certainly the caste system in India is an obvious obstacle. It fortifies the contempt and disgust for manual work prevalent in all social strata. Since an orthodox Hindu regards not only those who perform this work but everyone outside his own caste as beyond the pale, it also warps and stultifies ordinary human feelings of brotherhood and compassion.

While there is common agreement that greater equality should be a paramount goal for planning, the actual development usually goes toward increased inequality. In this situation a prevalent rationalization is then to postpone the realization of the goal to a stage where there has been substantial economic growth. It is held that increased inequality is natural in a "developing country." To support this thought, it is commonly observed that historically economic development has often led to a greater concentration of wealth and power; sometimes the inference is drawn that this result is inevitable. The Western and even the Japanese experience is often referred to in this connection. But by themselves these historical comparisons are not necessarily significant, because there are unique elements in the South Asian situation. Thus it is assumed that in South Asia development will be engendered by planning, and that this planning will be directed toward the realization of the equalization ideals.

The important question is whether there is a conflict between economic equalization and economic progress—that is, whether a price must be paid for equalization in terms of retarded progress. Even though there is still a lack of detailed knowledge about the relevant economic factors and their relationships in South Asia, it is possible to cite a number of conditions there that suggest, much more than in the Western countries, that an increase in equality would help rather than hinder development.

For one thing, economic inequality is among the causes of social inequality, and the reverse is also true. Thus a decrease in economic inequality should tend to bring about a decrease in social inequality, which would have a beneficial effect on economic development. Moreover, there is a similar mutual relationship between very low levels of living and low productivity of labor. Consequently, measures that encouraged essential consumption in the lower strata should increase labor input and labor efficiency, and raise production. The conventional postwar approach, which treats development simply as a function of investment, abstracts from both these important relationships, and this makes it possible to believe not only that development can take place without egalitarian reforms, but even that increasing inequality may be a condition for economic growth.

When the paramount goal of greater equality is retained at the same time as the development problem is approached in this biased way, the result is likely to be muddled, opportunistic thinking and the covering up of policies that are not in line with the egalitarian ideal. Even when reforms are ostentatiously motivated by that ideal, they have either remained ineffective or have even favored the not-so-poor. This is broadly true of various assistance schemes, of land and tenancy reform efforts, and of community development and cooperation programs. Certainly, in the long run, efforts to raise standards of health and elementary education should have equalizing effects. But even here, only a small part of the government's expenditure is earmarked for the neediest, and the school system in particular is ordinarily biased very heavily against the lower strata.

Fairly independent of their system of government, the South Asian countries are ruled by compromises and accommodations within and between the upper class and the various groups that constitute the bulk of the upper class. The fact that members of this upper class call themselves "middle class" is significant. Particularly in India, the government has tried by various means, including a progressive income tax, to limit the power and wealth of the maharajahs, the landlords, and the tycoons of industry and finance. The upper strata of landowners in the villages, the traders and the moneylenders, the ordinary industrialists, and the civil servants below the very top level look on these policies, which incidentally have not been very effective, as attempts to establish greater equality. In public discussions, it is commonly argued that greater consideration for the "middle class" would forward the cause of equality. The truth is, of course, that in the Indian setting, this "middle class" is definitely part of

the tiny upper class. It is the lower classes that need to be
aided if there is to be a real advance in equality.

What has been said of India applies to other countries
in the region as well. In Pakistan inequality, even without
the rigidity of the caste system, is just as pronounced.
Here the upper strata as a whole are relatively less concerned with social and economic justice—or at least are
convinced that it is unwise to stir up public opinion on
this issue. In Ceylon and Malaya, and in most other
Southeast Asian countries, the equality issue is complicated by the presence of Indian and Chinese minority
groups, some of whom occupy what appears, to the majority groups, to be privileged positions. Burma and Indonesia are committed to radical programs to promote
equality. But interest in this matter has waned in the face
of mounting internal and external political problems.

The ideal of political democracy is closely related to the
ideal of social and economic equality. By political democracy we mean a system in which an executive is
responsible to the people's will, as expressed by elections
with universal suffrage, an independent judiciary, and the
guarantee of a wide range of civil liberties. Part of the
attraction of greater social and economic equality was the
realization that without it political democracy would be
an empty achievement. But it was also often regarded,
especially in pre-independence times, as the principal
means of carrying out, or of making inevitable, a social
and economic revolution. In India, not only Nehru and
the socialist wing of the National Congress, but others as
well, firmly believed that giving the poor masses the vote
would result in radical reforms.

From the beginning the commitment to political democracy was commonly embraced by the leaders of all
countries in South Asia. The patterns they chose were
borrowed from the Western countries. The Western countries, in turn, regarded this choice not only as commend-

able, but as perfectly natural and normal—a strange example of ethnocentrism and lack of historical perspective.
During the days of South Asian emergence, there was
hardly any realistic discussion in the West about what
this pattern of political development amounted to,
whether it would work, and where it might lead. There is
little even now. Memories of what happened after the
First World War to the newly created democracies in
Central, Eastern, and Southern Europe might have occasioned some uneasiness. But if so, it was not expressed.

Little thought was given to the fact that the political
structure of the Western countries was quite different
when they were at a comparable stage of underdevelopment. Even today youngsters in West European democracies grow up with no clear idea of how restricted
suffrage was in their own countries only a few decades
ago, when a comparatively advanced stage of development had already been attained. At the time of their industrial revolutions, some West European countries had a
form of parliamentary government, representative of a
constituency of voters. But they were far from being
democracies in the modern meaning of the term. In fact,
history affords no example of a highly underdeveloped
country that has established a durable and effective political democracy based on universal suffrage. By the same
token, no country has ever attempted to realize the egalitarian ideals of the welfare state when it has been afflicted
with a degree of poverty and inequality comparable to
that of the South Asian countries.

Full democracy with universal suffrage has only been
successfully tried out at an advanced stage of economic
development, when there were relatively high levels of
living and literacy and a fair amount of equal opportunity. The ultimate arrival of universal suffrage was then
a triumph for education, popular agitation, organization,
and initiative. In South Asia, political rights had never
had to be fought for; they were granted from above with-

out the masses ever having demanded them. The stimulus from a fight to organize themselves for using the new rights to promote their interests was lacking. Today the South Asian states still face the daunting problem of how to assimilate the majority of their peoples and make them feel and behave as responsible participants in the nation-building process.

So the initial hopes that the newly independent nations of South Asia could establish full democracies or sustain them were not well founded. Four of these nations still have fairly stable parliamentary governments. The others have come under some form of authoritarian rule. In no country has there been far-reaching social or economic reform. At one extreme stands India, with a firmly established parliamentary government based on universal suffrage and a comparatively high turnout of the electorate. But in spite of this the masses are more the object of politics than its subject. They remain passive and inalert. They are not informed about their interests and not organized to protect those interests. They are not exerting power. India's democracy has proved remarkably stable, but it is largely the stability of stagnation, certainly in regard to the needed reforms of the country's rigidly inegalitarian structure.

For a time parliamentary democracy in Ceylon pursued an orderly course. But after the early 1950's it operated in an irresponsible and disorderly fashion. Politics became immersed in ethnic, linguistic, and religious emotions and a radical nationalism became rampant. That it did not come under a military dictatorship is probably largely due to the fact that its army is small and that it does not have the status that the armies have in Pakistan or Burma. Malaya and the Philippines are the only other countries in the region that have retained functioning systems of parliamentary government. But in Malaya political stability depended to a large extent on a contrived balance of interests between the upper strata of the Malays and the ethnic Chinese and Indian communities. Much depends on whether the Malays, who enjoy important political advantages and privileges, can better their own social and economic position before the more dynamic and better educated Chinese grow impatient with the secondary political position they now hold. Stability in the Philippines even more clearly rests on a highly unequal power structure. If articulate Filipinos are allowed to exhibit their zest for democratic freedoms and processes it is perhaps because as yet they have not seriously challenged the landed interests and allied oligarchic groups who control the levers of political power.

In other countries, for a variety of reasons, political democracy failed to take root and was replaced by some form of authoritarian regime. These changes were usually justified on the ground that political democracy, with its party systems, was ineffective, corrupt, and disruptive of national unity. A major cause of democratic failure in Pakistan was the fact that the Muslim League, unlike India's Congress Party, was not prepared ideologically or in any other way to handle public issues in a parliamentary manner. Many of the difficulties Burma and Indonesia experienced in trying to work out a system of parliamentary government are also traceable to similar initial unpreparedness. Thailand adopted a Western type of parliamentary government after World War II as an opportunistic adjustment to an external situation dominated by the Western democracies. The chances of its taking firm roots were slight in view of the country's authoritarian tradition. The peculiar character of French rule in Vietnam, Laos, and Cambodia and the manner in which the French were forced to depart gave little hope for political democracy in the successor states.

From the standpoint of modernization and economic development, the contrast between the countries that retained a democratic form of government and those that moved toward authoritarianism is more apparent than real. It is not possible to say that one form of government has proved more conducive to the application of policies of economic and social reform than the other. On the contrary, the various political systems in the region are strikingly similar in their inability or unwillingness to institute fundamental reforms and enforce social discipline. Whether democratic or authoritarian, they are all, in this sense, "soft states."

The movement toward authoritarianism in some South Asian countries actually owed little to outside influences. There has been little explicit ideological influence from Communist countries in this respect, although South Asian observers might have inferred from the experience of these countries that economic progress is possible without political democracy, in the Western sense, and perhaps impossible in a very poor country without a more authoritarian government. The fact that France, as a cure for her political instability, turned to de Gaulle, a military man, to restore effective government lent respectability to systems of direct rule that sidetracked elected assemblies. Nor did it go unnoticed in South Asia that this development in France was initially generally welcomed in other Western countries.

Basically, however, influence from abroad was not decisive in undermining political democracy in the region. One fundamental weakness of South Asian democracy is that it was handed down from above, without any struggle by a large section of the people. When democracy has faltered or failed in the region, it has never been because the masses have become organized to stand up for their interests and so forced the elite to take actions to safeguard themselves. In other words, there has been almost nothing in the pattern of political development in South Asia corresponding to Marx's model of class struggle. For the most part, the masses have remained apathetic and disunited.

This does not mean that the people are content with their present situation; this is far from being the case, particularly in India, Pakistan, and the Philippines, where the poverty of the masses is extreme. There is often sullen dissatisfaction among the underprivileged in the villages. But it is politically abortive. There is no avenue whereby the individual can make his protest effective.

In view of the difficulties the South Asian nations have experienced in trying to establish genuine Western-style democracy, it is worth asking whether they should not try instead to duplicate an earlier phase of Western development. Could they not try to establish a secure upper-class regime such as those which characterized the Western countries at the time of their industrialization? It might be argued that a system of representative assemblies elected on the basis of suffrage restricted by education, property, or income qualifications would stand a better chance of functioning effectively and producing a government that, by virtue of its stability, could afford a considerable measure of civil liberty. Simply restricting the suffrage to the literate could make an important difference. Furthermore, the development prospects for such a system are obvious, since a gradual widening of the franchise would naturally follow from an increase in the standards of literacy and living.

The short answer is that the tide of history cannot be rolled back to enable the new states of the region to experience the political evolution of the Western countries. There has been no attempt to restrict suffrage. And the idea of democracy has not been given up. Even when the ideals were poorly realized, their influence and prestige were such as to prevent a peaceful, stable upper-class state from coming into existence.

A quasi-democratic upper-class state of the West European type cannot be created once universal suffrage has been accepted as a moral imperative. The retreat from full democracy has to go all the way, and the franchise must be denied to everyone or made inconsequential by downgrading the elected assembly. Presumably, depriving only the lower strata of the population of their right to vote would be regarded as less "democratic"; it would be like standing for sin against virtue. The whole trend provides an illuminating example of the power of ideology, even when it is being distorted. Seen in the proper historical perspective, these dictatorships may be regarded as substitutes for what these countries do not have and cannot create—namely, stable upper-class regimes comparable to those of the Western countries when they began to industrialize.

What critics like Jayaprakash Narayan and former President Sukarno fell back on was some romantic idea of village democracy before the colonial area. Their thoughts on political reconstruction have been colored by golden-age myths about their people's special talents for mutual cooperation and harmony. Ayub Khan of Pakistan was almost the only opponent of the application of Western democracy to talk less about the "genius" of the people than about their political immaturity. As a result of these concepts, all manner of political systems—"guided democracy," government through consensus, indirect elections, and direct dictatorial rule—were instituted in place of representative government based on a restricted suffrage.

But stability of such a regime would presuppose the existence of a stable upper-class society with a ruling class confident in its status and power and feeling inner security. In India, the basis for such a society was weakened by the anti-feudal reforms enacted soon after political independence. More important, it was undermined by the spread of the ideologies of political democracy, equality, and planning. These ideals gained a certain hold over the ruling upper strata, at least to the extent of upsetting their confidence.

. . .

In every case where authoritarian rule replaced parliamentary democracy, the armed forces have been the instruments with which it was accomplished. It can be argued that there are merits in this. The armed forces, at least, must operate according to a rational plan, and they have a basis of discipline. If the military leaders of these governments are truly devoted to reducing social and economic inequalities that hamper progress, then a military dictatorship might well be preferable from the point of view of the modernization ideals. But military officers often come from the privileged classes or are scheduled to marry into these classes. And in order to govern effectively they are almost always forced to align themselves with the business and landowning groups and the higher civil servants. This too often results in a holding operation for the upper classes.

Whether a military dictatorship will work in the interest of development is thus uncertain. Nor is it easy to see clearly the direction in which the South Asian countries are drifting politically. All that can be said with any certainty is that the forms of democracy or authoritarian popularism they now have or will develop are crucially different from the systems of government the Western countries had at a similar stage in their history. *Once again we have to view South Asia as a third world.*

The reaction in Western countries to the fate of political democracy in South Asia has been inhibited and ambivalent, mainly because of cold war considerations. In Western countries, and particularly in the United States, there is a widespread fear that the South Asian, and indeed all, underdeveloped countries will go Communist. It is commonly assumed that if poor countries do not experience a fairly rapid rate of economic development, and if the fruits of that development are not shared by the masses, such an occurrence is highly probable. So when dictatorships make their appearance, some Western commentators are reluctant to criticize them for not being democratic, so long as they are anti-Communist. On more respectable intellectual levels, there has been a growing realization of the immense difficulty in achieving democratic ideals under conditions prevailing in South Asia. Western writers have been trying to be more neutral about the form of a regime and more interested in its efficiency from the standpoint of planning, though they continue to make manifest their preference for democracy. Nevertheless, the political issue most often discussed is still whether or not these countries are heading toward Communism.

We want to express our profound skepticism in regard to the validity of any forecasts about future political developments in South Asia, especially those based on glib notions about the behavior of the masses. We stress that it is easy to conceive of revolutionary events, or the absence of such events, that fit neither Marx's theory of revolution nor its amplification in the theory of a "revolution of rising expectations." It is perfectly possible, for example, that the lower strata in the Indian villages would remain supine in their shackles of inequality even if their living standards were to deteriorate still further. It is also possible that if they became deeply disturbed as a result of some influence from outside, class interests would supersede the present complex interest structure and lead to a popular uprising against the privileged. Under certain circumstances, outside forces would be more effective in stirring up the masses when the economy is stagnant or deteriorating. Under other circumstances, rising levels of living and literacy might provide a better seedbed for such revolutionary influences from outside.

If the "educated" unemployed increase in number, this particular "middle-class" group might provide the impulse for the organization of a mass protest movement. But it is also possible that the frustration of this category of the jobless would find an outlet only in manifestations of the surface: unorganized demonstrations, strikes, and riots. The distance between the "educated" and the masses is formidable in countries where menial work is despised and education is valued because it may provide an escape from physical drudgery. Again, international tensions and clashes, utilized by Communist propaganda from abroad, might serve to spark an organized rebellion. Under certain circumstances, nationalist fervor might be enlisted in the cause of revolution; under other conditions, the nationalist appeal might be used to quell incipient revolts, particularly if it is imbued with religion. Reactions to changes in these imponderables would be different in different countries and at different times.

When Communism is depicted as the "counsel of despair"—in the sense that it is said to win easier access to the minds of people who are very poor and who have little prospect of improving their lot than to the minds of those who are somewhat better off and optimistic about the future—this is a generalization that is not supported by experience and careful analysis. It is quite possible that in the long run several South Asian countries will waver more in the direction of Communism. It is also possible that the Western countries, by generous aid policies, may succeed in strengthening an anti-Communist regime, though sometimes without any favorable effects on the economic situation of the masses.

Whatever happens, the causes will be complex, and may be very different for the several countries. Poverty, inequality, and a lack of development have no foreordained or definite roles in the process. It is regrettable that Western writers, who should know better and who have a sympathetic regard for the downtrodden masses in South Asia, feel that they have to appeal to anti-Communist sentiment among their nations in order to get a hearing for their plea for more moral solidarity among the peoples of the world.

Chapter 11

SOUTH ASIAN SOCIALISM

While Communism, or open alignment with the Communist blocs, has not as yet succeeded anywhere in South Asia (outside the former French Indochina), "socialism" of some sort is the official creed in India, Ceylon, Burma, and Indonesia. The socialist ideology, in fact, tends to be respectable throughout the rest of South Asia as well.

Although adherence to socialism is widespread, the term has never been rigorously defined. Its meaning varies greatly, not only among but within countries, confusing the public debate. To a minor extent this confusion stems from the association of socialism with "Marxism," itself an indeterminate concept. What then emerges is an ideological compromise, be it "Islamic socialism" in Pakistan, "socialism a la Indonesia," "Buddhist socialism" in Burma, or "Sarvodhaya socialism" by Gandhians in India. It is regularly asserted that the ideals of socialism are immanent in the indigenous philosophy and even in village organization. The truth, of course, is not so simple, and the intellectual contortions engaged in to explain and

160

justify the indigenous form of socialism are likely to be no more than verbal jugglery.

The adherence to a socialist ideology, furthermore, has varied over time. Each country has undergone a variety of political experiences. But whatever the course of events, the concept of socialism has continually served to express a vague radical commitment. The vagueness is symbolized by the variety of expressions chosen to designate the socialist doctrine that is adhered to. Even India, where otherwise the ideological debate is on a higher intellectual level than in the other South Asian countries, has used a plethora of terms to describe the sort of society aimed at, with much shifting of meaning: a "socialist society," a "socialist (or socialistic) pattern of society," a "cooperative commonwealth," a "socialist cooperative commonwealth," or a "classless society," sometimes with the amplification that it should be established "by peaceful and legitimate means."

The vague leftist tendency everywhere implied has a common historical origin in the opposition among the alert intellectuals to colonial domination. It is therefore also closely connected with nationalism and especially with the egalitarian ideology that was an integral part of Asian nationalism. In nearly every case, the socialist ideology in South Asia spread as part of the independence movement. Its acceptance did not require the sophistication of a Lenin or a Hobson. The existence of large-scale foreign investment and the privileges enjoyed by foreigners who controlled management and banking strengthened opposition to colonialism and its capitalism. J. S. Furnivall offered a cogent comment on the line of reasoning that emerged under these influences:

> Yet they [the colonial peoples] have, I think, more sympathy with Communist *ideals* because they have seen too much of capitalist *practice*. From economic individualism they instinctively react in the direction of socialism, not necessarily, though not excluding, the text book socialism of state con-

trol over production, distribution, and exchange, but of socialism as the reintegration of a society ravaged by unrestricted capitalism—or, if you prefer the term—colonialism. And, much as they dislike and fear Communist methods and Communist domination, they will, and do, respond more readily to the claim of social duty rather than to the illusion of individual prosperity.

Intense resentment of the poverty and stagnation in their countries led South Asian intellectuals to charge private business, whether foreign or indigenous, with the failure to engender economic progress. Given the setting, it was natural that most leaders of nationalist movements demanded not only political independence but also liberation from what they conceived as the colonial structure of capitalism and sought an alternative system of economic organization.

In the Southeast Asian countries of Malaya and Indonesia, and in Ceylon, socialism has been influenced by a process of readjustment following the unstable situation in which these countries found themselves after the withdrawal of the Western overlords, with political power in the hands of indigenous groups but economic power often the preserve of alien minorities. In these countries there have sometimes been demands that the state take over ownership and management. But often this "socialism" is simply the displacement of minority aliens by indigenes.

In India, for one, socialism has often been equated with planning—on the assumption, of course, that its objectives will be those we have called the modernization ideals. In any case, it has been held that socialism will not be realized without planning. Or socialism is understood simply as the attainment of the "good society." In most instances socialism is merely a rather vague term for the modernization ideology, with an inherent stress on equality as a primary planning objective. Undoubtedly, this is the meaning of socialism for many of its adherents in

India—especially those who do not favor extensive changes in the structure of the national economy.

But such a formulation is not what Westerners mean when they talk about Asian socialism. What socialism heretofore has connoted, above all, is a commitment to nationalization and, more generally, to state ownership and management of a larger sector of the economy.

It should first be noted that in the economic application of socialism in South Asia, state ownership and management are contemplated, if they are considered at all, for only very limited fields of the national economy—public utilities, modern large-scale industry, mines, large plantations, banking, insurance, and, to some extent, commerce, in particular with foreign countries. Agriculture, crafts, and small-scale industry, whether modern or traditional, are not considered potential targets for socialization. Instead, in these vast fields of economic activity decentralization of ownership and management is the ideal in India, just as much as in Pakistan, Thailand, Malaya, and the Philippines. There is a consensus in South Asia about the policy of leaving them in the private sector and supporting individual entrepreneurs, as there is about the need for cooperation and all that is included under "democratic planning." The only difference is that in the countries claiming a commitment to socialism, these policies are assumed to be socialist.

Opinion in South Asia is equally unanimous that public utilities, on the other hand, should normally belong to the state. But again, it is only in the socialist countries that this line of policy is called socialist. The financial institutions created since independence in South Asia are mostly state owned. Each country in the region has established a Central Bank to create an independent money and investment supply that can be regulated to serve its own development goals. But all countries have also expanded the private banking systems inherited from their colonial predecessors. In the whole region there has also been frequent government intervention in trading and commerce, with the establishment of state export-import institutions. This intrusion in commerce and business has often been motivated by prejudice against foreigners, particularly the Chinese and Indian middlemen who are present to some degree in all the Southeast Asian countries. And in most of the region the state has been virtually forced to take over the essential item of food supply because, with the exception of Burma and Thailand, there is usually a food deficit. Thus there are many varied motives, many of them unrelated to socialism, that have prompted the state to assume more responsibility in trading activities.

Even with the above-mentioned activities, in most of the South Asian countries the issue of socialism does not arise or is irrelevant in a discussion of the largest part of the economy. All that remains is big modern industry, and in this we include mines, forestry, and plantations. Big manufacturing, even in India, continues to be a very small sector of the South Asian economy. However, there are two reasons for attaching special importance to big industry in a discussion of socialism. First, if the countries of the region, especially the poorest with their large and rapidly growing populations, are to have any hope of success in their development planning, a much larger part of the working force must eventually be employed outside agriculture. If big industry can best be promoted by state entrepreneurship, this becomes a valid argument for expanding government participation. Secondly, certain types of big industry are held to be "basic," usually with the implication that they make possible more industrial enterprise—either "basic" or "not basic." In planning, they then represent to the government a means of influencing the speed and direction of economic development. Throughout South Asia, with the exception of Malaya,

there have been, in fact, attempts, in some form, to organize state-owned industries.

The issue of government intervention in industry is
assumed, everywhere, to be crucial. The answer to it,
supposedly, will chart a country's course toward radicalism or conservatism. The choice is thought to be open,
hinging on the government's decision to proceed toward
a "socialist" or "free enterprise" society. The South Asian
countries, after independence, could undertake state
ownership of industry in three ways. They could:
   (1) inherit enterprises in the public sector;
   (2) nationalize private enterprises; or
   (3) establish new state industrial enterprises.
The South Asian countries, with few exceptions, inherited little industrial enterprise in the public sector
from the previous colonial regime. (Thailand was never
occupied as a colony.)
Nationalization of privately owned industrial enterprises in the region has so far touched mainly those owned
by foreigners. It has occurred in Burma, where the big
extractive industries were held by foreign concerns, and
in Indonesia. However, in the latter this was done in a
shadowy way that for the most part left foreigners in control of management, or as a political move not primarily
related to socialism; in some instances what was taken
over has since been handed back.
Of the three countries where the public sector is expanding, India has declared that promotion of public
large-scale industry is part of its socialist policy. But
Pakistan and the Philippines are officially free-enterprise
economies. In the latter countries, state undertakings in
industry are justified on two grounds: lack of sufficient
high-calibre private enterprise, and the accrual of benefits
to private enterprise—as they do from state-owned public
utilities—through increasing the supply of scarce goods
and creating external economies. But the same reasons are

advanced in India, ordinarily as arguments for the policy it chooses to call socialist.

In only one respect can India be regarded as more committed to socialism than Pakistan and the Philippines: the latter countries consider the public undertakings to be merely transitional. They have declared their intention to turn over state enterprises to private business as soon as this is feasible, and have partly carried out this intention.

Taking all the foregoing into consideration, there seems to be good reason for deflating the issue of the public versus the private sector as an ideological choice between socialism and free enterprise. The differences in economic policies and in accomplishments in regard to industrial development among the South Asian countries are not closely related to their ideological positions.

When Western scholars speculate as to whether India will allow much private enterprise, they are concerned with future actions rather than with present policies; this is also true in the main of the anxiety sometimes expressed in private business circles in India. By themselves the official policy declarations about a developing socialist economy hardly provide a basis for these fears in the future. Such declarations and ideas have abounded in India since long before independence. Although policy declarations have tended to become more radical, actual policies have given private business more of an entry into the sectors reserved for the state. India's recent difficulties and its increased dependence on foreign aid must be assumed to strengthen this trend.

Neither should the higher growth rate of investments in the public industrial sector give rise to concern about the future of private industrial enterprise, as long as these investments are concentrated in heavy industry. Broadly speaking, they, like investments in public utilities, can be regarded as stimulants to private enterprise. Nor is it realistic to fear that this public sector will strengthen the government's power to control private enterprise. To begin with, its growth is liberalizing to the extent that it overcomes scarcities. And once the government has control of iron, steel, and other products from heavy industry, it should have less need of other controls and should be able to give more opportunity to private enterprise. Finally, the political trend has been conservative, a fact that should also calm the anxieties of private business.

Of two things we can be reasonably certain. First, in India especially, the present patterns of action generate their own momentum and build up considerable resistance to sudden change. Secondly, the established socialist ideology and its practical interpretation will continue to influence future developments. Nonetheless, undue importance is commonly attached to ideological positions. Thus the future of private industry in Pakistan is much less questioned or even discussed, either in that country or in Western nations, although Pakistan's future course may be more uncertain than India's because the pattern of political life is not nearly as well established in Pakistan as in India. But again it must be said that predictions about the direction of policy in any South Asian country are hazardous in the extreme.

Chapter 12

DEMOCRATIC

PLANNING

"Democratic planning" is a term that is popular in South Asia. It embraces many ideas, but the most prominent are the following: First, "democratic planning" is held to mean that planning and the policies coordinated in the plans should enlist not only the support of the masses but also their active participation in preparing and implementing planning. Secondly, it is generally held to mean that this popular participation and cooperation should emerge voluntarily so that state policies can be carried out without regimentation or coercion. In everyday debate these two meanings are generally combined, and are blended with the other ideological elements already mentioned in Chapter 9.

The rationale of the quest for mass participation is simple. In abstract terms, we can say that economic development ultimately requires a change in the way people think, feel, and act. Individually, they will have to alter their attitudes toward life and work; in particular, they will have to work harder and more efficiently and direct their energies into more productive channels. Collectively, they will have to cooperate more to improve their society and thus the conditions in which they live and work. Behind this approach must be the faith that once the masses become aware of their miserable conditions and are shown how to improve them through state policies, they will respond positively by supporting the adoption of these policies and participating in their fulfillment. The quest for mass involvement is the central tenet of "democratic planning." The term "decentralization" is often used as a synonym, especially in reference to political self-government within units smaller than the state. The basic idea is that of organized cooperation between people in the same region or locality, or in the same industry or occupation.

Such cooperation can often easily be arranged in large-scale private business. But the attempt to foster cooperation in agriculture, crafts, and small-scale industry, almost all of which remain in the private sector, is assumed to constitute the essence of democratic planning. The essential element is that, below the national level, people everywhere should cooperate in their common interest. It is only then that planning actually becomes democratic planning.

But in assuming all this, several dilemmas are posed. To begin with, the masses, imprisoned by poverty and tradition, may not be ready to understand or accept the rationalist ideals of planning for development (and still less, the demand for greater equality generally implied). Maurice Zinkin, a Western writer who has been most sympathetic to the hopes of South Asia, put it harshly but well long ago when in his *Development for Free Asia* he wrote: "[The Democratic politician's] difficulty is that in most of Asia it is precisely the wishes and the prejudices of the electorate which stand in the way of development. They *like* their society static, or their handicrafts protected, or their children uneducated, or their pigs uneaten, or their cows kept alive, or their reproduction uncontrolled. The list of the prejudices, beliefs and attitudes which stand in the way of development in one Asian country or another (and, indeed, in Western countries too) is an endless one."

Up to a point, the planners have recognized this and have placed special emphasis on educating the masses through their own participation in the plans. In this, they have often tended to be over-optimistic about how difficult this can be and how long it can take. But without this optimistic bias, the ideology of democratic planning would disintegrate. According to the ideology, the plan should be initiated with the support of the people and carried through by their willing participation and cooperation. But planning cannot await support that is itself to be engendered by the educative process of planning.

There is a second main dilemma. It is generally thought that democratic planning should create greater equality in the interest of the masses. Economic and social equalization, it is assumed, assure voluntary mass support for planning, so that it can be carried out without resort to compulsion. But the power to elect the representative bodies of government that direct the preparation and execution of plans remains predominantly in the hands of privileged groups. And there has been a large-scale failure to achieve greater equality. To these and other dilemmas we shall return later.

The practical means of attaining democratic planning has generally been understood to be the establishment of institutionalized cooperation in various ways and in many fields. In this very inclusive sense "cooperation" embraces many diverse and often overlapping institutional arrangements—from local and district agencies for self-government to credit and other cooperatives, community development programs, agricultural extension, trade unions, and so on.

These ideas and programs stem largely from the ideological influences of the West. In fact, colonial governments tried to promote cooperatives and even to establish
local and district self-government. Even community development is not an entirely new idea. It is common in
South Asia, however, to claim that cooperatives and village self-government are age-old traditions to their
country or their region. These assertions echo the illusions
of a golden-age myth, although they contain an element
of truth, since every primitive, non-market economy has
some type and degree of cooperation and local self-
government, however different from the type of institutional infrastructure the South Asian countries are now
trying to introduce.

In the Western countries, and especially those the South
Asian leaders would like to emulate, highly developed
structures of local government, plus quasi-public and
private organizations that promote the common interests
of groups, have grown up as a result of pressure from
below, often in opposition to the state power used to try
to suppress them. In regard to provincial and local self-
government, the West could build on, and continually
modify, a well-established institutional pattern.

But the South Asian countries are in a hurry and need
the modern infrastructure in order to mobilize popular
support for planning and development. They cannot wait
for an infrastructure to emerge spontaneously from below.
In fact, if a modern infrastructure cannot be created by
state intervention, there is scant hope of any development
at all that might later generate the appropriate spontaneous response. There is no choice but to create the institutional infrastructure by government policy and to spur its
growth by government intervention. This raises a vital
question: is not the ideal of democratic planning rather an
illusion that will weaken the whole effort? These are serious questions and there are others that are equally
serious.

In the Communist countries the institutional infrastructure was created after revolution by political fiat. It was, and is, mainly used for channelling commands from above to the local and sectional levels. As we pointed out in Chapter 9, the ideology of planning in South Asia is in some respects closer to that of the Soviet Union, but the South Asian governments have not created totalitarian and monolithic states. The institutional infrastructure, however, has to be created by state intervention, because otherwise it does not develop. The big question then is whether, once created, it will catch on and have any life of its own to develop further. The hope of democratic planning is that it will.

Already it is apparent that even in regard to the institutional infrastructure the underdeveloped countries in South Asia are destined to constitute a third world of planning, different from both the Western and the Soviet pattern.

In attempting to create such an institutional infrastructure, India has been in the lead, both in planning and in the initiation of programs. The level and intensity of public debate on these efforts has been high, and India has also made by far the most penetrating evaluation studies of the results, particularly of the rural uplift programs.

From the beginning India stressed what it calls the national extension service and community development, which is a coordinated attempt to raise productivity and levels of living and to improve attitudes toward work and life in the villages. The community development program was initiated with great enthusiasm and expectations of rapid gains. But many evaluation studies under different auspices showed early that these expectations were grossly over-optimistic. In most Indian villages nothing has changed much.

To promote cooperation, India intensified the efforts begun in the colonial period to develop credit cooperatives. The number of these has substantially increased and the percentage of total funds that they supply has risen from 3 percent to more than 20 percent. Nevertheless, the countryside is still dominated by moneylenders, and the cooperative movement suffers from the same maladies as in colonial times. Many cooperatives exist mainly on paper. Many others are not true cooperatives; unsuccessful in their efforts to raise money from their members, they serve primarily as agencies for the disbursement of concessional finance. Many are insolvent and their management is often inefficient and corrupt. The Indian planners also encouraged the cooperative movement to enter other fields. But the "multi-purpose cooperatives" and particularly the farming cooperatives have suffered the same defects as the credit cooperatives, and their achievements have been even more modest.

In more recent years, India has emphasized the creation of a statutory basis for local self-government. A three-tiered pyramid of locally elected assemblies, beginning with the village panchayats and culminating at the district level, was established. It was hoped that these institutions would take increasing responsibility for planning and implementation and for general local administration and taxation. As yet, however, these panchayats have not contributed much to the realization of democratic planning goals.

Taken together, Indian policies designed to realize democratic planning are truly impressive in scope. But an appreciation of the magnitude of the work must not blind the observer to the seriousness of the inherent problems. For one thing, it was unrealistic, considering the initial conditions, to hope for *rapid progress* in these efforts toward democratic planning. The fact is, however, that rapid change is as essential as it is difficult to accomplish, while the potential dangers of failure are incalculable. Unfortunately, this is but one of the several dilemmas confronting India and the other South Asian countries in their efforts to accomplish democratic planning.

A second dilemma concerns the scope of the program and, in particular, whether *superficial coverage of the whole country* would be better than intensive efforts in selected areas. In India the latter would have assured more rapid success in certain areas, but most of the country would have remained stagnant.

A third dilemma concerns *aspects of life* with which the programs of rural uplift should be mainly concerned. Recently, the urgent need for more agricultural products has led to widespread agreement to increase farm productivity as a first priority. But since low productivity is related to educational and health conditions and to attitudes, this currently popular view may prove to be mistaken.

The simple truth is that India badly needs to make rapid progress in the whole vast countryside by changing all undesirable conditions. Concentrating on certain aspects of development now or on a few districts and settling for slow progress are both inadequate answers for a very underdeveloped country whose labor force is now increasing by probably 2.5 percent a year and must stay in agriculture if it is not to swell the city slums and shanty towns.

In their initial planning the Indian economists chose the *village* as the lowest basic unit on which to build their development models. Their faith was anchored in the belief that there was a legacy of community feeling in the villages. They believed that the villagers had a good understanding of their own local problems and were more socially minded than Westerners in their relations with each other. There was also the still more questionable assumption that there was a genuine identity of interests among the villagers.

But in actuality the type of self-government and cooperation that the Indian program for rural uplift has been trying to foster departs sharply from past or existing practices and attitudes. The new programs attempt to induce the villagers to be rational and to seek change and improvement, while traditional self-government and cooperation have, at best, been concerned with preserving established relations.

The Indian village is the very stronghold of the inequalities, conflicts of interest, and resistance to change—all the attitudes caused by and in turn buttressing stagnation that the policy of democratic planning must overcome. The romanticized view of the village as a unit with a harmony of interests is so strong, however, that very few Indian writers have dared challenge it, even on the basis of efficiency. It is certainly doubtful whether the village should be preserved as the basic unit. Perhaps forces for change can be mobilized only by integrating the village into a bigger unit right from the start.

A fundamental idea underlying democratic planning is that it should be a *"building from below"* and that, moreover, it should come into existence through the voluntary participation and cooperation of the people. The British were constantly criticized for being unwilling or unable to enlist the wholehearted participation of the people. Independent India, it was believed, would steer a new course. Hence the dilemma. For in the stagnant villages of South Asia, this voluntary participation does not emerge spontaneously as it did in Western Europe. The great poverty and the rapid population increase rule out gradualness; the alternative to rapid development is no development at all or even regression.

Certainly the state must step in to help in the creation of village leadership. But the question is whether this will touch off the force that will give self-government the chance to gather momentum as a truly popular movement. The governments have not wanted their people simply to follow their own inclinations but rather to follow the course of action these governments prescribe while participating in new institutions that should improve their living conditions. This means a tremendous change, and the stress on voluntary participation only makes it more difficult. The instrument for carrying out this social and economic revolution is necessarily the administration, which has to be enlarged, trained, and redirected. This is especially true since these governments do not have a fanatic and disciplined party cadre, as the Communists do. The ideological formula, so frequently reiterated, that self-government and cooperation should not be "handed down from above" but should spring from the wishes of the people is thus largely a self-deception; indulging in it is hardly likely to make the planning of rural uplift rational and effective.

Many of South Asia's organs for self-government were created more in the Western mold and intended to be the means by which the people asserted themselves, especially in India. But more often these organizations have been run by officials as central government agencies. The trade unions are a case in point. Throughout South Asia, trade unionism is confined mainly to large-scale industry and plantations; no serious attempts have been made to organize agricultural workers. There has been, in some countries, an effort by government leaders to help the workers as the weaker party in the labor-management struggle, particularly when the management is under foreign direction. On the other hand, there has been the feeling that work stoppages, the final resort in collective bargaining, would hinder economic development. Consequently, there has often been lip service paid to the Western concept of independent and assertive labor unions, while government efforts have actually been turned toward pulling the union into restraint on wages and cooperation through conciliation and arbitration. This leaves most of the trade unions in South Asia almost indistinguishable, ideologically, from those in the Soviet Union.

But all these efforts to create machinery for self-government, cooperation, and popular participation without changing the basic social and economic structure are essentially attempts to bypass the equality issue. And this attempt to evade the problem of inequality is in large part responsible for the failure of these reform policies. This issue is here presented as a dilemma—indeed the basic dilemma of the ideology and policy of democratic planning—because it is difficult to see how, given the political and social conditions in India and the other South Asian countries, a very different policy could have been followed.

In India many of the leaders who have embraced the tenets of Gandhi frankly recognize the inequality that prevails in the village structure. They even talk of the need for a full-scale revolution that would abolish caste and private ownership of land. But they have advocated achieving this without compulsion. Nehru understood the weakness of this approach, saying that instead of real change in the social order, stress was placed on charity and benevolence within the existing system and the vested interests remained where they were.

In discussions of the practical issues of rural uplift and democratic planning, it is often emphasized that the institutions for self-government and cooperation should embrace *all members of the villages*. The hope is that the democratic process will result in special consideration for the poorer and weaker; the privileged will be induced to forfeit their privileges and enter into truly democratic cooperation with the unprivileged. This line of thought can be said to be the official creed in India; it is supported by Gandhi's trust in non-violent social change, when the people can be brought to work together. But in the official debates, there have been publicly expressed doubts about all this. D. R. Gadgil, in his *Economic Policy and Development,* characterizes this type of Gandhism as "little more than revivalism." He holds that the failure of Gandhi's approach "lay essentially in not recognizing the need for thoroughly demolishing the older institutional and class forms before a new synthesis could be attempted."

In India's peculiar ideological situation, it is easy for the politicians and intellectual elite to make clarion calls for greater equality and the removal of injustice from the villages. But few of those making these pronouncements would back practical measures to realize these ideals. Directing development from above is contrary to *their* ideals. But, as Richard Bendix, writing in "Public Authority in a Developing Political Community: The Case of India," contends, the villagers are being asked to cooperate today, not tomorrow, "and today they are deeply divided by great economic inequalities and intense communal affiliations. The fact is that the 'public' does not possess that capacity for a village-wide solidarity and organization which may arise in some distant future if and when the conditions of village society have been transformed."

More important is the fact that rural uplift measures have themselves tended to benefit primarily those who are already better off than most. Although contrary to the objectives, this tendency is a natural, indeed a necessary, consequence of applying uplift policies in an inegalitarian society without prior or simultaneous efforts to break down the existing institutional barriers to greater equality. The whole system of administration encourages these tendencies.

The administration itself has a strong hierarchical inheritance that no amount of sermonizing will change, at least not rapidly. Douglas Ensminger of the Ford Foundation, an American expert who played a leading role in

India's community development efforts, warns against the caste-like attitudes of the civil servants initiating these programs. He complained that "all too frequently the village worker is looked upon, and treated, as a low grade peon, not as a co-worker" and that "the present caste system within the administrative hierarchy is a further major deterrent to the success of the community programme."

There are also frequent complaints about the social barriers and the aloofness many administrators raise against the lower strata. But this failure is not fully explained by looking only at the administrator's own actions and attitudes. Even if he were the most dedicated and energetic of men, could he really be expected to go into a village and rouse the untouchables to rebel against their exploitation? He would no doubt be driven from the village, or at best be discharged for incompetence. *He is not sent out to start a revolution on behalf of the government,* but to accomplish something practical. To do this, he naturally deals with the propertied class and the dominant castes. He can work with them, and they are more receptive, since they stand to gain most from his efforts. It is equally logical that the lowest classes consider him to be only a government agent, in no fundamental sense one of their own. The logic of the situation accounts for the exclusion of the poorer villagers from the program— except as potential voluntary laborers and recipients of a few crumbs. It also explains why the results are so insignificant and so delayed. Substantial rapid development would require especially that the backward groups begin to have their own ambitions, but the present political, social, and economic setting does not foster this change.

Western observers of this dilemma demonstrate much ambivalence toward it. They applaud the community development programs, partly because they approve of their conservative, basically anti-Communist thrust. Yet they also often feel that the conservative forces are

already too strong and that to avoid revolution the South
Asian countries must reform the inegalitarian structure of
the villages. They regret that more has not been done in
land reform and tenant protection. Yet there has been
very little determined criticism, and the equality issue is
studiously avoided when community programs are discussed. It is evident that diplomacy has been a major
concern in most of the writings on the various programs of
democratic planning.

The dilemma of "voluntariness" is often obscured by
the widespread confusion of three altogether different
meanings of the term. One meaning is that democratic
planning requires the people's participation and initiative,
not in a distant future, but as early as possible in the
course of creating the new institutions for self-government and cooperation. Fundamentally, the problem of
planning is how to induce people to participate and cooperate in remedying all the less satisfactory conditions
that make a country underdeveloped. A second meaning
is that the entire planning and development process
should take place within a democratic political framework. In all the South Asian countries, even those where
the forms of political democracy have been relinquished,
there is a pretense that the regime is "democratic" in the
sense that it attempts to conform to the needs and desires
of the people.

The third meaning holds that the participation and
cooperation of the people shall be sought without resort
to compulsion, by relying on persuasion and conciliation.
India has definitely leaned toward the latter choice, to an
extent that seems extraordinary to a foreign observer,
whether from a Western or a Communist country. The
other countries in South Asia have made a similar choice.
There is in all respects extreme laxity, and government
policy is continually trying to do things by using the
carrot rather than the stick.

It must be observed that this preference is not logically or factually identical with the two other meanings. It is obviously not identical with political democracy. All these countries have placed fewer obligations on their citizens and have enforced even those they have much less effectively than the Western democracies. This avoidance of compulsion is certainly not identical with the first meaning of "voluntariness." Instead of promoting cooperation, this abstention from establishing and enforcing rules only serves to increase the cynicism and disinterest of the masses. This is particularly true if they recognize the government's failure to enforce greater equality.

It is no exaggeration to say that in the whole region there is a systematic blending of the three meanings of "voluntariness." This has produced confusion, and the confusion has been increased by representing this unclear mixture as a stand against Communism and against terror and regimentation. The Western countries, whose policies call for aid and advice to South Asia, have applauded all this as evidence that the region is determined not to "go Communist." Ironically, it has also been tacitly accepted by the European Communist countries, who are eager to appear "democratic" and therefore reluctant to advise more compulsion. Further, these countries appear to believe that compulsion could not be applied in South Asia until after a revolution, and they are careful not to push that at this stage.

The real and very serious dilemma covered up by this verbal fuzziness about the ideal of voluntariness is that *there is little hope in South Asia for rapid development without greater social discipline.* To begin with, in the absence of more discipline—which will not appear without regulations backed by compulsion—all measures of rural uplift will be largely ineffective. In principle, discipline can be effected within the framework of whatever degree of political democracy a country can achieve; in the end nothing is more dangerous for democracy than lack of discipline. But the political and social conditions in these countries block the enactment of regulations that impose greater obligations. Even when laws are enacted, they cannot be easily enforced.

It should be possible, however, both for the indigenous intellectual elite who establish the region's ideologies and for the outside observer, to clarify concepts and to avoid concealing factual difficulties in romantically confused verbiage. To do so could be of practical importance, in terms of conclusions about how to overcome by government policy, purposively and gradually, the inhibitions and obstacles to effective reform, and even, in the best of cases, how to accomplish this without relinquishing the basic tenets in the accepted democratic ideology.

The several dilemmas touched on above are interrelated. They all branch out from the dilemma of voluntariness, which in turn is explained by the complex of social conditions that we have referred to as the "soft state." When we characterize the countries of South Asia as "soft states" we mean that, throughout the region, national governments require extraordinarily little of their citizens. Even those obligations that do exist are inadequately enforced. This low level of social discipline is one of the most fundamental differences between the South Asian countries today and the Western countries at the beginning of their development.

There is reason to believe that the South Asian countries, in pre-colonial times, had systems of obligations similar to those of the West in medieval and pre-medieval periods. Even in South Asia these networks of obligations ensured the upkeep of roads and canals and other community facilities. In the West, the growth of the community and the protective discipline needed to preserve it has been steady throughout the years; today everyone, rich or poor, is equally bound by the system of community control. South Asia has not experienced a similar evolution from the primitive and static village organization. Instead, colonialism ordinarily led to a decay of the ancient village organization without the creation of a substitute. In India Gandhi built a philosophy and a theory of political tactics on non-cooperation. In those South Asian countries that lacked a Gandhi or even a strong liberation movement, disobedience and non-cooperation were nevertheless a natural protest and defense against the enforced colonial power structure. The legacy is a set of anarchic attitudes with an ideological and emotional force deriving from memories of resistance against the colonial power. In the newly independent countries, this attitude is now being turned against their own authorities.

From a Western point of view, the obvious solution to widespread and serious indiscipline might seem to be that the government should rapidly establish a rational system of community rules and see to it that they are properly enforced. Indeed, this would appear to be the most essential element in planning for development. There are, however, a number of reasons why such advice is difficult or impossible to follow in South Asia. First, there is the historical legacy, in which colonialism generated attitudes of resistance to authority that have not disappeared with independence. The inauguration of a "strong state" is handicapped not only by the attitudes and institutions in the villages, but also by inhibitions of the rulers. Moreover, no South Asian country has an administration prepared to enforce new rules, even when these rules are not very revolutionary. Corruption, rampant at least on the lower levels even in colonial times, is generally increasing and takes the edge off commands from the central government.

There is also an important ideological element among the inhibitions. The new countries of South Asia have generally accepted the egalitarian ideals of the Western democratic welfare state and the Communist countries.

The fact that reforms in the interest of the underprivileged strata are largely thwarted on the level of both legislation and implementation must make precisely those members of the government and the intellectual elite who are most devoted to the egalitarian ideals wary of measures that would demand performance from the masses of poor people.

Nonetheless, it is beyond doubt that *rapid development will be exceedingly difficult to engender without an increase in social discipline in all strata and even in the villages.* It is therefore disturbing that all the plans are silent on this point. Even in India, where planning had been made a going concern and where successive plans did take account of such a variety of relevant issues, one has to scrutinize the plans very closely indeed to find a few references to the need for regulations placing obligations on villagers; even these are apparently presented without much conviction and are not acted upon. On the whole, the need for greater discipline is avoided in public discussion—much more in fact than in Gandhi's time, for he often upbraided his people for laziness, uncleanliness, and general lack of orderliness. The general pattern today is, instead, to pray for a new community "spirit."

Chapter 13

OPERATIONAL CONTROLS OVER THE PRIVATE SECTOR

The plans the South Asian countries have produced in the past for their development have been constructed as fiscal plans. It is true that many of them contain sections that call for legislation or administrative action that is expected to improve public services, provide land reform, support birth control, or make other large and structural changes in the institutions and attitudes that form the framework of their society. But since these reforms are only incidentally related to public expenditures, and as in any case only costs but not returns are accounted for, they are really not integrated into the body of the plans.

In addition, there is a whole system of what we shall call "operational controls" over the private sector. Within that system we include all the short-range policy measures applied by governments to influence people's economic behavior in some particular respect. Even

185

though similarities exist, operational controls are different from long-range reforms in that they are meant to be the levers of policy, the manipulation of which is needed to ensure that development proceeds from month to month and year to year as closely in line with the targets of the plans as is feasible in a context of change.

While policies intended to induce fundamental changes in institutions and attitudes, even if not rationally integrated, are often discussed at length in the plans, operational controls, and the way in which they should be handled, are usually not discussed at all. Little or no attention is paid even to such vital matters as interest rates and other credit conditions, the prices state-owned enterprises should charge for their goods and services, price controls and rationing, or the licensing of private enterprise and investment. In particular, the plans are silent on the crucial problem of how to achieve a rational coordination of controls so that *together* they direct development toward plan fulfillment. This means the plans are not "operational." The controls are not really planned in advance, but have to be improvised in an *ad hoc* fashion. They are certainly not analyzed as a system in the sense that the several controls are seen to be interchangeable or that one type of control makes other controls necessary. From the point of view of planning, the problem should always be viewed as the total impact of all the various controls on development.

We classify the operational controls as being in two broad groups: *positive* and *negative*. The positive controls are aimed at stimulating, encouraging, facilitating, and inducing production, investment, or consumption. We include in these controls educational campaigns aimed at clarifying the business situation and encouraging investment; the provision of technical assistance to the private sector, subsidies, tax holidays, and credits on easy terms; the allocation of products from state-owned enterprises at controlled prices; and protection by import controls and the provision of foreign exchange. The negative controls, on the contrary, are meant to prevent or limit production by means of bullying; administrative restrictions on capital stock issues, investment, and production; the denial of foreign exchange; rationing of producers' or consumers' goods; the imposition of excise duties; and so forth.

Although in common usage the word "controls" has a negative connotation, for want of a better term we have adhered to it to describe all operational state intervention in the economic life of a country. A more material qualification to be borne in mind here is that controls may often be negative and positive at the same time. For instance, state controls over foreign exchange allocations and imports is a negative control for some importers but a positive control for others, and certainly it is regularly a positive control in protecting domestic producers from foreign competition.

Another distinction between controls relates to how they are applied. If their application involves an individual decision by an administrative authority, they are called *discretionary*. But if they are applied automatically from a definite rule, or by means of price regulations, tariff duties, or subsidies given to a particular branch of industry without the possibility of discrimination in favor of particular firms, the controls are presumed to be *nondiscretionary*. This distinction is, on the whole, identical with that between "direct" or "physical" controls and "indirect" controls as described in many writings on this subject. There are instances where a general administrative ruling is laid down in such clear and specific terms that there is no room for discretion, if the ruling is strictly followed. But that case is rare in South Asia. Whenever administration gets its fingers into the pie there will ordinarily be opportunities for discretion and, consequently, also for discrimination.

In comparison with the developed Western countries, the countries of South Asia—with some considerable differences—are relying very heavily on administrative discretionary controls as opposed to automatically applied, non-discretionary controls. But the scarcity in South Asia of administrative personnel with both competence and integrity makes discretionary controls all the more difficult to execute with reasonable effectiveness, and also makes reliance on them more hazardous, even morally. With this consideration in mind, we derive the value premise that, on the whole, it would be desirable if non-discretionary controls were used to the maximum extent possible.

There are often in the South Asian plans general statements in favor of automatically applied non-discretionary controls, usually through policy measures affecting the price mechanism. Practice, however, is very different and planners apparently regard the use of administrative discretionary controls as standard procedure, indeed as the very essence of planning. In particular, one gets the feeling that South Asian economists and politicians of a more radical bent look upon the willingness of a government to employ discretionary controls as a particularly "socialist" trait. This confusion of thought is reflected by many Western writers who find in the plethora of administrative discretionary controls in South Asia an indication of a socialist or even a "Marxist" turn of mind. Business circles keep up a running fire of criticism against the government for interference in business, but this criticism is queerly subdued and very apparently not meant to be taken too seriously. The explanation for this is that the interests of business and particularly big business are, on the whole, greatly favored in the system of discretionary controls that is actually applied.

First a few words about controls in the agricultural sector, the largest by far in South Asian economies. After independence, the new governments found themselves with an agricultural sector in which formal markets were weak or even non-existent and where non-discretionary price controls were seldom effective or even applicable. There remained also a legacy of paternalism and authoritarianism, with the peasants expecting to have officials interfering to organize and direct their activities. But at the same time, they also demonstrated an inherited tendency toward sullen non-obedience, and an established pattern of trying to get away with as much as possible. In colonial times Western officials were conditioned to look on the villagers as disorderly, lazy, and unambitious children whom they had to look after without, however, getting involved too much, particularly in social problems. Administrative discretionary controls were exercised directly by these officials and their subordinates.

It was a natural ambition for native politicians who succeeded the Western officials to step into their shoes. The states that the new governments took over were "soft states," and this was particularly the case in rural areas and in regard to agriculture. In the present context the implication was that the independent governments found themselves even more constrained than the colonial governments from using non-discretionary controls.

However, one very big difference was implied in the coming to power of native political leaders. They, as well as the whole intellectual elite in the area, were committed to push for development implying fundamental change. In view of the conditions that existed in the rural districts, the governments felt compelled to exert an increased influence on community life. In the absence of effective markets and with price incentive foredoomed to remain weak, administrative discretionary controls were essential if this influence was to be exercised. All South Asian countries shunned negative controls that laid down specific duties on any class of villagers. This implied that the policies for rural uplift must be confined to the positive discretionary controls. Cooperatives and organizations for self-government became instruments for offering positive inducements, ranging from instruction to subsidies of all sorts. In the previous chapter we have discussed these policy measures and also pointed out how, in the absence of structural changes of land ownership and tenancy, they tended to favor the less poor in the villages and so increased inequality in the rural districts.

Positive discretionary controls, and particularly subsidies in various forms, also have another effect. As they multiply, so does the need to supervise those officials who administer them and, in turn, to supervise the supervisors. Rigidity, red tape, and bureaucracy easily become the *signum* of planning and reform. Undoubtedly, the large and growing volume of positive discretionary controls in the agricultural sector, with the need for even more discriminatory decisions, tends to lower the standards of administrative efficiency and honesty. Ineptitude and corruption, in turn, are apt to poison the spirit of the movement to promote democratic planning through local participation in organs for cooperation and self-government. This is a true dilemma that cannot possibly be solved in an ideal way. When attitudes and institutions are archaic and more fundamental institutional reforms are excluded for political reasons, little can be done in pursuance of a development policy by means of price policies and other automatically applied, non-discretionary controls. Negative controls are unworkable, as they also lack political and psychological backing.

Most of the discussion of the operational controls in South Asia and their implementation has been focused on the modernized industrial sector. The enterprises in this small sector, whether private or publicly owned and managed, tend, as in colonial times, to be enclaves amid a much larger traditional economy. Neither their supply of labor or other factors of production nor the demand for their products operates in anything like a perfect market. They also tend to retain many characteristics of traditional manufacturing. Thus nepotism and "connections" play a large role. It is nevertheless in this modernized sector, often called the "organized" sector, that price policies and other non-discretionary controls could be expected to be more effective, and we would assume that planners and governments would use this opportunity to the utmost, since it would minimize the need for state intervention of the discretionary type to attain the targets of the plans. The fact is, however, that even here administrative discretionary controls are used to an extraordinary extent.

During and immediately after the Second World War, all the Western countries were forced to impose commodity and price controls and to bolster these with rationing, licensing, and so forth. Those Western countries that had colonial territories introduced these same controls there. Thus the independent governments that came into power after the war often inherited most of their discretionary controls; in any case, the Western wartime controls provided a model for them to copy and develop further. In general, the Western countries tried to drop such controls as quickly as they could.

But in the low-elasticity economies of South Asia, the need for discretionary controls remained much greater and more enduring. Even in the organized sector, market conditions are still such that the governments must regularly apply discretionary controls to a much greater extent than the Western countries find necessary. This analogy points thus to a rationale for the control system applied in South Asia. The basic reasons are, first, the region's poverty and underdevelopment—which is reflected in the traditional character of business enterprises in an economy where bottlenecks and surpluses are more normal than a balance between demand and supply—and secondly, its interest in engendering and directing development. But the reliance on discretionary controls to the extent they have been used cannot be considered necessary.

· · ·

One of the major bottlenecks in most of South Asia (Malaya and Thailand excepted) is the scarcity of foreign exchange. If there were adequate foreign exchange, the imports that are needed to overcome shortages in the organized industrial sector could more easily be obtained. This scarcity of hard currency with which to buy abroad often can not be overcome to any substantial extent by price policies or other non-discretionary controls such as customs tariffs, multiple exchange rates, or import surcharges. Nor can devaluation be expected to improve the foreign exchange situation very much. Whatever the exchange rate, countries like India and Pakistan must hold tightly to their import controls. If they did not, they would be abandoning one of the most important tools in their planning armory. These import controls must be essentially discretionary in regard to the nature and quantity of goods allowed to be imported. Otherwise not enough foreign exchange would be left to import the essential consumer goods and those needed for development.

Such an import control has the incidental effect of affording protection to production at home of products that are prevented from entering the country from abroad. The tighter the import control is, which ordinarily means the less essential the products are, the higher the protection becomes. This perverse effect could be prevented by prohibiting the production of certain products which the government deems to be entirely unnecessary and by laying excess duties on the production of other products.

Such non-discretionary controls are ordinarily not applied, and never fully applied; this has the incidental effect that the pieces of paper by which the granting of an import license is authorized become an individual gift worth money. Apart from this, the reluctance to use the non-discretionary negative controls makes it then necessary to counteract the clearly irrational protective effects by a complex system of discretionary controls.

In India, new security issues of companies are controlled by the government. A government license is required for all new major undertakings in the industrial field or for changes in their locations or in the things they manufacture. The government also has the power to investigate the conduct of any industrial enterprise, and, if its directives are not followed, it can replace the management. Under the Essential Commodities Act, the Indian government can regulate the production and handling of all foodstuffs and raw materials. The Indian Tariff Commission fixes the prices of all the products of protected industries and can, if it chooses, limit profits to 8–12 percent of the invested capital. The State Trading Corporation has been given a monopoly on the import and distribution of important commodities with the object of insuring a "fair distribution at a reasonable price."

The result is that *no major, and indeed few minor, business decisions can be taken except with the prior permission of the administrative authorities or at the risk of subsequent government disapproval.* All these negative discretionary controls authorized are, of course, never utilized to the full. If they were, no part of the organized sector could be called "private" in any meaningful sense. From time to time the scope of those controls that are actually employed is altered by government or administrative decisions. But there is a narrow limit to what can be accomplished in this direction, as long as there is scarcity of foreign exchange and a reluctance to use nondiscretionary controls to master the situation.

In Pakistan, despite repeated assertions in the plans and by government spokesmen that administrative discretionary controls should be relaxed and more reliance placed on working through the price mechanism, the situation is broadly similar to that in India. Ceylon has been moving in the same direction. Burma and Indonesia have been pushed even farther toward administrative discretionary controls by the radical bent of their political development and the insurrections and civil wars that have marked their recent history. Malaya and Thailand have relatively few negative discretionary controls, though their positive controls—for instance, the granting of tax exemptions to new undertakings—are to an unusual extent a matter for political and administrative discretion. It should be noted that in all of Southeast Asia, as in Ceylon, discretionary regulations have been adopted partly because of the desire to discriminate in favor of majority groups against ethnic minorities and foreigners. This aim could not be pursued through non-discretionary controls.

In a system of operational controls of the Indian type, the application of one set of controls makes necessary the application of others, which ordinarily also have to be discretionary. To make fixed prices effective, allocation and rationing are needed. Often more far-reaching intervention on the supply side is also required. There is thus a self-perpetuating and expansionary tendency in every system of discretionary controls, especially when the economy is suffering from a shortage of domestic supplies and foreign exchange.

All economic planning in South Asia starts out from the idea that development should be pushed. More particularly, it is felt that private enterprise and, specifically, investment in production is in need of promotion and stimulation. This view is commonly held even in a country like India, where the growth of the public sector is pronounced as a prominent goal in planning.

A major consideration in fixing the prices charged by the public sector, for instance, has been that they should be kept low to encourage private enterprise. Various tax exemptions are given to encourage new business ventures, and the laxity of tax administration works in the same direction. Rates of interest in the organized capital market are held low, often lower than in the developed countries, in spite of the great scarcity of capital. Special credit institutions are created that often subsidize borrowers with cheap credits.

Even though the initial notion that there is too little private enterprise and that it needs to be encouraged is correct, it has actually become encouraged to the extent that it has had to be curbed. This is because supplies, particularly of foreign exchange, are not inexhaustible but very limited. Most of this encouragement is provided by positive discretionary controls. Administrative discretion is ordinarily exercised to determine who shall be serviced by the public sector and who shall receive loans at special rates of interest from finance corporations and, of course, who shall be allotted foreign exchange. As the positive controls are too strong, the result is a need for negative controls. Like the positive ones, they are given the character of administrative controls. In the process of both promoting and curtailing business, the government and the administration become directly involved in all phases of private enterprise.

An odd situation is thus created. While everybody talks about the necessity of encouraging private enterprise, and while a great number of positive controls are instituted with this in view, *most officials have to devote most of their time and energy to limiting or stopping enterprise* by means of the whole paraphernalia of negative discretionary controls exemplified above. This is like driving a car with the accelerator pushed to the floor but the brakes on. The need for a wide range of negative controls on a discretionary basis is to a large extent the result of applying excessive positive operational controls. The important point to stress is that encouraging private enterprise beyond practical limits makes necessary a gargantuan bureaucratic system of administrative discretionary controls to harness it, particularly as the positive controls mostly are of the discretionary type.

The abolition or relaxation of some positive controls would render some negative controls less necessary. The widespread existence of conflicting controls has the implication that there is need of *more* controls and that a *larger* part of them must be of a discretionary type than would otherwise be necessary. This is particularly unfortunate from a development point of view, as one of the most serious bottlenecks in the South Asian countries is the lack of administrators of competence and integrity.

The situation we are describing is undoubtedly in large part due to a lack of coordination, that is, to a deficiency in planning. The natural tendency of the planners and still more of the executors of the plans to set their sights high, but to not provide enough non-discretionary restraints to achieve their objective, leads to a system of controls full of internal conflicts, with the result that it becomes necessary to increase the volume of controls and make them discretionary.

As a result of the conflicting control pattern, those businessmen who can dodge through them stand to make extraordinarily high profits. The profits are "too high" in the sense that they are higher than needed in order to call forth the desired and possible volume of enterprise and investment. They are a consequence of the price system's not being conditioned to give entrepreneurs the inducements that are "correct" from the standpoint of plan fulfillment. The "too high" profits are, moreover, not very effectively soaked up by taxation; even when marginal tax rates are very high, South Asian tax laws contain convenient loopholes, and large-scale tax evasion is the rule.

To those businessmen who must find their way through the jungle of controls, the situation must seem inordinately complicated. They do complain about the proliferation of state interference, sometimes very loudly. But no observer can fail to note that these outcries are weak and, in truth, half-hearted. For one thing, private entrepreneurs have become so accustomed to the situation that they take it as much for granted as the climate, the observed caste rules in India, and many other conditions of life. Also, the individual private entrepreneur may be loath to protest a particular decision, as he knows that he will repeatedly have to seek the favor of the officials in charge. But the main consideration is, of course, that the stakes are high enough to make all the inconveniences very worthwhile. This means that all those who can make their way through the controls have a vested interest in continuing the pattern.

Another pattern is also obvious. Any system of administrative discretionary controls tends, against often proclaimed intentions to the contrary, to favor those already active in a field where permission of some sort is needed. Those already in business are better informed and they have better contacts with the officials. They are also more ready to give advice and cooperation when the government asks for it.

All this tends to restrict competition, favor monopoly and oligopoly, and pamper vested interests. In the present context this means that established businesses and, in particular, large-scale enterprises are greatly favored by the system of operational controls applied. This is in direct contradiction to stated policy goals. Also, the present system tends to place obstacles in the way of the birth of new firms or the expansion of small ones.

If big business has a vested interest in continuing these patterns of controls, the officials and politicians who operate the controls also have a vested interest in preserving them. We have already pointed to the power they acquire by virtue of the fact that so many controls are discretionary. This power is the greater as the controls are not integrated in the plans and the directives governing their use therefore tend to be vague. Application is a matter of administrative judgment, and there are often good reasons to decide in favor of established, large-scale firms, so they can preserve a good conscience.

But in a setting where caste, family, economic and social status, and, more generally, "connections" traditionally mean so much, the risk of collusion is great—and it extends from the upper strata in the capitals down to the villages. The result is often plain corruption. Indeed, the prevalence of discretionary controls invites dishonesty. As a United States Economic Survey Team sent to Indonesia wrote, "the problem of graft is the Siamese twin of direct controls."

The crucial role of South Asia's system of discretionary controls in undermining morality should not be underestimated. When the wartime Western world had to rely on a plethora of discretionary controls, even there black markets and corruption spread in spite of the very superior administrative machinery and personnel. In South Asia there is circular causation with cumulative effects in the sense that a corrupt body of administrators and politicians will have an interest in preserving and building up discretionary controls that give them the opportunity to enrich themselves.

In the Western world the price mechanism has increasingly become the servant of the policies chosen by the people through their democratic institutions. And the conditions under which that mechanism operates are continually changed to fit those inclinations better in a changing world. In this process the state has come to exert an ever greater influence on the course of events—a far greater one than in the South Asian countries, which are all "functioning anarchies," to use a term John Kenneth Galbraith has coined. But this influence in the West is, so far as possible, brought to bear by means of price and tax policies and other non-discretionary controls. The South Asian system of controls shows still less similarity with the policies of the Communist countries, which do not have a private sector to deal with. Again we face the fact that the South Asian countries are a third world of planning.

The analysis in this chapter has been based on the value premise that operational controls should to the maximum extent possible be of a non-discretionary type. This value premise is derived from the modernization ideals; it represents one of the points where in their own interest the South Asian countries should try to be more like the Western countries—if they do not opt instead for nationalizing the private sector and becoming like the Communist countries. But it should be conceded that the South Asian countries' reliance on discretionary controls is in part firmly rooted in necessity. The fragmentation or even absence of markets and the lack of response to price incentives make non-discretionary controls less effective.

Nevertheless, it should not be necessary to give such a tremendous preponderance to discretionary controls. If the operational controls were better planned and coordinated, there would be greater scope for non-discretionary controls and, in particular, it would be possible to avoid those controls that are the result of conflicts of policy. There are, however, strong forces working to preserve the structure of discretionary controls. One force is the ideological and attitudinal legacy of authoritarianism and paternalism. Another force is the vested interest of administrators, politicians, and big businessmen.

In no other field of South Asian economic policy is there such a lack not only of scientific analysis, but of systematic and specific knowledge of the empirical facts. The operational controls are not planned, they are clearly not coordinated, and the manner of their application is usually not disclosed in any detail. What we have tried to do is put together a "theory" that will provide a logically coordinated system of questions for further research.

Chapter 14

CORRUPTION—
ITS CAUSES
AND EFFECTS

The significance of corruption in Asia is highlighted by the fact that wherever a political regime has crumbled—in Pakistan and Burma, for instance, and in China—a major and often decisive cause has been the prevalence of misconduct among politicians and administrators and the resulting spread of unlawful practices among businessmen and the general public. The problem is of vital concern to the governments of South Asia, because the habitual practice of bribery and dishonesty paves the way for an authoritarian regime, which justifies itself by the disclosures of corruption and the punitive actions it takes against the offenders. Elimination of corruption has regularly been advanced as a main justification for military takeovers. And should the new regime fail to wipe out corruption, its failure prepares the ground for another putsch of some sort. It is obvious that the extent of cor-

ruption has a direct bearing on the stability of governments in the region.

Yet corruption is almost taboo as a research topic. It is
rarely mentioned in scholarly discussions of government
and planning, even by Western experts, revealing a general bias that we have characterized as diplomacy in
research. Embarrassing questions are avoided by ignoring
the problems of attitudes and institutions. South Asian
social scientists are particularly inclined to take this easy
road, whether they are conservatives or radicals. When
this bias is challenged, it is rationalized by certain sweeping assertions—that there is corruption in all countries;
that corruption is natural in South Asian countries because of deeply ingrained institutions and attitudes carried over from colonial and pre-colonial times; that
corruption is needed to oil the intricate machinery of
business and politics in South Asia, and is, perhaps, not
really a liability at all. These excuses are irrelevant and
transparently thin, and they are mostly wrong. They are
more often expressed in conversation than in print.

The problem of corruption, though not yet a subject of
research, is very much on the minds of articulate South
Asians. Particularly in the countries that have preserved
parliamentary democracy and freedom of public discussion, newspapers devote much of their space and the
political assemblies much of their time to the matter. In
all countries conversation, when it is free and relaxed,
frequently turns to political scandals. Periodically, anti-
corruption campaigns are waged, laws passed, vigilance
agencies set up, and special police establishments assigned to investigate reports of misconduct. Sometimes
officials, mostly in the lower brackets, are prosecuted and
punished, and occasionally a minister is forced to resign.
Yet the articulate in all these countries believe that corruption is rampant and that it is growing, particularly
among the higher officials and politicians, including the
legislators and ministers. The ostentatious efforts to pre-

vent corruption and the assertions that the corrupt are being dealt with as they deserve only seem to spread cynicism, especially as to how far all this touches the "higher-ups."

From the foregoing, two elements are clearly in evidence: what may be called the "folklore of corruption," that is, people's beliefs about corruption and the emotions attached to those beliefs; and public policy measures that may be loosely labelled "anti-corruption campaigns," that is, legislative, administrative, and judicial institutions set up to enforce the integrity of public officials at all levels. Both of these are clearly visible and should be easy to record and analyze.

The folklore of corruption itself embodies important social facts worth intensive research in their own right. This folklore has a crucial bearing on how people conduct their private lives and how they view their government's efforts to consolidate the nation and direct and spur development. It easily leads people to think that anybody in a position of power is likely to exploit this in the interest of himself, his family, or other social groups to which he feels loyal. A related question worth studying with this is the extent to which the folklore of corruption contributes to create a weak sense of loyalty to organized society. If corruption becomes taken for granted, resentment amounts essentially to envy of those who have opportunities for private gain by dishonest dealings. Viewed from another angle, these beliefs about corruptibility, especially the belief that known offenders can continue their corrupt practices with little risk of punishment, are apt to reinforce the conviction that this type of cynical asocial behavior is normal. The folklore of corruption then becomes in itself damaging, for it can give an exaggerated impression of the prevalence of corruption, especially among officials at high levels.

. . .

With public debate quite open as in India, Ceylon, and the Philippines, and with gossip flourishing in all South Asian countries, the facts in individual cases of wrongdoing should often not be too difficult to ascertain. The main research task is, of course, to establish the general nature and extent of corruption in a country, its incursion upon various levels and branches of political and economic life, and any trends that are discernible. What follows below is a very preliminary sorting out of problems for research. What is said is based on extensive reading of parliamentary records, committee reports, newspapers, and other publications and, even more, on conversations with knowledgeable persons in the region, including Western businessmen, as well as on personal observations. The fact that in the United States corruption has for generations been intensively and fruitfully researched should counter the notion that nothing can be learned about this phenomenon.

Concerning first the general level of corruption, it is unquestionably much higher than in the Western developed countries or in the Communist countries. If a comparison is made with conditions in the colonial era, the usual view of both South Asian and Western observers is that corruption is more prevalent now than in colonial times. In particular, there is the conviction that it has gained ground among the higher echelons of officials and politicians. As for the different branches of administration in the South Asian governments, it is generally assumed that public works departments and government purchasing agencies are particularly corrupt, with officials who control import and export licenses, collect customs duties and taxes, and manage the railroads running them a close second. It is apparent that whenever discretionary powers are given to officials, there will tend to be corruption. Corruption has sometimes even spread to the courts of justice and to the universities.

In the parliamentary and official studies of corruption, particularly those in India, there has been a general silence on the role played by Western business interests competing for markets in South Asia. Western business-men, naturally, never discuss this publicly. But in private conversations with us, many have frankly admitted that they have had to bribe high officials and politicians to conclude their business deals. Just as often, they have had to bribe officials, both high and low, to keep their enter-prises going without too many obstacles. These bribes, they say, constitute a considerable part of their total operating expenses in South Asia.

There is one specific difficulty facing researchers in their attempts to establish the facts about the taking and seeking of bribes, particularly on the part of higher offi-cials and politicians. Bribes are seldom given directly. Usually they go through a middleman. He may be an indigenous businessman, or an official at a lower level. Many Western firms find it more convenient—and less objectionable—to use a professional briber or fixer as their agent, who then pays off all those whose cooperation is necessary for the smooth conduct of production and busi-ness. More generally, when a business transaction is to be settled, an official somewhere down the line of authority will often inform the Western businessman that a minister or a higher official expects a certain sum of money. Even an indigenous businessman is occasionally placed in such an indirect relationship to the bribe-seeker. As the whole affair is secret, there is often no way of knowing whether the middleman is keeping the money for himself. Indeed, he may be using the weight of an innocent person's name to sweeten the deal and increase his take. This is, of course, one of the ways in which the folklore of corrup-tion may exaggerate the extent of corruption at the higher levels.

·   ·   ·

The folklore of corruption, the political, administrative, and judicial reverberations of these beliefs and emotions in the anti-corruption campaigns, the actual prevalence of corruption in the several countries at different times, and the present trends—all these social facts must be ascertained and explained in causal terms by relating them to other conditions in South Asia.

When we say corruption is more prevalent in South Asia than in the developed Western countries, we are implying a basic difference in mores—a difference in where, how, and when to make a personal gain. It is exceedingly difficult in South Asia to stimulate a desire for profit and market competition in the same sense that these now exist in the West. But it is equally difficult in South Asia to eliminate the desires for private gain from sources that have been largely suppressed in the West—the spheres of public responsibility and power. Certain actions that Westerners would not consider a source of profit are commonly for sale in South Asia. They have a "market," though certainly not a perfect one in the Western sense. These differences actually explain each other. Indeed, they are remnants of a pre-capitalist, traditional society. In South Asia, where there is often no market for goods and services and economic behavior is not governed by rational calculations in terms of costs and returns, "connections" must fill the gap. In such a setting, a bribe to an official is not considered any different from the gifts and tributes sanctioned in the old societies. Nor is such a bribe considered different from the obligations attached to a favor given at any social level.

Traditionally, South Asian countries were "plural societies" where basic loyalties were to families, villages, or groups held together on the basis of religion, language, ethnic origin, or caste rather than to the community as a whole, whether on the local or the national level. A wider loyalty to country, backed by firm rules and punitive measures, is the necessary foundation for modern Western and Communist mores, by which certain behavior reactions are kept apart from considerations of personal gain. In South Asia the stronger loyalty to such smaller groups invites nepotism, in itself a form of corruption, and in general encourages moral laxity. The prevalence of corruption is another aspect of the soft state and generally implies a low level of social discipline.

But this is a static view. It does not explain why corruption is spreading and increasing. Almost everything that has happened has tended to lead to more corruption. In themselves, the winning of independence and the transition from colonial status to self-government caused profound disturbances. The role of the politician greatly increased. At the same time, the corps of colonial administrators were called home, leaving few competent local administrators with the stricter Western mores. The number of official discretionary powers was increased by the type of controls applied over private business. This spread of corruption in turn gives corrupt politicians and dishonest officials a strong vested interest in retaining these discretionary controls. And the low wages of officials, especially at the middle and lower levels, makes corruption a great temptation. So corruption is caught up in the causal circle. It acts with special force as people become aware of its spread and know that effective measures are not being taken against it. Among the sophisticated grows the idea that corruption, like inflation, is an unavoidable appendage of development. The effect of this is to spread cynicism and to lower resistance to the giving and taking of bribes.

Corrupt practices are highly detrimental to any efforts to achieve modernization ideals. The prevalence of corruption raises strong obstacles and inhibitions to development. The corruption that is spurred by fragmentation of loyalties acts against efforts to consolidate the nation. It decreases respect for and allegiance to the government and its institutions. It often promotes irrationality in planning and limits the horizons of plans. The usual way to make money by corrupt practices is to threaten obstruction and delay in official functions. This causes a slowing down of the wheels of administration in South Asia to a damaging degree. The anxiety to avoid such delay produces the common commodity of "speed money." The bribe giver may often not be asking for any unlawful action by an official. He may simply be trying to speed up the movement of files and the reaching of decisions by government agencies.

The popular notion, expressed by Western students, that corruption in South Asia speeds up cumbersome administrative procedures is palpably wrong. Too often, when observers of South Asian affairs criticize the inherited faults of South Asian bureaucracy, they observe a taboo against citing corruption as a cause. Like so many who take part in the lively discussions of this bureaucracy, they avoid relating their observations to the prevalence of corruption, the frequent allegations of corruption, and the individual official's own interest in preserving cumbersome procedures (if the official is dishonest, these procedures better his chances of receiving bribes; if he is honest, they may serve to protect him from suspicion). When people become convinced, rightly or wrongly, that corruption is widespread, an official's incorruptibility is weakened. And should he resist corruption, he may find it difficult to fulfill his duties.

Consider, for example, the chief police officer we became friendly with in the district of New Delhi where we lived for a time. We once complained to him about the taxi drivers' habit of ignoring all traffic rules. "Why don't you order your policemen to enforce those rules?" we asked.

"How could I?" he answered. "If one of them went up to a taxi driver, the driver might say: 'Get away, or I will tell people that you have asked me for ten rupees.' If the policeman then pointed out that he had not done it, the rejoinder of the taxi driver could be: 'Who would believe you?' "

When one recognizes the very serious effects of corruption in South Asia, the problem is raised of what can be done about it. The important Santhanam Committee report in India has analyzed administrative procedures that create opportunities for malfeasance and has made recommendations for reform. The committee urges simpler and more precise rules and procedures for political and administrative decisions that affect private persons and business enterprises and also closer supervision.

A main committee theme is that discretionary powers should, insofar as possible, be decreased. It suggests that the pay of low-level civil servants be raised and their social and economic status be improved and made more secure. The vigilance agencies, including special police departments, should be strengthened. Laws and procedures should be changed so that punitive action against corrupt officials could be pursued more speedily and effectively. Measures should be taken against those in the private sector who corrupt public servants. The committee also proposes that income tax reports and assessments be made public and that more generally the practice of declaring public documents confidential be limited. It suggests that business enterprises be forbidden to make contributions to political parties, that persons making *bona fide* complaints be protected, and that, on the other hand, newspapers be prosecuted if they make allegations without supporting evidence.

The committee concedes that corruption is a long-term problem that requires firm resolve and persistent endeavor for many years to come. The big questions are whether the government will take action along the lines the committee suggested, and to what extent such action will be effective within a national community when what the committee refers to as "the entire system of moral values and of the socio-economic structure" has to be changed.

When considering the prospects of reform in countries where corruption is so embedded in institutional and attitudinal remnants of traditional society and where almost everything that happens increases incentives and opportunities for personal gain, the public outcry against corruption must be regarded as a constructive force. This holds true even when this reaction is basically only the envy of people who have become demoralized to the extent that they themselves would not hesitate to engage in corrupt practices had they a chance. As those people who can benefit personally from corrupt practices are a tiny minority, the public outcry against corruption should support a government intent on serious reforms.

Great Britain, Holland, and the Scandinavian countries were all rife with corruption two hundred years ago, but it is quite limited there now. It was during the liberal interlude between mercantilism and the modern welfare state that the strong state developed in these countries. One of the principal factors in this was an apparent strengthening of morals, particularly in the higher strata, together with salary reforms in the lower strata, often accomplished by transforming customary bribes into legalized fees.

Undoubtedly the South Asian countries could learn something from studies of the reforms carried out a little more than a hundred years ago in these Western countries. There is, however, a fundamental difference in initial conditions. The relative integrity in politics and administration was achieved in these European countries during a period when state activity was reduced to a minimum. When the state again intervened in the economy on a large scale, it had a political and administrative system whose high quality only needed to be protected and preserved. The South Asian countries, on the other hand, have to fight rampant corruption in an era of their history when the activities of the state are proliferating and when preference, even beyond what is necessary, is being given to discretionary controls. Again, South Asia stands out as a third world of planning.

Part Four

LABOR UTILIZATION

Chapter 15

"UNEMPLOYMENT"
AND
"UNDEREMPLOYMENT"

An extreme underutilization of labor is generally understood to characterize South Asian countries. The average output of the labor force is very low. It is low partly because much of the labor force is idle, either completely or for a large part of the day, week, month, or year. But even when members of the labor force are at work, their productivity is usually low. This is the result of many conditions, among them low labor efficiency.

This waste of labor is commonly discussed in terms of "unemployment" and "underemployment." Together, the "unemployed" and "underemployed" in South Asia are assumed to constitute a reservoir of untapped productive potential. This is conventionally explained by a lack of demand for wage employees or, in the case of the self-employed and the farmers, by the absence of opportunity for productive work. It is assumed that once these people

213

are presented with work opportunities, they will take them up. Both "unemployment" and "underemployment" are supposed to be involuntary and the low labor efficiency is kept from attention.

In the mainstream of economic theory, "unemployment" and "underemployment" on a vast scale are regarded as a primary cause of poverty in the South Asian countries. At the same time, the large volume of unused or underutilized labor possessed by the countries is thought to have a productive potential capable of creating capital and increasing production, thereby making possible higher levels of income and consumption—in short, a potential that can be used to eliminate poverty. The supreme task of planning is thus to drain this labor reservoir by channelling the "unemployed" and "underemployed" into productive work.

The focussing of interest on "unemployment" and "underemployment" and on the creation of jobs and work opportunities began, in the main, after the Second World War. In the earlier literature on South Asia, the paramount concern was usually the persistent shortage of labor encountered by colonial governments and private entrepreneurs. In perhaps no other respect has the modern discussion of economic problems in South Asia more sharply reversed that conducted in colonial times. The basic problem of labor utilization is now seen as that of providing demand and work opportunities for the "unemployed" and "underemployed" masses, whereas not long ago it was viewed as one of attracting wage laborers in sufficient numbers and raising their efficiency when working.

This dramatic reversal occurred when the South Asian countries became independent and began their struggle to plan for development. It was natural for their planners to regard idle or unproductive labor as, on the one hand, a curse and a cause of poverty and low living levels and, on the other, a potential resource for development. The practical problem was to devise ways to employ the labor force more fully. In this they were powerfully supported by the trend of thought in the Western countries, where, also since the end of the Second World War, full employment was declared a major goal of economic policy and a responsibility of governments. Western economists and their South Asian confreres—as thoroughly steeped in Western conceptions—applied to South Asia the ultra-modern view of unemployment in undiluted form.

Insistence by the Communists that the capitalist countries had not solved and could not solve their employment problems did not imply another view on labor utilization and underutilization. Their influence only meant that the post-war approach was strengthened in South Asia. There has thus been no encouragement to scrutinize the applicability in South Asia of the major assumption underlying Western concepts of "unemployment" and "underemployment": that idleness, above the set standards of work, was involuntary and that there was a reservoir of labor that could be tapped by increasing demand and augmenting opportunities for work. Labor efficiency was disregarded.

As in many other fields, economic thinking about the labor market in colonial times had originally been of a Mercantile type. According to a sixteenth- and seventeenth-century view of labor from the perspective of employers, a plentiful supply of cheap, docile, and disciplined labor was assumed to be in the public interest. The Mercantilists were not simply morally corrupt cynics, but men who argued and acted to advance what they conceived to be the common good, just as did the colonialists and business people who held power in South Asia in colonial times. Generally, the available evidence indicates that the new enterprises that grew up in the colonial era—whether plantations, mines, or urban industries—were often troubled by labor shortage. In any event, the new industries did not ordinarily encounter an enormous labor surplus, pressing for employment. As seen from this angle, the countryside did not by itself generate a large supply of readily available labor waiting to be tapped.

The difficulties experienced in recruiting labor—as well as the view held by employers and governments that new enterprises offered progress to a backward economy—gave force and sanction to policies that we have characterized as a branch of Mercantilism. The approach of governments and employers had a "factual" background; to them it must have seemed to correspond to actual circumstances and to be founded on experience. Ideologies, to those holding them, have always appeared to be simple, and indisputable, conclusions from obvious facts.

In the agricultural sector in colonial times, there was, of course, much idleness in the stagnant and traditional economy, particularly among self-sufficient agriculturalists and among the village craftsmen. Following a traditional bent, conditioned by poverty itself, people tended to be idle for much of what would be a normal working day from a Western point of view. Even when working they worked less efficiently. Though the masses of people were very poor, they were apparently not eager to improve their lot by increasing their labor input in agriculture and still less by offering their labor for wage employment. At the same time, there was an acutely felt labor shortage in the new dynamic sectors of the economy.

There was a colonial theory to explain this phenomenon. Its main theme was that the natives' tendency toward idleness and inefficiency, and their reluctance to seek wage employment, was an expression of their wantlessness, very limited economic horizons, survival-mindedness, self-sufficiency, carefree disposition, and preference for a leisurely life. They were not thought to be interested in raising their level of living. In these various respects they were assumed to be constituted differently from Europeans. This was commonly related to racial distinctions between the native stock and the white people in Europe.

Some other facts were woven into these explanations as well. It was commonly observed that the hot and often damp climate made sustained hard work odious and laziness inviting. Often attitudes toward work were also related to various observable elements in the social system. The many inhibitions to manual work imposed by social and religious customs and taboos were much commented on in colonial times. Often, it was also observed that undernutrition, and inferior levels of living generally, lowered stamina and ability to work intensively.

Although now more or less completely suppressed and never expressed publicly except in highly euphemistic forms, such attitudes, and particularly the racial inferiority doctrine, are still widely held by Europeans working in the South Asian countries and also shared by many individuals of indigenous extraction in the upper strata. They were, in particular, often shared by those few natives who in later times rose to higher positions in government service or who occasionally succeeded in becoming modern, large-scale entrepreneurs. This presents an important problem for systematic research, for beneath the conventional doctrine that there are no differences between indigenous and European people—which is now sanctioned by strong political and diplomatic interests both foreign and domestic—there survives a whole undergrowth of attitudes reflecting what we have here called "the colonial theory." This theory has its close parallels in popular views toward women not so many years ago and toward recent immigrants or toward Negroes in America.

In colonial times this theory gave rationalizing defense for the colonial power structure. It helped justify the popular concept of the "white man's burden" to govern those who in theory could not govern themselves. It supported the thought that nothing much could be done to raise income and living levels of indigenous peoples, because their plight was a consequence of the climate and immutable social and biological facts. This conclusion could be accepted with a better conscience because of another element of the colonial theory: the idea that the natives in their laziness and wantlessness were happy, perhaps more so than the Europeans whose ambitions drove them to exertions that often ended in frustration. The notion that the underprivileged are particularly happy is, as we know, an almost regular element in the rationalization of inequality by a privileged group; visions of the happy and carefree Negro, the happy and contented woman, the well-satisfied servant, etc., are paraded before us.

All knowledge, like all ignorance, tends to be opportune and to advance the cause of special interests. There is a convenience of ignorance that enters into our observations. Recognition of this fact does not, of course, imply that all our observations and inferences are faulty, but it does mean that we should scrutinize them carefully.

The post-war approach to the problems of labor utilization, which we have sketched and will discuss further below, *was a protest against the dominant theory of the colonial period*. Indeed, the fact that the post-war approach bears so much the stamp of protest makes an understanding of the dominant ideas of the earlier period important to study of present-day South Asia.

Implicitly, the colonial theory looked at conditions in South Asia from a Western point of view and measured attitudes and performances there against Western standards. Thus it derived its condescending, humiliating, and offensive character. But in point of view and standards applied, nothing fundamental distinguishes the older from the modern approach. Not only those South Asian intellectuals who identify themselves with the Western world, but equally those more aggressive nationalists who are positively anti-Western *must apply Western standards when they discuss labor utilization in terms of "unemployment" and "underemployment."* The colonial theory was put forward to explain the poverty of South Asia as well as to explain the lack of progress. Those South Asian intellectuals who now want to spur progress are *thus tempted to discount all those components of colonial theory that emphasized the impediments to it.*

By the accidents of history, the unemployment issue came to the center of Western economic theory and planning at about the same time the South Asian countries gained their independence and could start planning for their own development. Amid the outburst of interest in the problems of underdevelopment, development, and planning for development in the region, Western writers were inclined almost mechanically to think in terms that to them were familiar. South Asian economists were under much the same influence, as they had been educated to think in Western terms. In addition, the emotional load carried by the post-war approach in Western countries, through its close association with radicalism in matters of social policy, undoubtedly heightened its appeal to South Asian intellectuals.

More important, however, was the fact that the new Western approach refuted all the objectionable elements in the colonial theory. It said nothing, of course, about race. Perhaps a vague suspicion did linger that there might be something to the colonial assumptions of racial and biological inferiority, but such attitudes can no longer be part of a theory, whether on the scientific or the popular level, purporting to explain aptitudes and abilities of the people in South Asia. Equality in inherited mental traits between groups of people is now taken for granted and never challenged in the modern approach. This is unquestionably an advance toward greater rationality.

But at the same time the environmental facts, which had been stressed as different from the West's, were also thrown out. Differences in climate, for example, have never been of major economic significance in the temperate zones. Nowadays, climate is almost entirely left out of account in thinking about underdevelopment and development, although it played such a prominent part in colonial theory. And practically no research, either in South Asian or in Western countries, has been done on the influence of climate in labor utilization or on the possibility of controlling this influence. Neither does the post-war approach give much attention in its growth models to nutrition and levels of income and living and their relationship to labor input and efficiency. Even when these factors are considered in the South Asian context, they are considered only from the point of view of people's welfare and not their ability and preparedness to work or their diligence and efficiency when working.

Unemployment in the Western countries is understood as a situation in which a person has no job but is seeking one. There is a labor market and the workers have a knowledge of employment openings as they occur. From a planning point of view the unemployed and the disguised unemployed represent a "labor reserve." This can be regarded as a "readily available supply" waiting only for work opportunities. It can be mobilized by increasing the aggregate demand for labor. The planning problem in South Asia would be greatly simplified if we could regard the idle labor there as a reserve of unemployed constituting a readily available labor supply that could be tapped primarily by enlarging the scope of work opportunities.

The problem would be further simplified if we could legitimately disregard labor efficiency. In the West, the labor force is compartmentalized by skills. The length of the working day, and the number of working days in the week and the year, are fixed by collective agreements or legislation. Save for the exceptional asocial cases, those who are without work can be assumed to want a job under these standardized conditions.

In all these respects the problem is visibly different in South Asia. It is made still more complex by the fact that the very existence of much idle labor in South Asia has instilled an attitude resistant to measures which might raise labor efficiency. In some quarters, efficiency is regarded as detrimental to employment. The tendency—which is implied in the post-war approach and colors all aspects of plan-making—to disregard labor efficiency and place the responsibility for the waste of labor on the lack of demand for labor and work opportunities provides an escape from many awkward problems.

A further confusion in thought about the employment problem stems from awareness of the accelerated rate of population growth in the post-colonial era. As we shall show later, its implications for employment are not the most crucial aspect of population growth. At least within the perspective of the nearest decades—which is the perspective of all planning—the size of the labor force is not dependent on what can be done to lower fertility. Nevertheless, the population sector is commonly seen mainly as signifying a need to provide employment for a rapidly increasing labor force.

The post-war approach to the problem of labor utilization implies a number of assumptions about economic and social facts that are fairly realistic in the Western world but not in South Asia. Three of these are immediately apparent:

(1) that labor input can be discussed primarily as a quantity with little specific attention to its quality, i.e., labor efficiency;

(2) that a low aggregate labor input, i.e., idleness, can be treated as "involuntary"; and

(3) that, therefore, idle labor represented by "unemployment" and "underemployment" constitutes a "readily available labor supply" in the sense that the provision of work opportunities is the main condition necessary for the elimination of idleness.

These assumptions, implicit in the post-war approach, presume an abstraction from most of the peculiar and closely interrelated environmental conditions of South Asian countries—whether physical, technical, institutional, or broadly attitudinal—and, in particular, from:

(a) climatic factors;

(b) low nutritional and health levels;

(c) institutional conditions;

(d) attitudes that are molded by institutions, and, in turn, reinforce them; and

(e) the relative immobility of labor and the great imperfection of all markets and of the labor market in particular resulting from (a) through (d) above, but especially from (c) and (d).

In the general mold of thought shaping the theoretical economic discussion and reflected in the models and the plans, it is further assumed:

(4) that in the economic discussion political, administrative, and organizational problems can largely be bypassed; and

(5) that the general explanation for the failure of idle labor to be absorbed in work opportunities lies in deficient supplies of complementary factors of production.

As not only investment and working capital but also land and other complementary factors, such as managers, technicians, and skilled workers, are limited in quantity and an increase in their supply calls for investment, the explanation of the large-scale involuntary idleness—that is, in the terms of the post-war approach, "unemployment" and "underemployment"—can thus be reduced to:

(6) an insufficiency of capital from internal savings and foreign capital inflow.

The remedy implied is a heavier volume of capital input in the economy. A link is thereby established with the various economic models relating capital input to increases in aggregate output.

With the assumptions noted above, the elements of the modern approach can be fitted into a coherent system of thinking. In South Asia, the Western model in terms simply of employment and "unemployment" is supplemented by an appendage, which is thought to bring it into closer touch with conditions in the region—a theory of employed members of the economy, whether in agriculture or elsewhere. One implication of this doctrine and of the other assumptions made is that:

(7) the "unemployed" and "underemployed" together can be viewed as constituting not only a labor reserve, but at the same time a savings reserve. To the extent that they can be set to work without increasing aggregate consumption, and the costs arising from their employment—such as those for tools and other capital equipment—can be held down, the aggregate volume of investment can be increased without making claims on the organized capital market.

The post-war approach is here sketched in a highly simplified relief that does not do justice to the insights into South Asian reality which appear as occasional qualifications and reservations in the voluminous literature. The important point, however, is that despite these qualifications, this broad approach guides the economic discussion, the definitions of terms, the collection and analysis of statistical data, and the construction of the development plans.

A moment's reflection shows that these basic assumptions are badly tailored to a South Asian environment. South Asian societies have not experienced the processes of economic advance, integration, standardization, and rationalization that have made these assumptions useful in the West as starting points in aggregative economic analysis.

As the founder and chief of the Indian Statistical Institute, Professor P. C. Mahalanobis has had a major responsibility for attempts to throw light on the problem of labor utilization through statistical inquiries. He notes that only about 13 million persons, who work under government and public authorities or in private organized large-scale enterprises, have employment of the type usual in the advanced countries. The technical concept of "unemployment," he says, can be strictly used only in the case of those 13 million persons (out of a total labor force of 160 million); it is not applicable to the remaining 147 million who work in household or small-scale enterprises.

Even so, Mahalanobis attempted to estimate the extent of unemployment and underemployment in India in the manner of the post-war approach. This implies several unrealistic assumptions: a fluid labor market, standardized as to skill and efficiency, general awareness of opportunities, and that idleness of workers is really involuntary so that the supply of idle labor awaits work opportunities and will spring forward to grasp them. The figures he presents are, of course, not meaningful. Neither are other statistics on "unemployment" and "underemployment."

In the Western countries, the readily available labor supply and the labor reserve usually amount to about the same thing: a number of unemployed plus occasionally a fringe of disguised unemployment. This reserve can be mobilized by increasing the demand for labor, primarily through expansion of aggregate demand for goods and services. In South Asia, the readily available labor supply represents only a very small proportion of the real waste of labor. A massive waste of labor—whether because labor is not utilized at all, or is utilized for only part of the time or in an almost useless way—is one of the obvious facts of economic life in the region. In the present context, the important point is that little of this slack in the labor force can be taken up by turning on the tap of aggregate demand. Underutilization of labor vastly exceeds the supply that could be mobilized by expansion in demand.

Instead, the bulk of the labor force is embedded in a climatic, social, cultural, and institutional matrix that not only tends to perpetuate present low levels of labor utilization, but also resists rapid and immediate adaptation to new ways of living and working. Within an institutional framework that has perpetuated low levels of living and labor efficiency, the labor force that is wholly or partly idle or engaged in unproductive work cannot be considered as constituting a pool of readily available labor supply. Their employment situation cannot even be thought of in terms of the rationalistic conceptions of voluntariness and a fluid labor market. When one probes into what is known about the facts, the rationalistic assumptions applicable to Western countries and uncritically transferred to the study of South Asian countries break down entirely. The readily available labor supply assumed by the modern approach has thus been grossly exaggerated. Here the character of underutilization of labor is different, and the problem is a long-term one. "Full employment" is a distant goal and not one which can be reached via aggregative measures which leave attitudes and institutions unchanged. The limited scope of organized markets, among other things, makes aggregative measurement of the underutilization of labor far less possible.

When we use the concept of a readily available labor supply, we are asking a rather straightforward question: how much labor input would appear in response to an increase in demand for labor both in the wage labor market and in the sectors dominated by the self-employed? Essentially, we are then interested in establishing a behavioral fact, quite independent of the norms of outside observers. But even this apparently simple question does not permit a completely straightforward answer in South Asia. Workers themselves, on whose response the answer depends, may have difficulty in even imagining such a changed state of affairs, one in which they would find it attractive to take up new work, or work for longer periods, or work with greater intensity.

When we turn our attention instead to the labor reserve at the disposal of the planner, the problem becomes even more complex in South Asia. Here we are attempting to grasp the waste of labor from the point of view of an outsider concerned with reducing that waste. The labor reserve in his conception is the additional labor supply and input he would have at his disposal after having set various policy measures in motion—policy measures which would, both directly and indirectly, produce a variety of effects, including some changes in the attitudes of workers and in the institutions conditioning these attitudes. The standards of behavior he works with are thus different from those manifested and observable in the present behavior of the labor force.

The concept of a labor reserve becomes, therefore, a highly hypothetical magnitude, dependent upon the direction and intensity of all the planned policy measures. Millions of individuals must be induced to change their traditional attitudes toward employment and work, both directly—by education, propaganda, leadership, regulations, or compulsion—and indirectly, by creating changed conditions for work through such means as increasing capital investments, improving production techniques, and reforming the institutional framework in regard to ownership of land. In these dynamic policy terms, the available labor supply and the duration and efficiency of work become themselves functions of the policy measures adopted.

Every attempt to look upon the underutilized labor in South Asian countries as a labor reserve implies a policy assumption. The size of the labor reserve is a function of the policy measures to be applied. It cannot be defined— and therefore ascertained empirically and measured—in an "objective" way as merely related to facts and independent of policy assumptions. In general terms, the more far-reaching and effective the planned policy measures are, and the more sharply they are focussed on the specific objectives of increasing the available labor supply, input, and efficiency, the larger we should expect the labor reserve to be.

The thesis we here expound is this: under South Asian conditions, the labor reserve, for logical as well as practical reasons, must be conceived in dynamic and policy-determined terms. And the planner's reserve cannot refer simply to a single moment in time, but must assume a time span during which the policy-induced changes can take effect. In addition, the natural increase in the labor force during that period must be drawn into the analysis. Further, sensible policy cannot be directed solely toward increasing aggregate labor input. It must also aim at improving labor efficiency. As an ultimate goal, the planner and policy-maker must aim to absorb the total labor reserve by utilizing the labor force fully at higher levels of labor efficiency and still higher levels of labor productivity. Viewed in this sense, it is clear that the labor reserve available to the planner and policy-maker in South Asian countries is very much bigger than the readily available labor supply.

As a matter of fact, very little study has been devoted to the functional relationship between policy measures and the aggregate utilization of labor that we have named as the main problem for economic analysis. The literature is replete with unworldly statements about how much labor could be saved in peasant farming while yields were increased, and how much labor could be saved in many other occupations if production were rationalized. There is nothing wrong with the general drift of such assertions. The consciousness of their essential truth is the intellectual force behind the efforts at planning and policy-making in these countries. But unless they are supplemented by specification of the particular policy measures required in the actual circumstances of a South Asian country, they lack clear meaning.

In general, those who subscribe to the post-war approach have, instead, tried to define the labor reserve in static terms, as existing *per se* at a given point in time, and unrelated to any policy assumptions. In regard to those who work for wages, the usual procedure has been to accept as the labor reserve those workers who are idle but can be assumed to want employment. But the major effort has been to define and measure the amount of "underemployment," understood as surplus labor bottled up among the self-employed in farming and other family enterprises who are wholly or partly idle or who work at very low levels of productivity. This is undoubtedly inspired by a belief that the post-war approach needs to be adjusted to the very different circumstances of South Asia. Carrying out an analogy to the unemployment discussion in the West, this surplus is often called "disguised unemployment."

Though there are many variations on this theme, the basic idea behind the "underemployment" approach is a static one: it assumes that under unchanged conditions of capital equipment, production techniques, and institutional framework, and with only minor changes in the organization of work itself, the same total production could be obtained even if a part of the labor force were "removed." This static definition must be based on an external set of norms. In some cases, these have been based on performance on farms where labor is utilized more intensively; in other cases it has been assumed that a certain number of hours or days of work per year correspond to full employment. Sometimes it has not been made clear what standards have been applied and whether static conditions are assumed to be fully preserved.

This way of thinking is in line with the tradition in the social sciences, especially in economics, to "objectify" concepts and to reach politically meaningful conclusions without a value premise. In regard to labor utilization in

South Asian countries, the temptation to adopt this procedure has been strong. On the one hand, there actually is a tremendous waste of labor in the sense that workers are idle and, when they do work, they work very inefficiently. On the other hand, the cure for underutilization of labor touches explosive policy issues. Discussions about taxation, land and tenancy reform, and compulsory work arrangements, for example, are obviously highly charged with vested interests and emotions. The doctrine we criticize attempts to be "scholarly" in the time-honored way by a maneuver that is logically impossible: by defining and measuring the waste of labor while remaining innocent of how anything can be done about it.

Putting the observations of the facts in this theoretical Procrustean bed also leads to gross distortions of reality—distortions common to all theories based on the post-war approach. The attempts in recent decades to devise a concept, "underemployment," which would define a labor reserve in terms of a static comparison, and so permit accurate measurement of the waste of labor in South Asian countries—a situation once described in an earlier era as "overpopulation"—have been abortive. What we can attempt to study empirically is the readily available labor supply. Even though that labor supply cannot be precisely measured, the concept is at least consistent and clear. It refers to the way people would, or might, behave in a different situation and is not bound by *a priori* assumptions.

We know also that, from the viewpoint of the planner and policy-maker, the labor reserve in South Asian countries, unlike that in the West, is very much bigger than this readily available labor supply—if the planning is prepared to induce radical reform policies. This is one of the most crucial facts of South Asian economic life. But it cannot be established or measured within the framework of the post-war approach, which in this problem is static and attempts to work without value premises. It has to be studied realistically as a functional relationship between policy measures, on the one hand, and the input and efficiency of labor, on the other hand, during a period of time and in a particular situation.

We have rejected the post-war approach to the problem of labor utilization and so discarded the terms "unemployment" and "underemployment" as inadequate to South Asian reality. Thus we now turn to an alternative approach—one we believe to be logically consistent and adequate for the study of actual conditions in South Asia.

In this study we shall use the term "potential labor force" or "labor force" to mean the population of working age. The age limits of this force must be determined by realistic assumption consistent with the customs of the region. In discussion of policies, this assumption should also take into account the way these customs might be induced to change according to value premises that should then be made explicit.

The level of development and its rate of change can be indicated by the average *productivity* of the potential labor force. The problem of planning is to devise politically feasible and practicable policy means to induce changes that raise average productivity as much and as fast as possible. Productivity of the labor force can be increased by means of a higher total labor input and this depends on:

(a) The *participation* rate, or that portion of the labor force normally performing some work, at least when the whole year is taken into account. The participation rate is lower than one everywhere in the world but, for various reasons, it is strikingly low in some South Asian countries.

(b) The *duration* of work by those participating (according to the above definition), in terms of weeks and months per year, days per week, and hours per day.

~ These definitions permit us to determine the degree of *idleness* in the following way. The total labor input achievable through complete participation of the working force at an assumed standard of work duration can be calculated. The degree of idleness can then be established in two steps. First, the difference between the labor input obtained from actual participation and duration, and the labor input maximally achievable under the assumed conditions, can be established. Secondly, this magnitude can be expressed as a proportion of maximum labor input assumed to be achievable.

In the post-war approach, idleness is assumed to be involuntary. This volitional approach—implied in the concepts of "unemployment" and "underemployment"—to the problems of labor utilization in South Asia is unhelpful. People may not seek work because they believe none to be available; this in turn is a function of the lack of an effective market and of limited horizons imposed by life in stagnating and largely isolated societies. Moreover, social and religious institutions and attitudes have a forceful effect in making some people indisposed to work at all and others willing to work only if they can be self-employed or in a family enterprise. Even those of working age who would be prepared to work for an employer may be available only locally or only in the service of a particular kind of employer, or only for certain types of tasks. Thus their mobility may be restricted by where they might work and what they might do.

An essential point is that the scope of rational planning cannot be restricted to those who respond to an opportunity to work, assuming for the moment that the magnitude of the readily available labor supply could be defined and ascertained. It must also be directed toward raising levels of living and, in particular, toward changing institutions and attitudes so that more people will be willing and able to participate, to work longer hours and more days and weeks and months per year, and to work with greater efficiency.

The second major variable besides the quantity of labor input is average output per unit of labor input. It depends upon a number of factors.

(a) One is *labor efficiency*. This represents a qualitative dimension of labor output. We shall define it as the worker's productivity, when all the conditions under (b) through (e) below are given. Labor efficiency thus defined depends on the worker's physical and mental stamina—his health—which in turn is determined by available health facilities and, in addition, by nutritional and other levels of living; on his education and training for work at prevailing levels of technology; and on his attitudes toward life and work, as determined by climate, levels of living, customs, and institutions.

But the level of productivity is also influenced by a set of conditions that are not simply to be understood as qualities of workers. These are:

(b) occupational distribution of the labor force;

(c) natural resources;

(d) the volume of capital resources and their allocation; and

(e) technology.

The degree of labor utilization depends on the three components: participation, duration, and efficiency. Broadly speaking, the post-war approach has been preoccupied with the first of these ratios, and then in only a partial and unrealistically biased way, whereas all three are essential to an understanding of labor utilization in South Asia. And it must be appreciated that all three are connected. Labor efficiency is regularly lower when there is also much idleness and, more generally, when labor is abundant. Climate may also reduce both the duration and intensity of work. The same is true of low physical and mental stamina caused by bad health, which in turn results from low levels of living. Health deficiencies may prevent participation in work or cause workers to shorten their hours; poor health will usually also diminish labor efficiency during actual work. Improvements in labor efficiency may lead, at first, to increased idleness on the part of some. Large increases in participation could mean that the length and efficiency of work would be reduced. All these factors can be changed; indeed, it is the purpose of planning to accomplish the desired changes in a coordinated way.

The magnitudes referred to in our approach are all simply behaviorial and should be possible to observe and register. But as the efforts to collect statistical data have been guided by the unrealistic post-war approach, the possibilities to account for the underutilization of labor and its several components—participation, duration, and efficiency—are severely limited.

Even in regard to the minor part of the labor force which is employed in such sectors, where there is a semblance of similarity to a Western labor market and where we should be able to register workers as unemployed, the statistical base becomes very shaky throughout South Asia. In the Western countries, estimates of the volume of unemployment are generally prepared from two primary sources of information—unemployment compensation rolls and registration with the labor exchanges. The absence of any unemployment compensation schemes removes much of the incentive to register at the labor exchanges, which are usually also too few and too centrally located.

For the larger part of the labor force, the statistics on their idleness in terms of "unemployment" becomes entirely useless. The attempt to measure labor underutilization in terms of "underemployment" meets the logical difficulties referred to above. Indeed, the entire approach in terms of "removal" of a labor surplus in agriculture and crafts assumes that the supposedly superfluous workers have somewhere to go. This is consonant with the common, glib preconception that industrialization, by also giving employment to labor moving out of agriculture and crafts, is the main solution to the development problem in underdeveloped countries, even in the fairly short run. In the chapters that follow, we show that in South Asia industrialization, even if it were to proceed more rapidly, would not imply much more demand for labor for decades ahead and might even imply less employment in manufacturing.

Moreover, we will demonstrate that the labor force will increase very rapidly till the end of the century, regardless of any efforts to spread birth control. Since in South Asia industrialization does not provide much of an outlet under any conceivable circumstances, this increase in the labor force will have to find its place mainly in agriculture. The whole idea of "removal" is unrealistic.

Chapter 16

LABOR UTILIZATION IN TRADITIONAL AGRICULTURE

If development through sound planning is ever to succeed in South Asia, there must be a thorough understanding of how labor is used and what is accomplished by its work. Western concepts of labor utilization, of unemployment and underemployment, do not apply. They not only fail to illuminate the fundamental issues that confront economic advance in the region, but they actually obscure these issues.

We begin with labor in agriculture because this segment of the economy provides an income, however meager it may be, for the bulk of the population. Moreover, in the rural areas the characteristics of the South Asian economic structure that differentiate it most sharply from its modern Western counterpart stand out in bold relief.

Far more than in Europe or North America, the patterns of present-day agriculture in South Asia are reflections of the ancient systems in the region. In the areas of predominantly shifting cultivation, the economic system once was, and continues largely to be, self-contained, with the peasants geared to producing only the subsistence requirements of their families. In the zones of fixed cultivation, whether on dry or irrigated land, a much more stratified organization emerged in the past. A surplus beyond the family's immediate needs was produced, and much of this was transferred as tribute to the local chief. He, in turn, might have passed a further part on to an overlord or king. But whatever he did with it, the important feature of this arrangement was that part of the peasant family's output was extracted without payment. The peasant, for these offerings, was assured some rights in using the land and had some expectation of protection by the chiefs or king. Beyond his contribution to them, the peasant could dispose of the rest of his crops as he chose. But he could not dispose of the land he lived on. This belonged to the village or to the chief, as did all the land surrounding the village, whether or not it was tilled.

In the systems based on sedentary cultivation, it is important to appreciate that the village community—in which the basic rights to land were vested—was not a group definable geographically as a collection of people living in a certain locality. It was instead primarily a social and religious unit. Only those persons who were born within it and who shared its religion and its social customs enjoyed full membership with the privilege of working land on their own account. Outsiders were accepted as serfs or laborers, but their admission to full status in the group might take generations, if it were achieved at all. Even today, tribal people and untouchables in India are fighting to obtain full membership rights in villages where they have lived for centuries without the right to own land or even to use wells or roads. In Indonesia an effective distinction is still maintained between the original members of the village, who alone have the right to own agricultural land, and other villagers, who can possess only the compound on which their house is built. In many parts of Indonesia the village leadership as a body still has the power to decide whether an outsider can acquire first-class citizenship with rights to agricultural land.

There have been elements of continuity in the rural structure from those years until now. But three major forces for change have molded the traditional agricultural patterns into their present-day form. These have been the intervention of European colonial rule, the progressive introduction of money transactions, and the growth in population.

There is no doubt that major changes in the traditional agrarian structure would have occurred even if the Europeans had not come to South Asia. But colonial rule did act as an important catalyst for change. Foremost was the European attempt to superimpose on South Asian societies Western types of land tenure arrangements, even if it meant riding roughshod over the distinctions drawn in the traditional system between rights to occupy land, to receive tribute from it, and to dispose of it. Generally speaking, village lands not under permanent cultivation remained in collective ownership, but often with the important difference that the right of ownership was now transferred from the village community to the government. They were no longer village lands but "waste lands belonging to the Crown," and people who started cultivation on them were often considered "illegal squatters," whether they belonged to the local village community or not. For the arable land, on the other hand, the Europeans usually recognized a private owner, either the previous receiver of tribute or the present cultivator of the land.

One of the significant social consequences of the land tenure arrangements that evolved after European intervention was the breakdown of much of the earlier cohesion of village life, with its often elaborate, though informal, structure of rights and obligations. An equally serious economic consequence of European interference with traditional land tenure arrangements was the emergence in many parts of South Asia of a class of large private landowners whose activities were no longer circumscribed by custom. In addition to rent, the Asian landlord often received from the tenants traditional "gifts" at specified occasions, labor services, and various other payments. These remnants of the ancient tenure system sometimes became more onerous because of the increased opportunity for oppression provided by mounting population pressure.

Indeed, the big landlord in South Asia often managed to enjoy the prerogatives of a capitalist landlord without giving up the privileges of a feudal chief. At the same time, he avoided nearly all the obligations of both. Even now, he does not typically invest in improvements to the land, nor does he contribute to the working capital requirements of his tenants beyond sometimes supplying part of the seed. Nowadays the typical South Asian landlord not only pays much lower land taxes than do landowners in America or Europe, but he also mostly escapes taxation on income derived from the ownership of land.

Nor does he typically perform any agricultural work himself, even work of a supervisory kind. It was, and is, rare for a large landlord to operate a home-farm with hired laborers. Usually he lives in the town and turns over the working of the land to sharecroppers or other tenants. Only rarely does he himself collect the rents. Usually rent collection is delegated to local agents. In many cases, these intermediaries were granted permanent rights of collection against the payment of a fixed amount to the owner of the land. Especially in India and Pakistan, this process is known to be repeated several times over. Long chains of intermediary rent-receivers have thus developed.

. . .

By creating individual titles to land, European intervention produced an environment in which another agent for change in the rural structure—the moneylender—could flourish. Once the land tenure system had been adapted to Western concepts of private property, land became a negotiable asset. It could now be used as security for loans, and, in case of default, could be forfeited and transferred.

The force of these circumstances was heightened by another factor—the partial spread of money economy and commercial agriculture. This introduction of the money economy had only a limited effect in stimulating higher production or in promoting new lines of output among the masses of South Asian agriculturalists. But its effects on demand were more far-reaching. Economic contact with Europeans led to the introduction of a whole range of new goods—goods, moreover, that could only be procured with money. These phenomena, in combination, set in motion a chain of disturbances in the traditional agrarian structure in which the moneylender was to play an important role.

In subsistence economy, the moneylenders' activities were restricted to supplying the peasant with money to live on when he was in trouble because of a crop failure or when he needed money for a family wedding or funeral. But with commercial farming, money outlays for seeds, fertilizer, and other costs became needed for successful cultivation of most commercial crops. If the peasant's food crops were reduced to make room for cash crops, he also needed money for part of his food requirements. Generally, his cash needs became greater; since his land was transferable, he had a ready source of collateral, and the moneylenders were willing to advance even greater sums than before.

It rarely occurred to the peasant, and not always to the moneylender, that the rates charged for these consumption loans were ruinous when applied to lending used to finance commercial agriculture. This is not to suggest that present-day farmers in South Asia always use the loans they get for productive expenditures. In many places the moneylenders' credits are still used for the most part in the traditional way, particularly to support extravagant ceremonial expenditures. By charging exorbitant interest rates, or by inducing the peasant to accept larger credits than he can manage, the moneylender can hasten the process by which the peasant is dispossessed.

This erosion of the status of the peasant proprietor has by no means taken place uniformly. Ironically, it has been in the prosperous districts of commercial farming, rather than in the poorer subsistence farming areas, that moneylenders undermined peasant ownership. In the prosperous Punjab of India, in the fertile delta areas of lower Burma and Southern Vietnam, and in the richest areas of Indonesia, the problem of the moneylender came to overshadow other agricultural problems. In some areas, even the big landowners fell under the hold of the moneylender, with the result that whole villages were taken over by them.

Many countries of South Asia have set restrictions against the right of foreigners to own land or for it to be transferred to the moneylenders. But too often ways have been found to circumvent these restrictions. The peasants often allowed the land to be registered in their name. Or tenancy contracts have been drawn in which the indebted peasant leases out his land to his creditor at a low rent and then leases it back at a much higher rent. Thus the debtor is in fact transformed into a sharecropper on land that, by law, is his own.

Nor does the power of moneylenders in the rural structure derive solely from their position as financial intermediaries. Often it is buttressed by their ancillary roles as merchants or landlords. As trader and landlord, the moneylender has significant opportunities to raise the real rate of interest well above the nominal rate. He may set arbitrarily low prices on the products the peasant sells and excessively high ones on those he buys, or he may manipulate rents to the peasant's disadvantage. One of the most highly developed systems of this sort is the paddy *kuncha* system in Malaya. To an increasing extent, tenants have been obliged to make cash rental payments in advance. This has compelled them to borrow to remain on the land. At this point the paddy dealers, who are often landlords and shopkeepers as well, step in as suppliers of funds, and the tenant must pledge a fixed quantity of his crop in advance with interest rates often amounting to 100 percent or more.

In Moslem areas, such as Malaya, the local people are often restrained from entering such "commerce" themselves by their religious proscription against the profession of moneylending. Throughout Southeast Asia, much of the moneylending has traditionally been done by Indians or Chinese. Many of these have now been forced out, at least temporarily, by protective laws, but enough remain to make relations between the peasants and Chinese and Indian business interests one of the most explosive issues in Southeast Asia.

In addition to European intervention and the growth of a money economy came the third factor for change, the rapid growth of population in most areas during the colonial period. This growth could have meant a corresponding expansion of the cultivated area as new farmers appeared. But even where this was possible, the inhibitions of tenure and attitudes often held it back. The further subdivision and fragmentation of holdings was almost everywhere the result. These factors received reinforcement by the traditional Moslem and Hindu laws, which require that a whole estate be divided equally among all the heirs.

These traditions, combined with the pressures of the

moneylenders, kept bringing smaller and smaller farms. For example, in a village of the Poona district near Bombay, the average holding in 1770 was 40 acres. By the end of the First World War, it had shrunk to below 7.5 acres. In Ceylon, the same fragmenting pattern was found, with the added element of many heirs retaining ownership but moving into the nearby towns and letting some other peasant rent the land or sharecrop on it. In less extreme forms, the same process is going on all over South Asia. In all these countries land is still regarded as the safest and highest-yielding investment, and the prestige of land ownership is high. Moreover, there is often sentiment connected with owning land in one's native village—sentiment enhanced when, for economic reasons, land values are constantly rising.

The rising populations, and this constant reduction of plot size, has led to the steady impoverishment of many peasants. As the economic circumstances of these smallholders worsen, they become more vulnerable to complete loss of their lands, and an increasing proportion of the population is left landless. This trend toward landlessness is, of course, expressed in various ways—not only through growth in the number of sharecroppers but also through growth in the number of completely dispossessed who must resort to wage earning. Whatever its manifestations, it has acted to intensify economic inequalities and to promote a more rigid social and economic stratification in rural areas. These tendencies toward economic polarization have been augmented by the deterioration in rural handicrafts.

The imposition of European concepts of property, the rise of commercial elements in farming and the activity of the moneylenders, and the growth in population certainly reshaped the village structure. But it may be misleading to assert, as has often been done, that generally these trends led to the "disintegration" of rural society. Instead, adjustments were made that produced a type of social organization only partially different from the inherited one.

Two widely held misconceptions about the South Asian village structure should be disposed of. One is a view of the typical village as composed of a mass of poor tenants, united in opposition to absentee landlords and their local agents. The other is a view of the village as a typical collection of self-sufficient cultivating families, living harmoniously together. There are such villages, but the usual South Asian village structure is far more complex. More often it is a hierarchical system consisting of several groups linked by a network of economic and social relationships. Some of these relationships derive from age-old traditions that are highly resistant to change. Others have arisen from more recent economic and social developments that produced new and sharp conflicts of interest.

A number of groups with quite divergent interests are to be found in nearly all South Asian villages. At the apex of the village social pyramid are the landowners, of which there are three broad types. The first includes the big landlords, who are the remnants of the feudal-type structure, either inherited or created by colonial policy. The second is composed of non-cultivating owners of smaller plots, to whom rents from land are often not a primary source of income, but a supplement to other earnings. These two groups are usually absentees, living outside the uncomfortable and unpleasant villages, but the impact of their influence on village life is formidable. The third category comprises those landowners who actually live in the villages and are classified in most Asian statistics as "owner-cultivators."

Within this third group are two types. One, the peasant landlord, has enough land to rent out part of it. The other, the ordinary peasant owner, has only enough to keep himself and his family busy, though he may employ a farm servant and some casual labor in the peak season.

Large numbers of South Asian peasants have been forced to take land on crop-share or other forms of lease in order to bring their cultivated acreage up to a size sufficient to support a family. The distinction between ordinary peasants and sharecroppers is thus blurred in many villages by the effects of subdivision of holdings. But while there is considerable overlapping between these various groups, there can be no question that the lowest positions in the rural structure are occupied by those who own no land and are dependent on others for work.

Unfortunately, it is impossible to get a clear statistical breakdown of these categories in the villages. Rigorous inquiries have not been sponsored officially, and one of the main reasons may well be that the authorities, even after independence, have not wanted to risk stirring up demand for agrarian reform that the release of such information might invite. But broadly speaking, those who mostly rely for their subsistence on wages as agricultural laborers usually account for at least a third of the rural population.

The division of the village population into the basic categories we have described is more than mere occupational grouping. It also delineates a social hierarchy. The scale of values determining social ranking in rural South Asia continues to be a pre-capitalist one. To own land is the highest mark of social esteem; to perform manual labor, and particularly to do it for an employer, is the lowest. Considerable social status is attached to supervisory work, but the prestige enjoyed by people who abstain from work altogether is greater. The status of hired workers is substantially below that of persons who perform manual work on their own account, while those peasants who possess land but do not themselves till it enjoy the highest prestige. Yet the worker does not necessarily earn less than the sharecropper; in fact, the earnings of hired workers may exceed those of the average sharecropper. This is precisely because the lower social esteem attached to wage employment may make it necessary to offer somewhat higher economic rewards in order to attract hired laborers in sufficient numbers.

In India, the village structure is still strongly affected by the caste system. While caste does not ensure economic ranking, it does influence rights to land and attitudes toward owership. Some Brahman people are by religious custom prevented from plowing and they often interpret this very broadly as an indictment of all manual agricultural work. For this reason, some of the very poor among them lease their tiny bits of land to sharecroppers or have the work performed by farm servants. Through such strict observance of caste proscriptions, they are likely to sink still deeper into poverty, but this demonstration of orthodoxy may enhance the esteem in which they are held by the village people.

Generally speaking, each person is born into his place in the village hierarchy, although everywhere in South Asia—even in India—there are possibilities for movement, both upward and downward, on the social ladder. Unfortunately, landless sharecroppers and workers hardly ever move upward, unless the government grants them land, and even hesitant steps in this direction are likely to be resisted fiercely. The downward movements are easier to catalogue. Usually the process is a gradual one. The peasant who loses his land may have a pair of bullocks and some working capital. If he does, he can take a plot on a share-rental or even a cash rental basis by virtue of social connections with the landowning groups. But later on, crop failure may force him to sell his bullocks and to earn his living as a casual laborer. He may even sink down into the group of more or less bonded laborers who work as farm servants for their creditors.

There have been instances, particularly in the immediate years after the Second World War, when the poor have attempted to rebel against this pattern and take the law into their own hands. But in the main, the village structure has displayed a remarkable degree of stability and resistance to change. This is explained in part by the stigma against manual labor. The landed, however poor, manage to make adjustments that relieve the direct distress of the dispossessed. And the sharecroppers do not feel interest solidarity with the landless laborers.

Nor is there the level of resentment against the moneylenders that an outsider might expect. The moneylender is not always even an unpopular figure. Although when he is a member of a non-indigenous ethnic group he may be, and often has been, the target of violent passions, the functions he performs are welcome. Debtors may harbor grievances about his terms, but he provides services that alternative credit institutions offering more favorable conditions have not been prepared to duplicate, particularly for the landless.

Lack of real movement in the village structure is also fostered by the crisscrossing of diverse interests within the village itself, which tend to balance each other and stop the scales in the middle. For instance, peasant landlords, who supply a considerable share of the marketable output in many parts of South Asia, have obvious reasons for supporting high prices for farm products. Small peasants and sharecroppers, on the other hand, offer little for sale and may even need to buy supplementary food toward the end of the crop season. Their interest in food prices may be opposite from the landlords', and neither group has the same outlook as the landless laborers, who certainly benefit more from low prices. The same opposing interests affect the landless when it comes to wage rates. A sharecropper or renting tenant may himself hire labor, in which case he would want to pay as little as possible; in turn, however, he may hire himself to a neighbor part of the time, for which he would want the highest wages.

Even land reform itself has not polarized supporters and opponents. Peasants whose holdings are so small that they need have no fears of expropriation for land redistribution join forces with those opposing reform proposals that would confer land on agricultural workers. Often these peasants hire some workers in the busy season, and such redistribution would tend to push up wages. But noneconomic factors also tend to unite all members of the village hierarchy in opposition to ambitions of the landless workers to acquire land of their own. In India and Pakistan particularly, all but the lowest strata can make common cause in obstructing the achievement of status and dignity by the dispossessed, for such efforts are typically regarded as scandalous violations of caste rules.

So, in effect, the South Asian village has developed into a complex molecule among whose parts extreme tensions have been built up. Although the tensions crisscross in a manner that maintains equilibrium, it is conceivable that these tensions might reorganize in a way that would explode the molecule. This probably would not happen spontaneously, but as the result of a forceful onslaught from outside.

This evolution of the institutional structure of the South Asian village from the ancient feudal systems to the interlocked groups of the present has had a profound effect on South Asian social and economic conditions.

From what has been said it is clear that conditions in the region do not fit the usual model of Western economic analysis with its implicit premise that the bulk of the economic activity is oriented toward market transactions and that production and exchange can consequently be discussed in terms of rational economic calculations. The supporting or fixing of farm prices to stimulate production or improve the market, as has so often been done in the West, would be of little consequence in South Asia. Food crops are made available for sale to the non-agricultural population, but in general this does not come about through the agency of the price system. Instead, the landlord and the moneylender are the major instruments for extracting output from traditional agriculture. This does not generate incentives to spur productive efficiency. On the contrary, the pattern that has emerged has sapped much of the incentive for raising productivity through intensification of the input and efficiency of labor or through output-raising forms of capital investment.

The unfortunate consequences of the "quasi-capitalistic" structure of South Asian agriculture can be seen vividly if we consider for a moment the situation in which an important member of the rural community—the sharecropper—finds himself. The insecurity of his tenure robs him of much incentive to execute output-raising improvements. Even a relatively quick-yielding investment, such as the use of fertilizer, does not deliver its full benefit in the first crop. More important, the fact that the rent varies not with the net return, but with the gross output, means that the system has a strong built-in deterrent to intensified cultivation. Nor has the landlord any forceful inducement to invest, as he can obtain a comfortable return without doing so. In the main, these landlords are content with whatever their holdings produce, and disinclined to attempt to improve their yield.

Too often in South Asia, the transfer of land to a nonagricultural owner or to a peasant landlord has meant that it will be tilled by a sharecropper, who has less inducement and no greater ability to undertake improvements than the former owner had, while the new title-holder himself remains aloof. At the same time, the social status system in the South Asian village has impeded increased production through the efficient use of wage labor. The employer is loath to push his workers too hard because the stigma attached to manual labor makes it so difficult to hire them in the first place. Some persons prefer semi-starvation on a tiny plot of rented land to a higher real income obtainable from wage employment.

In combination, all these factors have tended to stifle

incentives for improvement in efficiency and productivity. They have fostered an environment in which rent-receivers tap the surplus from agriculture without providing the resources that would make possible an increase in that surplus. They have discouraged the intensification of cultivation that might have been accomplished with the labor resources at hand, even without increases in the supplies of cooperating factors. Considering the deterrents to effective utilization of labor and to intensification of agricultural production that we have noted, it is perhaps remarkable that the performance of South Asia's traditional agriculturalists is no worse than it is.

It is clear that the social and institutional environment of traditional agriculture in South Asia places a high premium on abstention from productive work. Again, statistical breakdowns of how many persons actually work, who they are, and their ages and sexes do not come easily. Some South Asian countries—for example, Indonesia and South Vietnam—have only the foggiest notion of the size of their populations. But even if our knowledge of the work participation ratios and the forces affecting them is still imperfect, it appears that the proportion of eligible participants who effectively engage in work is low, and, moreover, that this proportion may even have tended to decline in at least some countries in the region.

All farmers in the world are affected, to some degree, by the seasons. During some parts of the year, such as planting and harvesting, their work is longer and far heavier than during others. In South Asia, the planting and harvesting seasons are periods when even some who are not regular members of the agricultural labor force may be drawn into field work. But for all those connected with farming in South Asia, the work year has large periods of idleness. One Royal Commission, studying colonial India, found that most of the cultivators had at least two to four months of complete leisure in the year.

Another study, made in the mid-1950's, concluded that there is seasonal unemployment among Indian agricultural laborers from four to six months of the year.

Obviously, smallholders who work their own land and peasant landlords, who themselves hire labor only at certain times, have a higher rate of participation. In many instances, farm workers who are attached to a landlord to discharge their debts may be absorbed in household and domestic duties during the slack season.

In parts of South Asia the agricultural year is sharply divided by wet and dry periods. But even when agricultural production is dominated by the monsoon, the work pattern should not have to be completely governed by the seasons. The effect of the climatic cycle on labor utilization could be modified through changes in cropping patterns. Even where the harshness of the climate permits little flexibility in cropping patterns, much useful work can be done in the off-seasons to improve living conditions. The rural areas urgently need improvements in housing, roads, sanitation facilities, and water supplies, most of which could be made with small claims on the capital resources at the disposal of the planners. Farmers in northern climates of the West, even in the days when labor was relatively immobile, used the long, severe winters to improve their houses and roads, repair their tools, and practice traditional crafts. Their higher levels of living, even a hundred years ago, rested on the fact that the Western farmer was very much of an all-around man, trained to do many kinds of work for the family and the farm, and hence less dependent upon climatic conditions.

Large-scale idleness thus cannot be analyzed in terms of the seasonal fluctuations alone, as is often assumed. It must be related to the level of living, to cultural patterns, and to the institutions that obstruct changes in cropping and diversification of work. Important among these institutional impediments is a cultural pattern that claims a good part of the year for festivals, holidays, ceremonial occasions, and, in the case of Moslem farmers, a month-long period of fasting.

A few Indian leaders of the recent past have inveighed against peasant lethargy, and both Gandhi and Nehru have openly accused their countrymen of laziness. But for the most part there is surprisingly little criticism in India or in neighboring countries of the low level of labor efficiency and the short duration of the work day or week. This may be partly explained by national reluctance to discuss shortcomings, and partly by a more or less sophisticated understanding that the reluctance to work and work hard is not attributable to a lack of moral fibre, but is caused by institutional and other factors that are obviously resistant to change. In some areas, climatic extremes, in combination with low levels of nutrition, stamina, and health, are such that prolonged periods of rest are necessary or at least desirable. In the months of extreme heat and humidity, reserves of energy are often drained after only a few hours of physical activity. Yet climatic conditions cannot bear all the blame for the relatively short periods of works and the low efficiency in work, as throughout much of the agricultural area in the Great Plains of the United States, temperature and humidity in the peak season are not markedly less disagreeable than in South Asia.

Inefficiency and considerable idleness are also tolerated for another set of reasons. In the main, there are no institutional spurs driving people to work and work hard. Even aside from the institutional inhibitions, the incentive to work often vanishes once the minimal output that makes it possible to survive has been achieved. This attitude, which is typical of subsistence farmers throughout the world, is not completely irrational. The agriculturalist whose tastes are circumscribed by his isolated position has little incentive to acquire the additional income that would permit him to diversify and augment his pattern of consumption.

The net effect of these factors is that workers, even when ostensibly busy, do not in fact make a very useful contribution to output. This is one of the crucial facts about agricultural life in South Asia. Yet the post-war approach, via the concept of "unemployment" and "underemployment," obscures it. We are driven to the conclusion that capital and technology are by no means the only limitations on agricultural advance, despite the tendency of post-war models to treat them as the basic determinants of labor productivity. The diligence of labor is perhaps an even more crucial variable. Its behavior, however, must be understood within the context of a social and institutional environment where standards of nutrition, health, and stamina are low and there is little incentive to work hard.

The problem of raising output per person in agriculture cannot be approached simply by designing measures to raise one of the components of labor utilization independently. It would do little good to bring more workers into participation if this only spread the work and reduced its duration or intensity. Little is accomplished when one group in the rural community is forced to work harder or longer so that another segment can withdraw part or all of its work contribution.

Even in the present state of poor factual data and incomplete research into labor utilization, it is possible to reach several important conclusions about the malaise afflicting South Asian agriculture and the obstacles hindering its improvement.

There is no situation where yields, income, and levels of living could not be improved substantially by a larger and more intensive labor input. But the institutional mold in which agriculture has been cast is highly inimical to greater productivity through a better use of labor. The tenancy system—particularly sharecropping—is doubly iniquitous. Not only does it tend to give command over the agricultural "surplus" to a group of landowners who, for the most part, are not disposed to provide resources that might increase the productivity of the land, but it also erodes the initiative of those who actually perform farm work.

South Asian indigenous agriculture is indeed caught up in a "vicious circle" of poverty. The task of breaking through that circle is likely to be very complex and difficult.

Chapter 17

AGRICULTURAL
POLICY

The struggle for long-term economic development in
South Asia will be won or lost in agriculture. Not only do
most South Asians live by farming, but it is here more
than anywhere else in the South Asian economies that
social advances can be made independent of much outside
assistance.

We know that the labor of those who live by farming is
not utilized effectively nor utilized to the extent that it
could be. The importance of this seemingly simple diag-
nosis is heightened by the equally simple fact that the
agricultural population of South Asia grows daily and no
matter what success may attend government birth control
programs, the labor force in South Asia will rise at an
annual rate of around 2 or 3 percent until near the end of
this century, or throughout any period within the purview
of today's planners, and that most of these newcomers will
have to stay in agriculture.

The hope, so commonly expressed, that a large proportion of those who will join the labor force in the decades

to come will be productively employed outside agriculture is illusory. The rural population is so large that its increase will not decline greatly during the next twenty or thirty years as the result of any movement from the rural to the urban areas. From a planning point of view, speeding up migration from rural areas to the city slums is anyhow not a desirable means of reducing the underutilization of the agricultural labor force. For millions born in the country, there is no other career than the farm; there is nowhere else for them to go.

But for the planners there are elements in the situation that seem to brighten the outlook for the productive absorption of more labor in agriculture, at least for the near future. The chief among these is the fact that yields in South Asian agriculture are so extremely low that it should be relatively easy to increase production levels. In a broad sense, the explanation for the low yields and the failure to capitalize on the potentialities for higher yields must be the prevailing work practices. In other words, there is a failure to make effective use of traditional and well-known farming methods. *Without any innovations and even without any investment other than longer and more efficient work, agricultural yields could be raised very substantially.* This is demonstrated by the different levels of yield as between districts or even individual farms revealed by management surveys.

Still greater increases in yields could be attained by applying modern scientific agricultural technology. But it must be remembered that much of the modern technology was developed in the West and does not always fit South Asian farming. There are still many gaps in agricultural research in this area—for instance, research about climates and soils, of the localized and intensive type that has made possible the rapid rise in yields in the countries in the temperate zones. This research must be conducted in the knowledge that Western techniques, which were geared to an agricultural labor force that was declining rapidly, do not fit South Asia, where a huge and largely underutilized labor force will be increasing rapidly for decades to come.

The silver lining in this situation is that, contrary to popular belief, South Asian work practices in agriculture are now not "labor-intensive." The labor input is low and inefficient. Instead, South Asian agriculture is "labor-extensive." The low yield per acre is mainly a consequence of an underutilized labor force. The implication of this is clear: *a fuller utilization of the labor force and a higher level of agricultural production are not only compatible objectives but, indeed, are two aspects of the same thing.*

The crucial importance of increasing agricultural production has now been duly appreciated throughout South Asia. But with a few exceptions, the countries of the region have not fared well in their efforts to raise farm output. With this apparent, we must note certain peculiarities in discussing agricultural policies practiced in all the South Asian countries. For one thing, the underutilization of labor, particularly in regard to duration and efficiency, is generally ignored or dealt with as a separate matter, unrelated to the "extensiveness" of agriculture and the fact that productivity is low. Occasionally the connection is made, but the need to improve labor use has never become a main theme in the planning of agricultural reforms. The organization of public work investments in agriculture has often been discussed, but there have been no large-scale efforts in this direction except recently in Pakistan.

Unfortunately, there has been just as much neglect of institutional and attitudinal problems. Instead, there has been an increasing emphasis on technological reforms, and general statements outlining plans for greater production have been completely taken up by descriptions of these reforms. Western governments, like those of South

Asia, continue to support resolutions in FAO conferences and other similar inter-governmental assemblies urging land reform. But this is only a gesture. The United States, though it felt compelled to place conditions on its food aid, usually merely adjured recipients to institute technical reforms and to divert more of their public "development expenditures" from industry to agriculture.

Meanwhile, a few institutional economists kept hammering at the importance of what has been called "the human-factor-first approach." Their thinking is upheld by people with field experience, who know that technical advice will bring results only up to a certain point, after which the cooperation of the cultivators is the limiting factor. Many Western economists who happen to touch on the problems of underdeveloped countries also often naively assume that these countries could stimulate agricultural production by simply raising farm prices. Western experts who have studied the South Asian agricultural situation are more careful. Like their South Asian colleagues, they do not count much on price support as a means of raising agricultural production.

We are not suggesting that agricultural reformers have been altogether unaware of the interdependence of technical and institutional changes, but rather that they have been biased to play down the latter. During the colonial era, governments were reluctant to interfere with the life and customs of indigenous populations, though they put aside their scruples when their interests demanded it, as in the case of land rights, the collection of taxes, and the recruitment of labor for European employers. A frontal attack on the deterrents to labor input and efficiency that were built into the traditional agrarian structure was precluded by considerations of expediency and expense and by the general colonial policy of *laissez faire*.

Ironically, this attitude has largely persisted since independence, though undoubtedly far more energy has been poured into the promotion of institutional reforms than in the past. The bias in favor of technical solutions has been strengthened by the post-war approach to planning, with its large-scale evasion of the problems implicit not only in institutions but also in attitudes and modes and levels of living and its faith in the ability of capital investment to raise output. It has been further reinforced by a vision of the "miracles" to be wrought by the application of modern science and technology. And it has been buttressed by the reports of Western agricultural planners acting as advisors who—though they often mentioned the importance of institutional reforms—usually confine their comments to the safer and supposedly more neutral subject of technological reform. This emphasis may merely reflect the fact that while trained in technical matters, these experts have little knowledge of attitudes and institutions in South Asia and how they might be changed.

Generally speaking, the increase recorded in South Asian agricultural production in recent decades has been due more to expansion of the cultivated area than to a rise in yields per acre. But there is general agreement among agricultural planners that further expansion of this area would be quite limited in scope and, in most instances, expensive to achieve. So it is generally accepted that increasing the yield per acre should be the most important pillar of any program aimed at rapid transformation of South Asian farming.

This is not because there is no more land to be cultivated. From a crude quantitative point of view, in the South Asian countries no more than 10 to 20 percent of the total land area is under cultivation. In the Indian subcontinent, this figure is only about two-fifths, though in India proper half the total area is tilled. The statistical data supplied by the FAO would suggest that at a minimum the cultivated area of Southeast Asia could be roughly doubled. Nature would permit the employment of perhaps two or three times as many agricultural workers in Southeast Asia, even with presently utilized techniques. In the Indian subcontinent, the possibilities for extending the area under cultivation are more limited, but by no means negligible, particularly if methods other than the traditional ones are used. But in too many of these areas, expansion would mean the need for heavy mechanical equipment and the expenditures of huge sums, much of them in precious foreign exchange.

Yet if nature has not set rigid limits on South Asia's agricultural population, other forces have obstructed the full utilization of tillable land. Landowners, having an interest in high rents and low wages, often display little enthusiasm for an expansion of the cultivated area. This is particularly true in India, where the problem is complicated by the opposition of the higher castes to lower-caste families or tribal people settling on waste land and acquiring ownership rights. Some governments have also sometimes been reluctant to encourage cultivation of village waste land for fear of increasing the danger of soil erosion.

The cultivation of untilled lands at a greater distance from the villages involves resettlement, and most South Asian peasants have been extremely reluctant to leave their homelands, no matter how crowded these have become. There are great areas of Sumatra and large parts of the smaller Indonesian islands that could be settled and developed. But a combination of the enormous costs implied and government ineptness in organizing migration have kept these programs at a disappointing level. Malaya has been methodically opening new lands for plantation cropping. But this has been a slow and cautious procedure. Many South Asian countries have rigid controls on squatters. If these were eased, many areas might be quickly opened up for cultivation with little public investment apart from the building of roads. This movement, however, would have to be protected by the government to prevent rich landowners and contractors from sending hired labor in to occupy these lands.

Much that is relevant to a complete evaluation of the scope for expansion of the cultivated area—particularly in regard to the quality of the untilled lands—is still unknown, and in most South Asian countries the planners' interest in the problem has faded in recent years. We can at least say that the capacity of the land area has not yet been thoroughly tested. The social and institutional structure and the traditional agricultural techniques have not encouraged—and in some cases have not permitted—expansion of cultivation to acreages that in other circumstances might have have been broken for tillage.

One of the cheapest and most promising ways to increase the area available for effective cultivation would be to reduce the number of farm animals. Uncontrolled pasturing is one of the factors responsible for the low quality and efficiency of South Asia's domesticated animal population. The demands of animals on space are most serious in India and, to a lesser extent, in Pakistan, which between them now possess not far from a third of the world's bovine population. In both countries there is roughly one cow for every two members of the human population.

Experts have been pointing out that traditional methods of feeding cattle on pasture are totally unsuitable in areas with a high population density. The same number of animals could be much better nourished on tilled fodder crops commanding only a fraction of the acreage now under pasture. René Dumont, a close student of conditions in the region, has suggested that if cultivated fodder crops were to replace traditional village grazing on common lands, one-fifth of these common lands would probably give more fodder than all of them did before.

A reduction in the total size of cattle population has also long been recommended. An American team of experts has concluded that at least a third, and perhaps a half, of India's cattle population should be regarded as surplus in relation to the feed supply. Resistance to cattle slaughter is not, of course, based solely on religious prejudice in India. Cattle are potentially handy sources of power, fuel (manure for burning), fertilizer, and foodstuffs. But agricultural experts believe that a much smaller, better-fed cattle population would increase the power available from draft animals. Moreover, a Ford Foundation team has reached the conclusion that "more dung is produced when a given quantity of food is consumed by one animal than when it is shared by two animals." In nearly all of Southeast Asia, cattle and buffalo are little used either for milk or for meat. Where milk consumption in the cities has become more widespread, as in Singapore and Djakarta, much of the supply is imported, in powdered or canned form. Apart from some outworn draft animals, the main sources of meat in Southeast Asia are goats, poultry, and, in non-Moslem areas, pigs.

The substitution of tractors and other farm machinery for animal power would be expensive initially. But much better cultivation would follow and, according to studies of farm management in the Punjab, if properly organized the use of tractors would be no more expensive than the use of bullocks and could be considerably cheaper. But such a rationalization of farm practices cannot be accomplished without changes in the institutional and attitudinal matrix. It cannot proceed very far when fragmented holdings, low incomes, and the tenancy system either rule out acquisition of machines or preclude their economic use. If these fetters could be broken, the cumulative effects of the introduction of tractors would be much greater because of the phenomenon of circular causation.

Great hopes have been placed by many planners on expanding South Asian farm production through irrigation. A constant water supply not only reduces the frightening dependence on the monsoon, but it could also permit the growing of more than one crop a year, if the peasants were willing to work that hard. Much has already been done toward increased irrigation in many South Asian countries and more is planned. But many of the results to date, particularly the major irrigation works, have been disappointing. Broadly speaking, the farmers have not been quick to make full use of the facilities offered. The actual cultivators have too often looked on irrigation as a form of insurance against monsoon failure rather than a device to increase their yields and perhaps plant more than one crop. Even the seasonal floods that bring rich deposits of silt have not been utilized to the extent possible.

A good part of the blame for the failure to utilize these existing opportunities to the full must be placed on the inherited institutional system. Farmers are often disinclined to avail themselves of the water placed at their disposal and in particular to shift to double cropping. They resent change in their accustomed rhythm of life, and in the existing agrarian structure they sometimes have solid economic reasons for resisting it. When the landlord, the water authorities, and the hired laborers all insist on the same rate of payment for the second planting as for the first, and when the second usually yields less and requires more labor, the sharecroppers in particular easily become skeptical about the whole thing. But certainly there have been conspicuous cases where irrigation has advanced agricultural output considerably, even when the advantages have not been fully utilized.

It must be remembered that irrigated crops regularly require large amounts of fertilizer. A clear case can thus be made for an increase in the use of chemical fertilizers. South Asia lags far behind in this also. Japan, for instance, uses more fertilizer than India, even though its cultivated area is only 4 percent of India's. And Japan's cereal yield per acre is almost five times that of India. But the important point is that fertilizers, like other agricultural aids, will yield maximum results only if applied in the context of over-all improvement in farming methods. The output of an agricultural commodity is a joint product that reaches its maximum only if irrigation, fertilizers, and other beneficial agents are applied simultaneously, in doses appropriate to local climatic and soil conditions. This clearly implies a need for complex research as guidance for the planners and policy-makers.

Meanwhile, it has been a difficult matter to bring about a change in even one agricultural practice. The following passage, from McKim Marriott, is a revealing explanation of why this is so: "Let me list some of the objections which farmers in my village, and in other nearby villages, have raised against the improved wheat seed. It is true, they said, that if the Lord pleases, one will get a better weight of fat wheat from the field sown with Government's improved seed: the yield in weight is really very good. One or two farmers have tried it. However, they had no intention of doing so again. The operator of the seed store was an impossible man. He gave the seed at a low enough rate of interest, but he demanded that it be paid back on a certain date, which might not be at all convenient if one had other debts to pay after the harvest. What was most unreasonable, the seed store operator demanded that the seed should be grown and returned pure, not mixed with the barley, peas, gram, and oil seeds that guaranteed against complete crop failure in a bad wheat season. Aside from these impossible conditions governing the loan and use of the seed, look at the resulting crop! The grain is indeed big—so big and tough that the women cannot grind it well in the old stone flour mills. Dough made from the new flour is difficult to knead and hard to bake into good bread. The new bread, which is all a poor farmer would have to eat, does not taste like the good old bread: it is flat and uninteresting (the explanation being in part, of course, that it does not contain that potpourri of barley, peas, gram and mustard seeds that 'wheat' contained in the old days). Next, look at the cows and bullocks! They do not like to eat the straw of the new wheat; they will die of hunger if we grow it. The straw is worthless, too, for thatching roofs. It does not even make a good fire to warm our hands in winter."

The absence of rapid progress, even when a wide range of improvements were introduced in areas where conditions were deemed to be particularly propitious, suggests that the advance of South Asian agriculture is slow not only because improvements are technically interdependent, but also because they often elicit an apathetic response from cultivators. But whenever a technical improvement is accepted, particularly if in combination with other improvements, attitudes are changed in such a way as to make further progress easier. The spread of literacy and education can play a catalytic role in such development.

We have shown earlier that South Asian agriculture is, for the most part, labor-extensive, not intensive. There is a frequent waste of manpower and a low level of productivity as a result. Among the many inhibitions against improvement is the belief that new methods of farming will reduce the number of farm jobs. This is not true. Advanced technology does not decrease the opportunity to improve labor utilization. On the contrary, it increases it. Indeed, the one thing practically all technological reforms have in common is that they require a greater labor input, for which the motivational urge must be created.

The South Asian countries need a new technology founded on a profound knowledge of local soil and climatic conditions and designed to take full advantage of the fact that the labor force in agriculture is severely underutilized and will grow rapidly for decades to come. At this stage in our knowledge, the point that must be underscored is that not even mechanization need be associated with less labor-intensive agricultural practices, as it has been in Western countries. When the possibilities are carefully examined in South Asia, some types of mechanization will be found essential to the intensification of agriculture.

Another and more serious obstacle to the spread not only of mechanization but of all the technological improvements of agricultural practices we have discussed is, as we have repeatedly stated, the cultivators' reluctance to embrace innovations that would change their work and life. Often technical experts fail to recognize the force of this reluctance. Promising technological innovations call for intensive programs of training and education, the facilities for which are inadequate everywhere in South Asia. Even when technical personnel are recruited and trained, their failure to work in the field, to overcome the sense of degradation associated with soiling one's hands, and to share the discomforts of the village life often renders the mission a failure. Ambitious and technically sound blueprints for reform have come to naught for this reason, and it would be folly to minimize the risk of similar failures in the future.

Today many of the opportunities for increasing agricultural production are in the nature of public works and require official "organization." It has increasingly become a passion to reduce the problem simply to one of organization. This is an opportunistic device. It serves as a means of bypassing the serious social and political inhibitions and obstacles to the assimilation of innovations and the community action that is supposed to be "organized."

In the years since they gained their independence, all South Asian governments have attempted some degree of land reform and most of the new governments pledged themselves to carry out agrarian reforms when they came to power. But the amount of land actually redistributed as a result of legislative action by these governments has not been very large. Most South Asian regimes have abstained

PART FOUR: LABOR UTILIZATION

altogether from the more radical land reform measures. Their intervention has, instead, been limited to protective legislation for all or some of the paddy-growing tenants, plus attempts to encourage cooperation and community development.

The failure of a consensus to emerge on radical land reform measures must be understood in the light of the complexity of interests concerned with land tenure. The wide diffusion of land ownership even among the urban upper and middle classes and non-cultivators in the rural areas, with both groups including many government servants, creates a formidable anti–land-reform bloc, powerful not because of its voting strength but because it embraces a substantial share of the literate population.

Part of the reduced ardor for radical reforms in the era since independence must also be attributed to the pressure on the national governments to consolidate their power and to create some semblance of order and stability in the nearly chaotic situations they inherited. But larger economic concerns have also encouraged caution. It was generally understood that the benefits from land reform would only come slowly, while the new governments were all preoccupied with immediate problems. Also, they attached a high policy priority to industrialization; in some influential quarters it was feared that the rate of industrialization might be slowed by radical land reforms because, in the short run, they might reduce the volume of marketable foodstuffs available to feed a growing non-agricultural population. Whatever its serious weaknesses in other respects, an agrarian structure heavily weighted with tenancy and burdened with debt does provide devices useful in extracting marketable foodstuffs from the poor in agriculture. Cultivators who might otherwise consume most of their crops are obliged to release a large part of them to landlords and moneylenders, who make the food available for sale in the towns.

South Asian governments are thus in an awkward

dilemma. If they fail to undertake land reforms, their attempts to raise agricultural output substantially will be thwarted. If they press major land reform programs with vigor, they run the risk of at least temporary cutbacks in the supply of marketable foodstuffs. Moreover, the larger part of the articulate and politically influential strata are against a more thorough land reform. Even if they play lip service to it, they will try to emasculate any enabling legislation or prevent its enforcement.

In India and Pakistan, the intermediaries, the semi-feudal landlord class that developed through British modification of the land tenure system, were particular objects of post-independence hostility. Efforts were made in the beginning to eliminate these landlords, who owned almost half of pre-independence India. But after an ambitious start, the usual forces of compromise and evasion prevailed and many of the intermediaries managed to hang on through the device of classifying themselves as personal cultivators.

Put bluntly, the abolition of the intermediaries in India and Pakistan was also not intended to give land to those who actually till it. It was meant instead as a policy to reinstate the original class of "peasant cultivators" who had lost their rights under the early British land settlements. The land went to members of the "cultivating" castes in the villages and the higher-caste families whose income had traditionally been drawn from land ownership and who had been granted the rights of privileged tenants by colonial tenancy laws. Those among them who actually worked the land had already before the reforms more incentive to improve cultivation than had ordinary sharecroppers because increases in their output were not directly and immediately associated with increases in rent.

The reign of the intermediary as a semi-feudal chief has ended. A side result is that, in general, power in the villages is passing from the old absentee landlord class and its agents to an upper middle class composed of merchants, moneylenders, and peasant landlords often living in the villages. A basis has been laid for the possible development of Indian agriculture along capitalist lines; those who favor such a development are not disposed to support further changes in the tenure systems. On the other hand, for those who want to see Indian agriculture develop on more egalitarian lines, the abolition of intermediaries was only the beginning of agrarian reform. Yet it was an important beginning. The elimination of big feudal landlords by parliamentary means was no small achievement in the first decade of independence, even though weakness and corruption in administration may permit the old rulers to exercise considerable influence for some time to come.

Considering the consequences of ownership ceilings and land redistribution measures, several tentative generalizations can be advanced about South Asian experience to date. There have been no revolutionary disturbances in property relationships within the agrarian structure. Long-standing inequalities within the village structure have scarcely been touched. The fact that these measures have not lived up to their advance publicity has contributed to a growing climate of agrarian frustration. Meanwhile, it is far from certain that favorable economic results have developed from the minor adjustments attributable to government action on agricultural property holding. In no South Asian country have any sizable numbers of tenants become owners of the land they till. Thus the security of tenancy continues to be a crucial problem. All the South Asian governments have pushed legislation to provide more protection for some, if not all, tenants and to limit the landlord's claim on the harvest.

It is important to appreciate that these tenancy laws, if they were to be effective at all, would have had to both prescribe maximum rents and guarantee a tenant's security of occupancy, which they have obviously not done. Also, compliance with the law has been difficult to attain. Too often these laws have been showpieces full of loopholes or bulky, extremely complicated documents that a tenant, even if he were literate, would have difficulty understanding. In post-independence India, the sharecroppers, in the usual pattern, have remained at a distinct disadvantage. They usually pay much higher rents than privileged tenants, and landowners have a special interest in preventing them from obtaining rights as protected tenants. As a result, the institution of sharecropping survives in virtually all of India and Pakistan. Even when they are technically covered by the law, sharecroppers, having no security of tenure, are in too weak a position to have legal rates of rent enforced.

Failure effectively to include sharecroppers in the category of protected tenants has grave implications for agricultural development. Unfortunately, in the economic and social setting of an agriculture where sharecropping prevails, injustices cannot be prevented simply by including the sharecroppers among the tenants to be protected by a strong tenancy law or by those laws that might limit the amount a landlord may take from them. In rural areas of South Asia where a rapid increase in the labor force is raising the demand for land, laws setting maximum rents may even have unfortunate social and economic effects when they are enforced. Too often a tenant is tempted to sublet his land at a rent much higher than the one he pays himself, and at the bottom of the tenancy pile remains the sharecropper.

Another great weakness of tenancy legislation in India and Pakistan and in the countries of Southeast Asia is that its administration has been in the hands of civil servants, who often lack both the qualifications and the integrity necessary for the job. Ceylon attempted a different approach by assigning administration of tenacy legislation to local committees elected by the peasants for this specific purpose, but the initial experience was disappointing. Only a small percentage of either tenants or landlords turned out to vote, though many tenants probably abstained more from fear of reprisal by landowners than from lack of interest. As a result, elections had to be cancelled in many villages.

The failure of land tenancy laws has thus not been because there were none, but because those that were adopted were not implemented. Besides the illiteracy and ignorance of most tenants, which make them easy prey for landlords and their agents, they are beset by the dual role of many owners as both landlords and moneylenders. When tenants are indebted to a landowner, they have to put up with his encroachments on their rights.

The tenant in turn receives no support from the peasants who are small landowners nor from the hired workers, who have no reason to care about them. The tenants themselves are too heterogenous and in parts of South Asia are too divided by caste distinctions to protest in mass against evasion of the law. It is also typical that the tenant regards the landlord with awe and reverence and lacks the moral courage to oppose him, even when he is breaking the law. The official who administers those laws too often is even more in awe of the landlord and cautious about moving against him.

A proven weapon for farmers in their running battle against the soil, the weather, and the market has, in many parts of the world, been the cooperative. Through such organizations farmers can buy in wholesale lots the seed and fertilizers they need, borrow money, provide mutual help at harvest time, and, through cooperative efforts, move their produce to market at more advantageous prices. Unfortunately, the attempts at various types of cooperative societies in South Asia have yielded little, and one of the primary reasons is the basic social inequality in so many parts of the region.

Programs for local cooperation have often been presented as if they were revolutionary and in themselves likely to create conditions leading to greater equality in the villages. Unfortunately this is bound to have been an illusion. While land reform and tenancy legislation are, at least in their intent, devices for producing fundamental alterations in property rights and economic obligations, the cooperative approach fails to incorporate a frontal attack on the existing inegalitarian power structure. Indeed, it aims at improving conditions without disturbing that structure and represents, in fact, evasion of the equality issue. If, as is ordinarily the case, only the higher strata in the villages can avail themselves of the advantages offered by cooperative institutions—and profit from the government subsidies given for their development—the net effect is to create more, not less, inequality. This will hold true even when the announced purpose is to aid the disadvantaged strata.

Like the cooperative movements, the community development programs that most South Asian nations have attempted to promote have been animated by the equality ideal, and stress has been given to the needs and interests of the lower levels in the village hierarchy. As things have worked out, however, there has been a tendency, particularly in India, to favor not only the wealthier in the villages, but also the wealthier villages and districts. Hopes that community development projects, instituted after independence, would produce a massive uplift throughout the region have clouded. What mass support there was in the beginning for these programs has largely faded. In particular, participation in the voluntary work programs —which was never impressive—appears to have fallen off, especially in India. Community development can no longer be regarded as a means to aid the lower strata's efforts in self-help. It has become, in fact, a device for channelling government assistance to the not-so-poor.

While community development suffers from the weaknesses in the land and tenancy laws and their implementation, it has itself increased the obstacles standing in the path of these other reform efforts as they were originally envisaged in India. The agricultural extension service got a vigorous start at a moment when the peasant landlord group had been strengthened by the elimination of intermediaries. At least some members of this group learned that money could be earned by the modernization of agriculture and that liberal aid could be obtained from the government for this purpose. Having absorbed that lesson, peasant landlords are less disposed than ever to agree that their holdings should be broken up for the benefit of less fortunate villagers.

Cooperative farming, a more complex approach to community participation, has been tried in some South Asian countries. At first glance, a cooperative farming scheme would seem to have much to recommend it in a country like India. With cooperative farming arrangements it might be possible to consolidate small and fragmented holdings into operational units to which rational principles of soil managment and land use could be more easily applied. At the same time, larger farming units offer better prospects for the introduction and intelligent application of output-raising techniques, such as irrigation and the use of improved seeds and fertilizers, and for economies in the use of work animals, tractors, tools, and machines.

In short, cooperative farming is often viewed as capable of transforming the entire institutional matrix of the South Asian agrarian structure and overcoming the long-standing obstructions to efficiency, improved productivity, and a fuller utilization of labor. It is only in India where an attempt at cooperative farming has been made on any large scale. But the Indian village, as it presently exists, does not constitute a favorable environment for the development of the type of social harmony necessary. A basic element in the general lack of success of Indian

cooperative farming was the failure to change the structure of land ownership. So far, the cooperative efforts
have produced virtually no change in the status quo. Even
absentee landowners support the cooperative farming
idea in India, because individual title to land is retained
and they have benefitted from what government preferences and aid have been offered. But perhaps the most
unfortunate result of preoccupation with the cooperative
solution is that it has diverted attention from the tough
problems of fundamental structural reform.

In the last decade and a half, virtually all economists,
Western or South Asian, who have studied agricultural
problems in the region have called for the mobilization of
labor to build roads and bridges, irrigation systems, and
other elements that would improve the rural infrastructure. It has been pointed out that these "investment"
activities require few additional resources to complement
the labor needed. But they all presuppose collective action, and every effort to organize underutilized labor has,
in most parts of South Asia, failed or been a near failure.
It has been proven virtually impossible to persuade
people to work when it is not for their own direct benefit.
The landless workers and sharecroppers in India, for
example, have no motivation for working without wages
on improvements whose benefits will accrue to the higher
strata who own the land.

One often hears the cry that there must be greater
leadership at the top and greater discipline among the
middle leaders to promote these self-help projects. More
often the explanation is offered that the possibilities for
mobilizing underutilized labor are more limited in a democracy than under a Communist regime. This reference
is sometimes nostalgic; more often it is stated proudly that
compulsion should not be resorted to, even though this
implies that less can be achieved. Generally, there is,
however, in most countries in South Asia, and definitely in

India, a greater readiness than in the Western countries to recognize that the Communist system relies on more than compulsion when arousing the masses to collective efforts. There is recognition that it relies also on radical equalization and on intensive education, propaganda, and organizational work carried out by a single-minded cadre.

A more tangible difficulty, for South Asia, is the lack of organizers. The bottleneck is not least the scarcity of competent and technically well-trained persons who can take command and direct work on the local level. Occasionally the army is suggested as a final resort. Indeed, with India forced to maintain a large army for defense against both China and Pakistan, it would be quite possible to provide some training toward public works. In Indonesia the army has been using its "civic action" programs to organize and aid peasants in public works. But even if the military, or persons they had trained, should be turned toward directing public works, they would confront the same difficulty that all those concerned with rural uplift encounter—the fundamental fact that the villages, like the states and the nations, are deeply split by differences inherent in the inegalitarian agrarian structure.

The catalogue of disappointments in the post-war struggle to uplift South Asian agriculture is lengthy. Perhaps the only conspicuous result of policies after independence has been the strengthening of the upper strata in the villages and a corresponding reduction in the position of sharecroppers and landless laborers in the lower strata of rural society. At the heart of this is the perpetuation of economic and social inequality throughout the region and the stultifying preoccupation with status.

The political consequences of the post-war trend of events are far-reaching. The evidence suggests that the opportune moment for a radical reshaping of the agrarian structure has passed. Sweeping changes might perhaps have been accomplished in the revolutionary environment of the immediate post-war years. But if consent for a fundamental change in property and tenancy rights might have been won then, it is not possible now. The piecemeal reforms that have been accomplished have bolstered the political, social, and economic position of the rural upper strata on which the present governments depend for crucial support.

As long as working and earning an income jeopardize status, while landholding and partial or complete abstention from productive work raise it, aggregate output is held well below its potential. If, on the other hand, measures to reduce inequalities can succeed in removing deterrents to work, aggregate labor utilization and production may be simultaneously advanced. Unlike the situation in Western countries (at least as it is conventionally diagnosed), the South Asian case may thus be one in which *the promotion of social and economic equality is a pre-condition for attaining substantial long-term increases in production.*

Success with such an approach to policy would by no means be easy to achieve; it depends on a host of complementary conditions. But it can at least be said that policies for agricultural reform that ignore the problem of inequality are not likely to achieve major and, especially, lasting results. This oversight is perhaps the gravest shortcoming of efforts at institutional change thus far launched by South Asian governments. Even measures that, on paper, have seemed to deal with the issue of equality—for instance, cooperatives and community development—have in fact failed to come to grips with it.

In many discussions of alternative patterns that might lift South Asian agriculture, land redistribution is ruled out at an early stage on the grounds that it would simply create small uneconomic holdings and sacrifice the efficiency of the present larger units of cultivation. These fears are, in fact, vastly exaggerated. It must be borne in mind that there is an enormous difference between the units of ownership and the units of cultivation in South Asian agriculture. The "farm" in South Asia bears no resemblance to farming units found in North America or Europe. The South Asian farm is not an economic unit composed of a house for the operator, a garden, and a collection of buildings for storing crops and sheltering animals and machinery. The farming unit is simply a piece of bare land or, more often, a number of scattered small strips, barren of fixed investment other than perhaps a well or, at times, some terracing and drainage or irrigation channels.

From the point of view of labor utilization, a radical land redistribution has an impressive recommendation. It holds out the promise of creating the basis for a major transformation in the psychology and attitudes of the rural labor force by cutting through the deterrents to work that have long been entrenched in the traditional pattern of inequalities. A radical land redistribution might encourage those who acquired land in their own right to work more intensively and use slack periods in making output-raising improvements. In particular, it might cut through the debilitating influence of the prevalent share-cropping system. Meanwhile, cultivating peasants whose holdings were reduced by such a redistribution might work more intensively to recover at least part of their lost income.

It has also been argued that land redistribution would bring in new owners whose inexperience might cause reduced yields. But sharecroppers and other tenants, and landless workers, the group that would profit most by the redistribution, are experienced cultivators. Even if the new owners were less qualified as cultivators than the ones they displaced, a heavier input of labor on their part might well outweigh any negative effects of their inferior qualifications. As we pointed out earlier, much scope remains for the intensification of agriculture with no more

than traditional methods that are either well known or
could be promoted by extension workers, who would get a
better response when the tillers owned the land they were
tilling. Nor is the argument that new landowners would
lack capital a forceful one. This could be overcome by the
pooling of needed equipment and by genuine cooperation,
including credit, which might be more possible in a more
egalitarian social and economic structure.

Radical land redistribution would certainly not remove
all the obstacles to agricultural advance. Much would
have to be accomplished through technological improvements and better use of labor. But land redistribution may
create a climate more receptive to the assimilation of
these innovations. The same might be true of cooperative
movements. Even cooperative farming would have more
of a chance if it could be made more genuinely cooperative.

But in the longer perspective, there is still another and
greater problem to be taken into account. In the absence
of protective measures, it would be erroneous to view
redistribution of land as a satisfactory long-term solution
to the problems of South Asian agriculture. The titles
transferred to the actual tillers might just as easily be
eroded by the same forces that now prevail. To be a
permanent improvement, a radical land redistribution
would have to be supplemented by an equally radical
elimination of past debts to moneylenders plus a prohibi-
tion on any new borrowings from them, and legislation
prohibiting the mortgaging and sale of land. Such measures would obviously make the radical land reform still
less acceptable politically. Moreover, legislation designed
to block future subdivision or fragmentation and prohibit
the sale of land might collapse under pressures from the
increase in the labor force in agriculture. At best, a radical
land redistribution could thus only be thought of as a
once-and-for-all change in the land tenure pattern, one
that by virtue of its shock effect might cut through the

obstacles to more intensive labor utilization that exist under the present system of inequalities.

If a radical redistribution of land to the tillers is not only unrealistic politically, but afflicted with certain practical defects, a nationalization of landholdings might seem to be a more favorable alternative. The problems of fragmentation and dispersion of small holdings could be overcome; rational land use and planning could be introduced; and the technical capabilities of irrigation could be better exploited. But consideration of the option of a radical land consolidation, though of interest in itself, has no political relevance. Such a policy could only be executed after a Communist revolution. And the results in South Asia would be even less satisfactory than those recorded in the Soviet Union or China, where a considerable period of organization and preparation preceded the acquisition of power by Communist governments and their consolidation of landholdings. Communism, even in theory, does not seem to provide a viable treatment for the ills of South Asian agriculture.

We have grave doubts that any program can be devised that could be regarded as ideal from all points of view. We are satisfied, however, that the approaches to agricultural policy presently being followed, and the alternative courses most prominently discussed, are not likely to produce the type of transformation so urgently needed. With considerable hesitation, we shall advance a tentative framework within which a fresh approach to agricultural policy might profitably be considered. We are thinking, in the first instance, of a country like India.

To date, agricultural policy has courted the worst of two worlds: equality has not in fact been promoted, with the result that people have become discouraged and cynical, while efficiency has not been adequately recognized and rewarded.

In this situation the first conclusion is that the government should lay down a definite policy and see to it that that policy is really carried out. The second conclusion is that—as neither the political will nor the administrative resources for a radical, or, for that matter, any fairly effective land reform are present—it may be preferable to make a deliberate policy choice in favor of capitalist farming by allowing and encouraging the progressive cultivator to reap the full rewards of his enterprise and labor, while approaching the fundamental issues of equality and institutional reform from a different angle and by different policy means.

A policy supporting the development of agriculture on capitalist lines must be sharply distinguished from one of *laissez faire*. Indeed, it calls for a major transformation of the *status quo*. As we have demonstrated elsewhere, indigenous agricultural practice in South Asia is typically a form of quasi-capitalism combining the least favorable features of capitalist and feudal patterns of economic organization.

For one thing, a genuinely capitalist path of development cannot tolerate passive and parasitic land ownership on the part of persons who sap the surplus of the agricultural sector but contribute nothing to its productive performance. Sharecropping should be abolished. It will not be easy to eliminate the abuses of absentee land ownership, and, for that matter, of resident ownership on the part of persons who claim to be "cultivators" but in fact are not. But much could be accomplished through a tax system that placed severe penalties on the income of non-participating landowners and through laws prohibiting the future transfer of titles to non-farming non-residents.

Laws of the latter type are in existence in many democratic countries, of which Sweden is one, even though the evil absenteeism there is infinitely smaller. The reform we have in mind would not take anything from anybody, but would outlaw purchases of land by persons who were not prepared to become cultivators and would, in particular, prohibit land acquisition by urban residents. It is, indeed, an indication of the power situation in South Asian countries, and its reflection in shaping ideologies, that, *though there have been plenty of radical pronouncements along the conventional pattern of a "social and economic revolution" and "the land to the tillers," such a straightforward, practical line of reform has not been seriously debated.*

Although considerable laxity in enforcement is inevitable, and we have no illusions about this, such an approach would still have much to recommend it over the policies promoted in the post-war years. By and large, post-war policy on agrarian reform has used the *size* of agricultural holdings as a basic criterion. Our proposal offers the criterion of *functional use* of land as a substitute. Large-scale ownership *per se* should not be regarded as an evil if it provides genuine gains in efficiency and productivity. Functional tests of efficiency and of genuine work participation would be far preferable to the static test of size of holdings.

An honest attempt—even if only imperfectly implemented—to imitate the controlled and restrained pattern of capitalist practice that has gradually evolved in Western countries would offer some considerable advantages over the policies and practices now prevailing. It would at least channel thinking in a more consistent direction by stripping away the deceptive facade of a "socialist pattern" that is not only far out of touch with the realities but arouses insecurity among the "haves" and expectations that, when dashed, give rise to debilitating disillusionments among the "have-nots."

As we have argued, there is no necessary conflict between the goals of intensification of agricultural production and absorption of heavier labor inputs. Nevertheless, it must be recognized that such a competition may occur in some cases—for example, in the uncontrolled introduction of mechanized processes. But if mechanization should threaten to have unfavorable labor-displacing effects, its use could be checked by determined government control.

The development of a genuinely capitalist system of production does not imply the preservation of the *status quo* but, as we have pointed out, is to be recognized as a quite radical land reform, though of a different species from the schemes usually discussed. It must be designed in such a way that the landowners are encouraged to become cultivators, at least in the sense of being genuine agricultural entrepreneurs. In particular, such a policy must be directed toward the gradual abolition of the sharecropping system. Looked at from the opposite point of view, agricultural workers should be given a respectable place in the capitalist agricultural system. Without question, *long-term agricultural uplift in South Asia cannot be accomplished unless the traditional distaste for diligent manual work and, in particular, for work as a wage employee is weeded out of the economic system and the minds of the people.*

In implementing this type of "land reform" it is, moreover, as important to devise measures to protect agricultural workers as to create incentives for genuine entrepreneurship on the part of landowners. Through such measures, this system of agriculture could gradually acquire the characteristics of "welfare capitalism." High priority in this scheme should be accorded to a program *to give a small plot of land—and with it a dignity and fresh outlook on life as well as a minor independent source of income—to members of the landless lower strata.* Even in the most densely populated countries in the region it would be possible to give the landless at least small plots on acreages that are now uncultivated waste. In some cases land is available for the landless in the vicinity of existing holdings. The existing pattern of cultivated holdings need not be seriously disturbed—in some places it would not need to be disturbed at all. In the most crowded districts, some reallocation of population would be necessary.

A modest redistributive scheme drafted along these lines, far less radical than the land reforms generally discussed and to an extent legislated, would have two important things to recommend it: first, it would offer a minimal form of social security to the dispossessed in the agrarian structure by allowing them to produce a modest income in kind; secondly, and more important, it would attack the institutional and attitudinal problem of status and dignity at its roots. It would be essential in such a scheme of limited redistribution, however, that *inalienable and unrestricted right to own and use land pass into the hands of the landless individuals.* If village cooperatives were to control it in any way, as in the Indian program, its central purpose would be frustrated. Very limited land redistribution would not immediately solve the problems of the underprivileged. They would still need supplemental income from other sources—either through agricultural wage labor or through other types of work in the countryside. Laborers, however, would bargain from a position different from the one they now occupy. And, having once been elevated in status, they might well adopt a more positive attitude toward their work.

In any event, long-term advances in agricultural output and efficiency can only be achieved if South Asian peoples can be brought to accept the fact that wage employment is a normal and healthy feature of progressive economies. After all, the bulk of the population in all the developed countries gains most of its income by working for someone else. By the same token, the people of South Asia must learn that wage earning need be neither offensive nor degrading. But before this lesson can be effectively absorbed, it will be necessary to confer—through land ownership—a dignity on those who at present are denied it. This proposal amounts, in effect, to a non-monetized social security and social advancement system of a type adapted to the environment of South Asian countries. It would offer some promise that one of the basic institutional and attitudinal deterrents to progress could be alleviated and a course toward progress more clearly charted. If it succeeded in promoting agricultural advance, it would lay a basis for more formal types of labor organization in the future, even in agriculture, that would better enable workers to defend and advance their own interests. Gradually, as levels of income rose, modern forms of social security as developed in Western and Communist countries might then also become possible and effective.

The course of action we have outlined calls for a selective adaptation of some of the methods for promoting agricultural advance that have succeeded in Western countries, although in combination with policies specifically devised to cope with the peculiarities of the attitudinal and institutional situation in South Asia. It represents a modified form of "welfare capitalism" for agriculture. What we are suggesting is less pretentious than most of the reforms discussed nationally or in the United Nations. But practically our proposal would be far more radical than anything yet accomplished in South Asia and probably far more effective for the purpose of raising productivity in agriculture and moving toward greater equality and mobility in the economic and social structure.

Politically, the prospects for steering agricultural policy along these lines are far from bright. The most probable development in South Asian countries is undoubtedly a continuation of the present course. Under the banner of a "social and economic revolution," land reforms and other institutional changes of a radical character will be talked about and, occasionally, enacted into law in some form. Very little reform will actually be accomplished and even greater inequality may result from both government policies and developments beyond governmental control, such as the increase in the labor force. A state of insecurity about the future of land ownership will be maintained, and that itself will tend to suppress improvements in production.

Not the least harmful effects of the prevalent radical ideological pretensions, when they are devoid of practical accomplishment, is that they have obstructed realistic thought and debate about pragmatically sound radical policies. Yet the need for such policies is great; that they are becoming necessary in order to avoid disaster should be clear from our analysis here and in other chapters of this book.

Chapter 18

LABOR UTILIZATION OUTSIDE TRADITIONAL AGRICULTURE

The non-agricultural sector of the South Asian economy was deeply affected by the colonial era, just as the agricultural sector was. The Europeans brought with them their own types of light manufacturing and, in larger numbers, their agricultural processing industries. The force of these was not great, but they did tend to put some pressures on the traditional urban handicrafts. There was not only new competition from machine-made products, but a parallel decrease in the support for national crafts that had persisted under the pre-colonial rulers. Although it deteriorated as a result, traditional manufacturing did not disappear. It is still by far the dominant form of manufacturing industry in all South Asian countries, particularly in terms of the part of the labor employed.

These craft industries have tended to take on many of the latter-day characteristics of indigenous agriculture. Contemporary craftsmen, like their predecessors, work largely by hand, with only crude implements. And like the farmers, many craftsmen who produce for a market are often in the clutches of moneylenders, of suppliers of raw materials, and of middlemen who purchase and market their product. Many South Asian craft enterprises are family affairs. They often hire labor to supplement the work of family members, though hired workers usually form a minority of the labor force. In many cases, these laborers sleep on the premises and their position is similar to that of personal servants; they help not only with production, but also with household duties.

Most of the more highly organized forms of business enterprise that can now be found in South Asia have, from the beginning, been initiated, financed, and managed by Europeans or by aliens, such as Chinese and Indian businessmen. More recently, many of these activities have been taken over by local people or by national governments and in some instances South Asians themselves have initiated some fairly complex business ventures. But Western forms of economic organization, even when established in the partial isolation of the old colonial enclave, could not be completely insulated from the influence of the indigenous social and institutional environment. When transferred to South Asia, Western economic institutions and practices had to undergo considerable adaptation, and their impact on labor utilization in South Asia often differs substantially from what it would normally be under Western conditions.

For one thing, the difficulty the Europeans had in recruiting, and retaining, local labor in colonial times led to extraordinary measures. Compulsion in some guise was often employed to mobilize a wage labor force. Wages were often so low that men were forced to leave their families behind in the villages. This may have saved an employer something in wages, but it also created a very unstable work force. Working hours, in those years, were onerous, and working conditions just as bad. Since independence, many South Asian countries have adopted laws to improve these circumstances. But throughout South Asia, a large gap remains between conditions prescribed in the laws and regulations and those which actually exist. No more than a casual inspection of the living conditions of the majority of industrial employees at some randomly selected industrial enterprises is needed to discover that existing standards of housing, health, and nutrition are not conducive to maximum efficiency. Nor is it clear that government regulation of hours of work has been effectively enforced.

Broadly speaking, managerial practices in South Asia also failed to create an environment conducive to high labor efficiency. In several important respects, the large-scale entrepreneur, whether he was a European or an Asian, tended to take on some of the attributes of the big absentee landowner. Though these men were more disposed to invest in the enterprises under their control than is the typical absentee landlord, they might still be almost as withdrawn from direct control over current operations. Many functions that would be performed directly by management in Western economies were often delegated to intermediaries, who were given wide discretionary powers.

Quite apart from its effects on the growth and expansion possibilities of the modern sector of the economy, the pattern of management practices has had another, though less obvious, influence on labor efficiency. In modern Western conditions, the trade union movement has emerged as a potent instrument in increasing standardization of working conditions. In South Asia weakness is the dominant trait of the trade union movement in the

modern sector of manufacturing. Although many interdependent factors underlie this—among them the difficult
bargaining position of workers when they are so far removed economically and socially from their employers
and there are so many jobless—it must be ascribed partly
to the managerial practice of delegating responsibilities to
native jobbers and foremen. Acting as powers unto themselves, these jobbers have a stake in perpetuating high
rates of labor turnover. The strategic position of the
jobber also frustrates the formation of a solidly based
labor organization, because the jobbers themselves—who
in a different environment might have turned their un-
doubted talents to organizing trade unions—have a vested
interest in the *status quo*.

It is apparent that even in the "modern" or "organized"
sector of industry the forces governing the utilization of
labor and affecting its performance are vastly different
from those now typical in advanced economies and those
presupposed in Western analytical models. Despite its use
of capitalist techniques and modes of organization, much
more highly structured than those of indigenous economic
institutions, the modern sector cannot escape the influence of its broader environmental setting. Most modern
enterprises, despite an enclave existence, cannot detach
themselves completely from South Asian social and economic life.

Most South Asian countries also have a third group of
economic activities outside agriculture and mostly carried
on in urban districts, sometimes labelled "informally organized." This embraces a wide range of heterogenous
activities that have only one attribute in common: a set of
institutional properties differing from those observed
either in the more formally structured Westernized units
of production or in the traditional, mostly rural crafts.
Most, however, have tended to perpetuate traditional
patterns, such as an emphasis on the family as the central
unit of productive organization. The services, in South

Asia, account for a far larger proportion of the urban labor force than do all varieties of urban manufacturing. The crowded field of retail trade, with its itinerant hawkers and peddlers, makes up another large portion, although when this field is filled with aliens, as it is in many parts of Southeast Asia, it is better organized. Characteristic of all these occupations is that the labor input is low and insufficient.

Broadly speaking, most forms of economic activity outside traditional agriculture lack the institutional checks on the duration and efficiency of work characteristic of modern Western economies. Although more highly organized undertakings are able to exercise more control and discipline over work performance than can either traditional manufacturing or the other loosely organized pursuits that engage most of the urban labor force, there are still serious restraints on the effectiveness of their efforts. In large-scale manufacturing, for example, efficiency is greatly retarded by the generally low levels of nutrition and health, to say nothing of the effects of miserable housing conditions on physical effectiveness and labor turnover. In general the physical well-being of plantation employees is higher. But their situation is basically different from that of other workers in advanced economies, in that they are often denied effective freedom of movement. Even when they are not tied by long-term contracts, many of them are caught in an alien environment without the resources to move to other employment.

A basic distinction should, at this point, be drawn between the forces in South Asia and in the West that may affect the long-term problem of worklessness. South Asians dismissed from jobs in the organized segment of the economy simply cannot afford the luxury of "unemployment." In a society that provides no dole, those who cannot go back to the villages or be sustained by the charity of their friends and relatives must find some work to do in the multitude of more or less casual economic activities in urban areas. The same is true of the very much larger part of the labor force that has never been employed in the organized sector.

Over the long run, though, the strongest influence on the availability of non-agricultural jobs is the mounting size of urban population. If this trend were due to an increasing demand for labor in the cities, workers could simply be fitted into these new jobs. But the migration to the cities of South Asia has been caused, in part, by the decline in peasant ownership of land and the recession in traditional rural crafts. In another part, it has been stimulated by the lure of the cities as an escape from the drabness of village life. South Asian planners have assumed that this migration to the cities will continue. Some have regarded it as an inevitable result of the process of economic development, comparable to what happened in the West during the Industrial Revolution. But it is highly doubtful that this comparison can be made. This point is partially conceded in official thinking when it is argued that new employment opportunities must be provided in urban areas if the volume of unemployment is not to grow alarmingly. Many systematic and detailed studies are urgently needed to illuminate the causes and effects of this migration. Unfortunately, official attitudes that presuppose that rural-urban migration is a normal and healthy by-product of industrial expansion do not create an ideal climate for such research.

In one important respect—the duration of work—the analysis of aggregate labor utilization is more straightforward outside traditional agriculture than within it. Seasonality, which exercises so great an influence on prevailing work patterns in agriculture, generally affects far less the duration of work in the economy. Outside of agriculture the institutional environment has much more bearing. Increasingly, the length of the working day and week in the modern and organized part of the urban economy is being standardized and subjected to regulation. But in contrast to the situation in Western countries, organized protests by the workers themselves have played very little part in efforts to shorten and regularize the work period in South Asian manufacturing industry. Spontaneous labor organization has been weak and ineffective, and the initiative for improving and standardizing conditions of work has been taken mainly by governments. And though official regulations have proliferated, their enforcement has been very spotty.

In some enterprises in the unorganized sector the work period is undoubtedly long. This is true in many craft activities. Often heavily indebted, and driven by the pressures of economic distress, artisans are known to put in long hours, the length of their work day being limited only by the number of hours of sunlight. Yet the essential truth is simple and obvious: there is often much idleness and the intensity, skill, and diligence with which the labor force as a whole works when it is working are, as a rule, low and do not generally show much improvement. This fact is widely acknowledged and has indeed often been remarked by South Asians themselves.

In view of the institutional setting of economic activity in South Asia, the basic reasons for the existence and persistence of low labor efficiency, even in the organized sector, are not difficult to comprehend. The bulk of the labor force is unaccustomed to a rhythm of sustained and diligent work, and management has often been lax in instilling discipline. Indeed, it is commonly felt that rigid work standards which raised efficiency would threaten job opportunities, and would therefore be anti-social. Hence employers frequently tolerate slack performance on the grounds that it provides a form of social insurance to workers who would otherwise be left defenseless and without means of support. And as long as wage scales remain low, employers have no strong inducement to economize in their use of labor or insist on high standards of work performance. The trade unions, which are not usually very effective in bargaining for better conditions, come to life readily enough in protesting any changes in established practices. These attitudes are in conformity with the more general traits that mark these countries as "soft states."

While in the West employers have a greater incentive to raise the efficiency of work performance and highly mechanized operations impose a certain rhythm and pace that cannot be easily varied, these same processes do not generally yield the same results in South Asia. When comparisons are relevant, it appears that output per worker in South Asia falls substantially below the norm in the West. Often the same machine is run at a slower pace in South Asian countries, though this differential may tend to narrow as skills and techniques are developed through practice. This state of affairs is hardly surprising. An inexperienced worker—particularly one who is below par physically—is at a serious disadvantage in comparison with his counterparts in more advanced countries.

In some South Asian countries fear of substitution of machines for labor has generally been acute and has had an impact on official policy. In India measures have been taken by the government to minimize the displacement of labor that results from competition between higher and lower techniques. The bulk of investment in machinery budgeted for in the plans has been allocated to new industries, a procedure that by-passes the resistance to productivity-increasing measures found in established industries. Western industrial experience was never complicated by the special factors that inhibit efficient utilization of labor in much of South Asia. Caste, religious, and ethnic stratifications impose artificial rigidities on occupational mobility in urban areas as well as in tradition-bound villages. Employers have at times been obliged to forego rational organization of the work pattern in order to adapt to these prejudices. One of their effects is to deny the employer a free hand in promoting an efficient worker or rewarding him in other ways. Unless he wants to risk serious labor disturbances an employer cannot confer upon an employee a status that would elevate him beyond his position in traditional society. Similarly, work assignments may have to be accommodated to the prejudices of the work force.

Another factor, the occupational distribution of workers, helps explain the low average levels of productivity achieved by those who are economically active. The share of those engaged in services and commerce is exceedingly large compared with those in manufacturing. Productivity in the crowded services and commercial trades is generally low. The crowding of the workers in the cities is caused most often by new entrants to the urban labor market rather than by skilled or disciplined workers temporarily out of industrial jobs. Another deterrent to efficiency is the constant demand that the governments take on more employees, especially those who would otherwise remain in the ranks of the educated unemployed.

The considerations advanced in this chapter permit us once again to observe the contrast between South Asian conditions and those typical in the West. Even in the modern segment of the South Asian economic structure much prevails that is alien to the environment of advanced economies. Indeed, the forces governing the utilization of labor in the region lie quite outside the experience of the West in modern times. Differences in institutions and in the attitudes that shape and are shaped by them are so profound that Western conceptual schemes based on a rational approach to employment and on the assumption that the institutional structure will automatically tend to produce diligent work at high and standardized norms of work duration are out of touch with the basic realities. These institutional and attitudinal contrasts, in turn, must be understood against the background of a South Asian economic environment in which labor is ill rewarded, and both leisure and waste are thereby encouraged.

At the risk of over-simplification, labor utilization in the region may be said to have as its fundamental attribute a peculiar combination of "mollification" and rigidity. On the one hand, a variety of institutional pressures have coalesced to induce spreading of the work load and, on the other, both traditional and modern factors have operated to restrict the members of the population regarded as legitimate job claimants. At the same time, many practices have been tolerated that frustrate diligent effort on the part of those who are nominally at work. The net effect of these forces has been to suppress growth in output per head.

Maurice Zinkin, writing in his *Development for Free Asia,* has pointed out: "If these societies want to be better off, they must put more emphasis on work, less on leisure. There must be less factory absenteeism caused by long leave to go home for harvest or marriages. There must be more weeding and harrowing and less sitting on a cot under a tree, less talking in coffee houses and more study, less theory and more actual field work."

Another Western observer, Woytinsky, writing in *India: the Awakening Giant,* says, in part: "the main source of India's weakness lies in the human factor: not a lack of innate abilities or technical skill in the people, but a lack of initiative, of interest in improving their economic status, of respect for labour. . . . If it were possible to transplant overnight all the factories of Michigan, Ohio, and Pennsylvania to India without changing the economic attitudes of her people, two decades later the country would be about as poor as it is now. On the other hand, if by some magic the psychology of 150 million employers, self-employed persons, and employees who constitute

India's labor force were overnight transformed after the pattern of modern industrial nations, India would be covered two decades later with modern mills, power stations, and speed highways, and her per capita income would have increased many times despite scarcity of domestic capital."

Again, it is necessary to realize that attitudes do not exist in a vacuum but are enmeshed and fortified by social institutions.

Members of one group—the "educated"—have preserved a singular position in the labor market, keeping them apart as a separate and different part of it. They have displayed a remarkable ability to sustain themselves even without gainful work, largely by relying on family assistance and support. While the educated demonstrate a high degree of geographical mobility as between urban areas, their functional mobility is negligible. They are looking for non-manual work and are not prepared to accept work that "soils their hands." It should also be remembered that even persons who have merely acquired some degree of literacy by going through primary school or who have dropped out of secondary school before graduating often consider themselves educated and exempt from any obligation to work with their hands. The number of these educated unemployed has risen steadily since independence. In India, at the beginning of the 1960's, it was estimated that there were more than a million of them.

From a rational planning point of view, these attitudes toward manual work are obviously highly detrimental to development. The attempt to build up a modern industrial structure is hampered by the lack of skilled workers who can calculate and work according to written instructions and work-sketches. It should be noted that ordinary workers in Western (and East European Communist) countries are as a rule not less, but more, educated than most of those called "educated" in South Asia. The tendency of even graduate engineers to expect desk jobs and to recoil from the prospect of physical contact with machines aggravates this obstacle to development. The waste involved in this underutilization of manpower is tragic.

But the issues involved in the status and attitudes of the educated in South Asia extend far beyond the relatively straightforward matter of economic waste. At least equally serious are the broader social consequences of the alienation of this group from the bulk of their countrymen and from the real development problems of their nations. The more successful among them are swallowed up by government bureaus and business firms; their detachment from the harsh realities of existence as they affect the mass of the population minimizes their potential contribution to the task of development. Everyone who has visited the South Asian countries can testify to the strange make-believe atmosphere that prevails in the higher echelons of the educated class. In the lower strata of the educated employed, and unemployed, there is even less sense of identification with national interests.

The problem of how to integrate the rising number of educated unemployed into the working community has occasioned much concern, particularly in India, Pakistan, Ceylon, and the Philippines. But recommendations for practical reform have usually emphasized the creation of more jobs of the type educated persons will accept—that is, non-manual jobs. The force needed to change prevailing attitudes would require an equally radical change in the whole educational system, and that system is deeply rooted in the social structure of South Asian countries. The practical reformer must concentrate his efforts on breaking down the monopoly of education held by the upper strata, by broadening and redirecting schooling.

Chapter 19

THE INDUSTRIALIZATION ISSUE

Throughout South Asia there is a clamor for industrialization. When the intellectual elite say their countries are underdeveloped, they mean that they have too little industry. Thus spokesmen for the South Asian countries frequently use the terms "pre-industrial" or "under-industrialized" as synonyms for "poor" or "underdeveloped." In this view, the growth of modern industry will provide employment for an underutilized labor force now bottled up in agriculture as well as in the traditional and the loosely organized sectors of non-agricultural pursuits. Industrialization is held to be crucial to development strategy also because it will radiate stimuli throughout the economy and lift it out of stagnation.

South Asia's intellectual leaders, like their counterparts in the West, believe the present high level of development in advanced countries is the result of changes set in motion by the industrial revolution. A further important influence on the ideology of industrialization in South Asia has been the recent rapid development of industry through government planning in the Soviet Union. In Communist ideology, industrialization embraces a theory and a program calling, in particular, for the setting up of a fairly comprehensive industrial structure based on heavy industry in every country and, indeed, every large district. This pattern is now often accepted as a natural one for any underdeveloped country to imitate. Virtually all the non-traditionalist intellectuals in the region have been decisively influenced by the Communist doctrine of planned and directed industrialization as a technique for engendering development. To them all, Soviet successes in planning convey lessons they would like to apply when charting their own course of development. There is added appeal in the Communist doctrine that true political independence from colonial dominance can only come through planned industrialization.

This interpretation of history contains enough apparent realism to win wide acceptance among South Asian intellectual leaders far outside the Communist fold, just as in much the same form it is now widely accepted by Western economists. More generally, the Communist view is also influential in breeding suspicion of Western governments and their attitude toward the order of priority of industrialization in planning.

The ideology of industrialization has also been stimulated by the concern over the relative decline in world demand for the raw materials South Asia has traditionally supplied and the gradually mounting awareness of the implications of accelerated population growth. South Asia is faced with the exceptional problem of its agriculture having very real difficulties in coming anywhere near fully utilizing its labor force, which is also continually and rapidly increasing. In modern industry larger and more rapid advances in productivity should also be possible, partly because it would be easier to circumvent attitudinal and institutional obstructions to effective utilization of labor. Moreover, in industry there are no limiting factors analogous to the availability of land in agriculture to impede the realization of increasing returns. Nor can there be any doubt, despite the poor quality and number of South Asian statistics, that labor utilization and labor productivity reach higher levels in modern South Asian manufacturing industries than elsewhere in the region's economies.

Part of the attractiveness of industrialization stems from its promise to bring modern techniques to a backward economy and to embody them in power and machines, particularly in heavy industry but also in industries producing consumption goods. For the most part, machinery used in South Asia must in the beginning be imported from the advanced countries, and once the direction of industrialization has been chosen, there is little latitude in the choice of techniques. Some scope remains, however, for varying the proportions in which capital and labor are combined. This is especially true of such operations as the handling, packaging, and shipment of raw materials and finished products. In South Asia these tasks can easily be, and for the most part are, performed by labor-intensive methods, with liberal use of workers, even when the direct processes of production are themselves capital-intensive.

For the immediate future, countries of the region have mostly only the alternatives of using technologies of the highly developed countries or rejecting modern machines altogether, except for one possibility that has hardly been touched: that of developing a trade in second-hand machinery from the advanced countries. Although there has been some discussion of such trade in Western circles, the South Asian countries have been less than enthusiastic about this prospect—partly because procedures for valuing used equipment have not been perfected, partly because of uncertainties about the continued availability of spare parts, and partly because the suggestion that they should accept "second-best" goods offends their sensibilities.

All South Asian countries face the challenge of a largely unskilled labor force and a small and inexperienced managerial force. This adds plausibility to the argument that large and highly mechanized industries are better suited to the maximum use of what skills and technical education do exist. This policy appears to be rational, provided there is also a policy to encourage the rapid increase of skills and to overcome the social restraints on their effective use. On the other hand, such a policy may not be uniformly favorable if modern technology is used to evade the social and institutional obstacles that have long inhibited economic performance and perpetuated low levels of labor utilization.

Part of the support for rapid industrialization is based on a conclusion that is obvious: in the larger and most populous countries of the region, substantial improvements in average levels of living by the end of this century—when the labor force will probably be twice its present size—are out of the question unless a considerably larger proportion of workers are engaged in productive activities outside agriculture. This is true no matter what advances are made in agricultural productivity. Even in Burma, Thailand, and Malaya, where there is more land and better opportunities for raising the levels of living, the long-range outlook demands that substantial industrial expansion must take place to improve conditions for a rapidly increasing population.

This simple conclusion in itself provides *a rational basis for the strivings of these countries to industrialize as rapidly as possible.* And although we shall be concerned with the conditions limiting an industrialization drive, with the restricted possibilities it offers for raising labor utilization in the near future, and with the very compelling need for development efforts in many other directions, this discussion should not be construed to mean that South Asian countries should forego industrial expansion. Analysis of the hazards and limitations points rather to the importance and urgency of overcoming the obstacles to successful industrialization.

In the literature on the development of South Asia and of underdeveloped countries in general, it is usually taken for granted that industrialization has a substantial impact on employment, even in the short run. The "creation of employment" is a major preoccupation of planners in all countries of the region. It must be remembered, however, that the objectives have been very modest—surprisingly so in view of the priority given to "full" and "fuller" employment in the general planning goals—and that achievements have usually fallen far short of targets.

The unorthodox view we shall expound is that *in South Asia the employment effects of industrialization cannot be expected to be very large for several decades ahead,* that is, until the region is much more industrialized. Generally speaking, the impact of industrialization on the growth of direct demand for labor in manufacturing is a function not only of the speed of industrialization but also of the position in the economy already achieved by modernized industry. Even a very rapid rate of industrial growth will not for a considerable time generate sufficient demand for labor to increase substantially the percentage working in the industrial sector. The labor force is growing too rapidly. For a considerable time the net employment effects may even be negative, if and when modern industry is out-competing traditional labor-intensive manufacturing. These dimensions of the problem are overlooked in the vision that sees industrialization as the remedy for "unemployment" and "underemployment."

The relationships involved may be seen more clearly if we consider a hypothetical example: Let us assume that one percent of the labor force is employed in modern industry at the beginning of a planning period and that no traditional manufacturing exists. Let us also assume that the population of working age is simultaneously increasing at 2 percent per year. In these circumstances, a 10 percent annual expansion of employment in modern industry—which *per se* is a very considerable increase not reached in any South Asian country—would mean that direct employment in that sector would absorb only 5 percent of the increment in the labor force. In other words, 95 percent of the entrants to the labor force would be obliged to find a livelihood in some form of economic activity outside it. Given these assumptions, the task of absorbing in modern industry the full natural increase in the population of working age would, in the first year, impose the unreasonable requirement of tripling the number employed in industry in a single year. The proportionate rate of increase required would, of course, decline over time, but for a lengthy period this decline would be very slow.

In this hypothetical example, we have ignored the likely backwash effects on existing manufacturing industry. Traditional manufacturing is affected in the backwash when new enterprises, using up-to-date techniques, turn out goods competing with goods produced in small-scale enterprises and crafts. Also semi-modern industry already established would be forced to attempt some degree of rationalization. Rationalization normally implies that less labor is used to produce a given quantity of output. Through planning, traditional and less modern manufacturing can be shielded from much of this backwash. Nevertheless, there is a real risk that for a considerable time the slight increase in opportunities for labor in new modern enterprises will be more than offset by reductions of jobs in earlier existing industry and in traditional manufacturing.

Backwash effects such as these do not occur when

newly formed manufacturing units either produce import substitutes or direct their output to export markets. But, as we have noted, export expansion by South Asian countries is extremely difficult. Import substitution, by contrast, is open to new manufacturing industry without risk of internal backwash effects, a fact that adds to its appeal. But if new or enlarged industrial enterprises are brought into direct competition with the remnants of the traditional crafts or with producers in other non-modernized units, the over-all effects of industrialization on job opportunities may for a considerable time be negative.

The problem of backwash effects on labor demand raises several other important issues. It provides a strong supplementary argument for restricting both new industry and the modernization of existing enterprises to sectors that produce export goods or import substitutes. Heavy industry is a particularly safe bet, as these countries began their independence with no modern capital goods industry worthy of the name. But even a country like India, which for compelling reasons has stressed heavy industry, cannot possibly channel all its modernization efforts to export-oriented or import-substituting manufacturing.

In this situation, planners and governments face a serious dilemma. Their long-term goal is to use industrial expansion as a device for modernizing the entire economy. But their short-term interest in preventing serious deterioration in traditional manufacturing, and particularly in crafts, conflicts with this long-range objective. India has attempted to resolve this dilemma not only by concentrating as much new investment as possible in import-substituting large-scale industry but also by protecting traditional crafts and by imposing restrictions on rationalization in certain lines of large-scale manufacturing that compete with traditional handicraft production. Measures of the latter type are particularly welcomed by workers, and concern for their interests has led the government to seek "rationalization without tears"—that is, without depriving anyone of a job, though the size of the work force may shrink when vacancies created by normal attrition are not filled.

But new enterprises are not subject to such restraints. And their awareness of the government's interest in protecting employment and of the risk of friction with workers should they later attempt to reduce the work forces gives entrepreneurs an added inducement to adopt capital-intensive, labor-saving techniques from the start. This creates a gap between techniques used in new and old establishments. The gap is widened when, at the same time, investment in older establishments is suppressed by governmental policy.

The planners in most of South Asia have not entirely overlooked the possibility of modern industrialization having only a small direct effect on employment in its early stages while the backwash effects may be considerable. Yet this has had little impact on the general acclaim of industrialization as the means by which the underutilized labor force in agriculture and elsewhere can be absorbed. But the conclusion stands that, in the absence of spread effects, industrialization can produce only a very small immediate expansion in demand for labor when it is not decreasing net employment. This situation, of course, is an inescapable consequence of the low base from which modern industrial expansion begins and the backwash effects that are certain to occur unless the output of modern industry is directed exclusively to newly created markets, either in foreign countries or in home territory.

When a start must be made from such modest beginnings, as it must in all South Asian countries, even a big push toward industrial expansion cannot for decades ahead be expected to provide employment opportunities directly for more than a very small fraction of the increase of the labor force, and even that gain may be partly, wholly, or more than wholly offset by backwash effects. This point needs to be strongly emphasized in order to dispel the quite unrealistic expectation still widely entertained that a rapid transformation of the occupational structure will come about once an industrialization program is launched.

If planners in South Asia have tended to overestimate the employment effect of new industries and to underestimate the likelihood and the impact of backwash effect, they have also tended to exaggerate the force of expansionary stimuli radiating from industrial starts—the "spread" effects hoped for from industrialization. This tendency has given rise to excessive optimism and has distracted attention from the rigidities and inhibitions likely to swamp potential spread effects. This bias is not very difficult to understand. Post-war theories, as adopted in South Asia, have encouraged unrealistic expectations about the indirect effects of industrial starts.

We have started from the propositions that no substantial development in South Asia, especially in India, Pakistan, and other high man/land–ratio countries—is possible *over the long run* unless these countries can employ a much larger part of their labor force in modern industry or other productive non-agricultural occupations. But there is a widespread view that such a change is possible without great delay and that, in particular, *even in the shorter run,* the launching of an industrial buildup will radiate powerful expansionary forces penetrating throughout the economic system. Very little analysis, even on the abstract and theoretical level, has been devoted to clarifying the mechanism through which the momentum expected from industrial starts is transmitted.

The crude vision of the quick side effects of industrialization has been based too often on a loose analogy with the early experiences of Western economies. There the industrial revolution began with a number of small and, occasionally, some large industries. The success of these bred conditions that made further new starts possible and they, in turn, spurred still others. The cumulative development touched all aspects of economic and social life. But on closer inspection, this image of Western economic history appears over-simplified and idealized. In retrospect it is easy to overlook the uncertainties, setbacks, and delays that attended success. But even so, conditions prevailing in the West a century and a half ago were more favorable to strong and effective side effects than are the conditions prevailing in South Asia today.

If industrial expansion could be brought about as the planners hope, one type of spread effect to appear would be "logistical." New plants must be constructed, and there must be extensions, in most areas, of the power, transport, and communications facilities. Demand for raw materials and other essential inputs would be increased. Not all of these new demands could come from domestic resources, of course. But some stimuli would certainly be felt locally. At the same time, the process of industrialization would create added potential for expansion in other sectors of the economy. On the supply side, industrialization would also have spread effects through the reduction of costs that occurs as growth gains momentum. Through all these changes new incomes would be generated. Unless restrictions on imports could be effectively imposed, part of the increase in consumption demand would at first probably be met by imports. If imports were curbed, heavier demands would be imposed on local producers of consumer goods.

There is nothing mystical about this transmision of spread effects through new demands. Reduced to its essentials, it is a cumulative process of expansion triggered by new domestic and production investment. The process of economic uplift, once initiated, thus should tend to become self-perpetuating. If sustained industrial expansion is planned for—indeed merely expected with some confidence—additional investment may be induced.

The general structure of South Asian economies suggests, however, that the inhibitions and obstacles to the effective spread of growth-inducing impulses through increased demand are formidable. The economies of the underdeveloped countries in South Asia are low-elasticity ones and there are bottlenecks everywhere. Even if all the economic stimuli resulting from industrial starts could be retained within the domestic economy—which, realistically, is not completely and sometimes not even largely possible—the spread effects would still be likely to be weak. Through intelligent planning, though, the bottlenecks and other impediments can eventually be solved.

There is a need, in all segments of the economy, for specific policies to foster spread effects that appear when there are increases in demand. Nascent manufacturing enterprises face the risk of early death for lack of sufficient market. Supply does not create its own demand, while demand does not call forth its own supply. But certainly the existence of a robust demand and new supplies would encourage efforts to overcome deficiencies. To become effective, all policy measures take time to become implemented. Meanwhile, however, the propulsive force toward expansion may have been spent.

Further, in South Asia it cannot be assumed—as it can be with reasonable assurance in Western countries—that economic stimuli for expansion will be automatically accompanied by favorable behavioral responses. The broader social situation is an even more basic obstacle to spread because of rising demands and supplies. Societies that have for long accommodated themselves to stagnation cannot be expected to readapt dramatically to unfamiliar opportunities. Even in the more highly organized modern industrial sector of the economy, where market sensitivity is greater, the response mechanism may be inhibited by an institutional structure that has failed to encourage dynamic entrepreneurial zeal.

This is the fundamental reason why the Keynesian model does not apply to these economies. Thinking in terms of relationships between aggregate supply and aggregate demand is less relevant. In particular, when bottlenecks have caused inflated prices soon after the first injections of additional incomes, South Asian governments —and particularly the Indian government—have used direct and indirect controls to block the initiation of some enterprises. They have thus checked forms of secondary expansion that might otherwise have taken place. This amounts to an unintentional killing off of spread effects. Underlying these measures of restraint is, however, the necessity of a "ceiling" that limits the volume of aggregate demand the economy is thought capable of tolerating.

The bottlenecks that make the economies low-elasticity ones take many forms. When new industries are created there are often strains on transport systems and there are shortages of skilled personnel. On the other hand, the capacity of the new industries can often not be fully utilized. Effective planning can reduce many of these impediments. But planning of a purely aggregative type cannot be expected to accomplish the desired results. Policy intervention must be directed to specific bottlenecks in individual sectors of the economy.

One of the difficulties faced by planners in trying to calculate the possible spread effects of industrialization in other sectors of the economy is the fact that an increase in economic activity would not necessarily be followed by an increase in job opportunities. In the service trades, for example, the problem is especially intricate. Such secondary effects on the demand for labor as might occur could easily be met by extending the work periods and efficiency of those already engaged. If the number of workers in the service trades increases, this is more likely to be the result of pressures from workless or underutilized labor, particularly migrants from the rural areas, than of impulses stemming from industrialization.

A major flaw in many planning calculations is, indeed, the implicit assumption that the influx of population to urban areas is a response to an increased demand for labor, which in turn is assumed to emanate from industrialization. The urban labor force is certainly swelling everywhere in the region, but this would in all probability happen without any industrialization at all. In fact, it would be possible to sustain a degree of industrialization far greater than any now occurring in South Asia simply by using the present urban labor force more fully and efficiently; no new workers from rural areas would be needed. Urbanization in all probability will continue, but this urbanization will not be to any large extent the result of industrialization.

Apart from these effects of industrialization through rises in demand and supplies, there are other spread effects that could be important. Industrialization is expected to instill a new spirit of rationalism, enterprise, discipline, punctuality, mobility, and efficiency.

People will be stirred to become mechanically minded and to master unfamiliar skills, not merely within the new industrial enterprises but elsewhere in the economy as well. More competitive and more perfect markets will be called forth and superior commercial and financial institutions developed. All in all, the organization of work and people's attitudes toward it will be altered in ways that raise the efficiency of work performance throughout the economy. Bottlenecks will be more easily eliminated and the potential for diffusion of spread effects of the logistic type will be extended. The stimuli radiating from new industrial starts will induce agriculture and traditional manufacturing sectors to tighten their slacks. All these happy results are expected to follow as a direct consequence of industrial expansion. Similar qualitative changes in the outlook, attitudes, and skills of the population are believed not to be obtainable from other forms of initial economic expansion, say from the development of agriculture.

Whether external economics such as these will quickly appear and spread through South Asia is uncertain. To begin with, the effects within the new industries themselves should not be exaggerated. Deeply ingrained rituals leave their stamp on work arrangements. For instance, the many traditional holidays will continue to be honored and the daily work schedule may be interrupted in deference to religious observances. As the majority of even the new factories cannot be air-conditioned, climatic disadvantages will cause interruptions and lower intensity of work.

The spread effects outside the new industries are still more uncertain and doubtful. The institutional structure and the prevailing attitudes inhibit changes conducive to substantial effects of this type. *The extent to which spread effects along these lines can be transmitted is, in fact, a function of the cultural, social, and economic levels already attained.* Poor countries with a long history of economic stagnation and fairly static social conditions thus face formidable obstacles when they attempt to achieve a higher level of development. Potential spread effects of all types are easily smothered.

This lesson has been forcefully demonstrated in the limited experience of South Asian countries with rationalized and highly organized modern industries. The small islands within which Western forms of economic organization have been imitated have not made much lasting impression on the sea of traditional stagnation surrounding them. In colonial times, the few modern industries developed in South Asia were not notable for transmitting stimuli to other segments of the economy. They remained enclaves. *There is an obvious danger that industrial starts now planned will perpetuate this colonial pattern.* Every open-eyed visitor to South Asia must notice that primitive modes of living and traditional patterns of work prevail within a few miles of cities where there are modern industrial establishments, as well as in the huge slums in those cities themselves.

Nor indeed have modern industries always succeeded in producing permanent changes in attitudes toward work or in the standards of skills of laborers they have directly engaged. Typically, little provision has been made for training, and the bulk of the labor force has remained with few skills. Moreover, among those who have returned to their native villages after a period in wage employment, the effects of contact with more intricately organized forms of economic activity and more regular work discipline have regularly been short-lived.

When thought through, the industrialization ideology fails to lend convincing support to the belief that institutional and attitudinal changes of types healthy for economic advancement will be produced *because* of industrialization starts. The appropriate inference is rather that specific policies in all fields—even far outside the industrial sector proper or even in regard to what is called the economic factors—must be pursued if spread effects are to be both forceful and sustained.

From the foregoing, several broad conclusions that stretch beyond the industrial sector and concern the economy as a whole can be reached.

Given the rapid and accelerating increase in the labor force in these countries, there is no prospect that incomes and levels of living can be substantially improved, or even that deterioration in standards thus far achieved can be prevented in the longer run unless a much larger proportion of the labor force can be effectively utilized outside agriculture and especially in modern industry. But modern industry, even if it grows at a rapid rate, cannot absorb more than a small fraction of the natural increment in the labor force for decades ahead. In the initial stages of industrialization, it may even be difficult to keep the absolute size of the labor force engaged in all types of manufacturing from falling. Only at a later stage can modern industry begin to increase its claim on the labor force.

But the South Asian countries should not give up their industrialization drive. On the contrary, the fact that industrialization will have an important effect only gradually, when it has reached a much higher level, means that these countries should industrialize as soon and as fast as they can. However, it also means that they should complement the industrialization drive with vigorous policy measures aimed at raising labor utilization and productivity in the other sectors including agriculture, which is the largest and most important of all.

Little confidence can be placed in the efficacy of favorable spread effects automatically emanating from industrial starts. Generally speaking, the extent to which stimuli for change and improvement can be assimilated is a function of mass education and the ability to change attitudes and institutions in which they are rooted. South Asian countries, now as in colonial times, run the risk of creating petty islands of more highly organized Western-type industries that will remain surrounded by a sea of stagnation.

Focussing the industrialization drive upon exports and import substitution is, of course, rational because it minimizes the backwash effects of modern industrial growth on established traditional manufacturing. But clearly, industrialization in this form is not enough to accomplish a significant change in the economic structure of these countries and to give real momentum to development. Indeed, if not accompanied by direct interventionist policies toward other sectors of the economy, it would merely bolster the enclave pattern of colonial economic experience.

By itself, industrialization can do little to raise labor utilization in the more tradition-bound sectors of the economy, especially in rural areas. These problems must be attacked in their own right by specific policies designed to promote reform. Success with these reforms requires, in turn, a major push in the direction of health and educational improvement. Such measures are necessary not only to compensate the rest of the economy for the absence of sizable automatic spread effects from industrial starts, but also to support the industrialization drive itself. The causal circle must be completed and joined. In particular, the modern industrial sector cannot thrive unless increasing quantities of consumption goods—particularly foodstuffs—can be produced and made available for sale.

The magnitude and pervasiveness of these problems naturally raises questions of priorities. Too often this is discussed solely in terms of the competition of different sectors of the economy for the same resources. It is misleading to regard such aggregates as savings and investment as significant and unambiguously quantifiable. This thinking is reflected in those plans that add investments in industrial plants and expenditures for agriculture, education, health, and community development together and juxtapose them as "investments" and "development expenditures" against available financial resources. This conveys the false picture that internal savings and funds supplied from abroad are substitutable for one another. Reductions in consumption at home, for example, cannot create foreign exchange—particularly in countries like India and Pakistan, where few consumption goods are now imported, other than those essential to survival.

The post-war approach also lends itself to another misconception. Many policy measures—especially those pertaining to rural areas—require the implementation of institutional reforms and enthusiastic efforts in health and education, but need only limited amounts of funds, which can often be mobilized within the rural areas themselves without imposing any burden on the modern industrial sector. In essence, it is clear that considerable unexploited scope remains for pushing industrial drives without jeopardizing development in other sectors of the economy. One of the most serious shortcomings of policy in those countries where comprehensive planning has been undertaken is the failure to plan more ambitiously and on a larger scale, and to supplement the industrialization drive with equally determined efforts in other fields.

Undoubtedly, the industrialization drive, which meets very little resistance from vested interests, has often served as an excuse for not pushing harder for reforms in other fields. What these countries need is a program that will induce changes simultaneously in a great number of the conditions that hold down their growth. Fundamentally, the task of planners is to coordinate all these changes in such a way as to spur development. It is easy to lose sight of this when goals and targets are assigned priorities.

Chapter 20

THE CASE FOR CRAFTS AND SMALL-SCALE INDUSTRY

Industrialization as an imperative of economic policy has not gone unchallenged. The rival traditionalist ideology does not demand an industrial revolution; rather it seeks to preserve and strengthen forms of traditional economic organization. Both ideologies, however, protest against the results of colonial economic experience. Those who support the industrialization ideology complain principally that modern industrial growth was hampered by the colonial powers' policies—or lack of policies. The traditionalists, on the other hand, are obsessed with the deterioration of the ancient crafts caused, in their view, by imports of manufactured goods, and partly also, at a later stage, by the local production of machine-made products.

Contrary to the champions of modern industrialization, they urge that the development of village crafts should be the primary means for achieving economic and social betterment and national self-sufficiency.

This traditionalist ideology exists in a number of variants and does not lend itself to succinct summation. But traditionalists of all shades share several convictions. They believe that village crafts should be encouraged, that measures should be taken to promote self-sufficiency at both the village and the national level, and that modern industrial products—particularly imported consumer goods—should be viewed with suspicion.

This type of traditionalist ideology has been highly articulated in India. Here the craftsmen suffered a harsher fate during the colonial era than did their counterparts elsewhere in South Asia. The losses sustained by the village economy were offset to a much lesser extent in India than elsewhere, and the rigid caste structure lacked the adaptability needed for a successful adjustment to changes. Village revival through village crafts was used successfully as a propaganda weapon in the liberation movement, and this was an important element in shaping the traditionalist ideology. As part of the nationalist struggle, Indians were urged to reject not only Western products but Western styles. *Swadeshi* (the Hindu term for preference for the products of one's own country) was elevated to a moral principle.

Going beyond rejection of European products and modes of economic behavior, this ideology has had positive implications for a future pattern of Indian economic life. This is the lasting legacy of Mohandas Gandhi, whose ideas still form a powerful force among traditionalists in today's India. There was in this thinking a certain animosity against machines. Modern industrialization was also seen by Gandhi as an enemy of village crafts. Urbanization he considered an evil that sucked the lifeblood of the villages.

Another important strand of thought woven into the traditionalist ideology is the concept of the moral superiority of self-employment over working for wages. In South Asia, and most particularly in India, the view that self-employment has special virtues is reinforced by the rigidity of a social structure within which a wage laborer is treated with contempt. This particular variant of the traditional ideology cannot without reservation be considered a true legacy from Gandhi, who stood up against the caste system and stressed the dignity of all labor.

Like the ideology of planning in post-independence days, *Swadeshi* implied a refusal to accept prevailing economic conditions passively. With the aid of such emotional preparation, independent India's efforts in planning have encountered little opposition of a *laissez-faire* liberalist variety. Ironically, *Swadeshi* thus came to lend ideological support to national economic planning and undoubtedly contributed to an autarkic approach to that planning.

In other South Asian countries some of the same themes recur, but the traditionalist ideology has been weaker here than in India. The supporting framework is not Gandhian. Nevertheless, an ideology favoring the strengthening of the traditional crafts did emerge, particularly during the struggle for independence. As in India, the return to traditional dress played a part in the tactics of the nationalist movements. Moreover, the revitalization of traditional handicrafts—particularly in the production of clothing—was given impetus by the exigencies of the Japanese occupation during World War II. Both the cutting of imports and the demands of the occupation forces stimulated the output of certain indigenous manufacturing enterprises.

Once independence was gained, the proponents of traditionalism had to shift to the more sobering restraints of national planning, into which the cottage and small-scale industries must be fitted. Those governments committed to modernization had, on their side, to make some compromises to accommodate the traditionalists. But it is frequently overlooked that protection and advancement of craft enterprises do not always conflict with the aims of rational planning putting the emphasis on industrialization.

We have stressed that even if it is entirely rational to build up as quickly as possible a modern industry, it would not for a long time create much new employment, and it might for some time imply a net decrease of the workers given employment in manufacturing industry in its broader sense. Meanwhile, the population is increasing at a rapid rate. Under these conditions the economy is likely to remain stagnant unless steps are taken to increase labor utilization and productivity both in agriculture and in that very large portion of manufacturing which consists of cottage enterprises in the villages.

The demand for village craft products depends largely on the level of incomes in agriculture. But even assuming that agricultural policy is much more successful than it has been to date in any South Asian country, a necessary element of economic policy must be to protect and if possible advance the position of village artisans. Since industrial expansion in exports and import substitution does not have backwash effects on the types of manufacturing the traditionalists want to protect, there is a fundamental compatibility between the goals of industrialization along those lines and of protection for cottage industry.

There are two ways in which cottage industry can be sheltered from modern industrial competition. First, the planners can channel development of new industries in such a way as to limit this competition and at the same time subsidize cottage industry to hold its costs down. Second, the government can help increase village craftsmen's protection by providing new equipment and organizing them into marketing cooperatives. These policies can be defended on the ground that they ease the adjustment of distressed and economically defenseless groups to a new situation.

Such policies meet great difficulties. As for the cottage industry workers themselves, there is no prospect of any large-scale adjustment for them for decades to come, particularly as the labor force will increase rapidly until the end of the century. And as industrialization progresses, it will become more difficult to hold off the products of modern industry that can be produced cheaper and more attractively. This is compounded by the fact that as incomes rise, there will be a greater demand for these products instead of for those of cottage industries. Nevertheless, as a holding operation the encouragement of the industrialization drive in directions that imply less competition within the crafts, and even subsidizing crafts, can be reliably motivated as part of planning.

In the South Asian policy discussion this straight argument in favor of protecting and subsidizing crafts has become complicated and even confused by introducing the idea that "small-scale" industry should also be favored. Usually, the thought was that it should be located in rural areas. Many traditionalists have been brought to support this view, and actually to extend their pleading to embrace "village crafts and small-scale industry."

This doctrine is, of course, a far cry from original Gandhism, though its proponents dispute this. Small industrial plants are understood to employ hired workers and to produce modern lines of output by modern machine techniques. There have been no consistent definitions of exactly what small-scale industry is, but it is clearly a question of enterprises bigger than the household enterprises, and sometimes much bigger.

When, nevertheless, many of the traditionalists have come to regard small-scale industry as an acceptable middle step between cottage crafts and large-scale industry, the ideological thread connecting it with cottage craft is the notion that industry should be "decentralized," or, more specifically, that plants should be dispersed in the rural areas. However, in all the South Asian countries not only has small-scale industry sought out the cities and indeed, the big cities, but often government support schemes have favored this. Without a well-developed power and transportation system, it is difficult to foster industries in rural areas, and it would be foolhardy, at this time, to alter the natural tendency to locate them in the cities. But this should not preclude future policies that would push them out into the smaller towns and even into the villages. Although such policy goals have often been stressed and even overstressed, no South Asian country has made noticeable progress in attaining them.

It has been argued in all the South Asian countries since the very beginning that small-scale enterprises deserve support because they need a lesser capital investment than big industry. But there are valid challenges to this contention. Studies have shown that in some but not all instances, even when the smaller plants are modern and mechanized, the capital/output ratio is lower than in large units. It can also be said that "capital" applied to small-scale industries is actually in the form of machinery and equipment that more often can be produced at home without drawing on foreign exchange. Similarly, a larger part of the capital employed in small-scale industry may be working capital, "waiting" only while stocks of materials and products are accumulated or until payment for the latter is made. But even taking such reservations into account, the capital-saving argument does not seem to carry much weight as a general reason for supporting small-scale industry.

There are other, more compelling reasons for aiding small industry. The spread effects from smaller industries should be greater than those from large-scale manufacturing. The experience gained from working with machines in smaller industries and from managing them would be wider among the labor force. And quite aside from the problem of attaining a regional balance in their industrialization, the South Asian countries face the problem of achieving balance between large and small production units.

It would be very unfortunate to have an economy consisting of a few big enterprises and a vast multitude of farms and craft enterprises. Under the level of big industry there should rationally be a layer of smaller industrial enterprises. The larger and smaller factories could complement each other in two ways. First, the big units could subcontract to smaller units the production of parts and service work. Second, the smaller enterprises could look to the larger for much of the materials they process into finished goods.

Small-scale industries can be protected from overpowering competition from large-scale manufacturing, just as cottage industries can be. Import and investment restrictions can be used to provide considerable market shelter. Measures to modernize and improve productivity in small industries can be used in the same way as in cottage industries. The advance of small-scale firms on a broad front presupposes a widening of markets, but—particularly if the field of export production is closed—this will occur only if there is a general rise in production and income in the country.

In assessing the progress made by South Asian countries in promoting expansion of small-scale and cottage industries, we must bear in mind the severe handicaps under which those who seek to improve matters must operate. Ultimately, all of these handicaps are the result of underdevelopment and the lack of a vigorous thrust forward. In this respect, India provides a good illustration.

The policy of sheltering cottage industries in itself can be little more than a defensive measure. To bring about a substantial improvement in the village craftsmen's economic position it is necessary to increase the quantity he produces and sells. The market's ability to absorb more of his products depends, however, on whether general production advances and incomes in agriculture rise. Village artisans must also upgrade their products if they are to capture more of the urban market. For this reason, policy efforts have been made to help workers improve the quality as well as the quantity of their output. But it can be fairly expected that cottage industries will come to face stiffer competition, no matter how much they are protected. At the same time, with more money to spend, the people often shift from traditional craft products to the newer, and often cheaper, products made by large-scale industry. Further, positive measures taken to increase productivity in cottage industry can, in the short run, threaten technological unemployment by putting the less efficient enterprises out of business.

In India, production in the spinning and weaving crafts increased very substantially during the first three planning periods, and in view of the problems discussed, this advance must be considered impressive. But most other village crafts fared less well. The costs of promoting cottage industry have been heavy and seem to have risen with time. Indian officials estimated that at the end of fifteen years of planning, cottage industry had failed to increase substantially the number of people employed in it and had not added noticeably to the wealth of rural communities. It should then be remembered, however, that in this period there was a marked population increase, while agriculture was relatively stagnant. Taking these factors into account, it appears that the government's policy nevertheless has been of very considerable value. Without it the problem of underutilization of labor would have become even more acute and the craftsmen's levels of living would have been depressed even further. Simply holding the line in traditional manufacturing in rural India, even if only for a time, is an achievement of no small importance.

All South Asian countries have tried to shelter and protect their small-scale industries. But in their planning, most South Asian economists have considered these production gains mainly in terms of their effect on employment. In this they have restricted their analysis to participation and largely ignored the other two components of labor utilization—how long and how well work is done.

We do not know how work duration and efficiency had been influenced by policies on cottage and small-scale industries. However, from what we know about the interrelationship between participation, duration, and efficiency in labor, we would assume that anything that increased the opportunities to work would also tend to raise the amount and effectiveness of this work. On this basis, enrolling village craftsmen in cooperatives where they will be subject to community discipline, training them by extension services and other means, and equipping them with tools and machines should lead to increases in the time they work and their efficiency.

But we know that in many instances things have not worked out this way. In the first place, the depressed levels of living of most village workers and craftsmen and their age-old habit of passive adaptation to conditions of low labor utilization are themselves formidable obstacles to improvement. These cannot be altered quickly, especially with a rapidly-growing labor force. In addition, many craftsmen, like the farmers, are in some form of bondage to middlemen or moneylenders. These intermediaries have an obvious stake in perpetuating the *status quo* and thwarting reforms. Their destructive power can be broken by vigorous policy measures, but it would be folly for reformers to underrate the force of this opposition.

The case for protecting and promoting the craft industries in the villages of South Asia is a strong one, particularly in the poorer countries. In the villages there is no alternative employment for most of the craftsmen, and the only possible way to improve their lot and, indeed, prevent a further deterioration in their living levels is to give them as much market protection as possible, and at the same time improve their productivity. This will minimize the costs to the nation of providing them with sheltered markets, but it will also increase their need for such markets. There is little hope for the establishment of large-scale industry in rural areas. Even so, the case for encouraging small-scale industries to locate in the cities as well is strong. The small-scale industries, because of their size and the stronger spread effects we anticipate from them, can prevent the industrial growth in South Asia from being confined to a few enclaves of modern large-scale enterprises as it was in colonial times.

The preservation and promotion of cottage industry and a similar policy toward agriculture implies that the underdeveloped countries of South Asia for a long time to come will have two distinct economic sectors: a small, but gradually growing, fully modernized sector of large-scale and small-scale manufacturing enterprises and a vastly larger sector that will use labor-intensive techniques not too different from the traditional ones and continue to give work to the larger part of the rapidly increasing labor force. Since modernized industry will economize on labor and the labor force will continue to grow rapidly until the end of the century, this pattern will have to be accepted, not as a transitional one but as one that will prevail for many decades.

Under these circumstances it is imperative to induce urban small-scale enterprises to modernize as fast as possible. The primary function of the most progressive small-scale enterprises should be, not to create a maximum amount of employment, but to expand their operations and thus speed up industrialization.

To accept the idea that agriculture and the crafts—and often small-scale enterprises as well—must remain technologically backward, and to confine planning efforts to building up enclaves of modern large-scale industry, is to invite failure on a grand scale. There was an essential element of rationality in Gandhi's social and economic gospel, and the programs for promoting cottage industry as they have evolved in the post-war era have come more and more to represent purposeful and realistic planning for development under the very difficult conditions that prevail.

Chapter 21

THE POPULATION
PROBLEM

We have often pointed to the definitional difficulties of applying concepts from developed countries to the social reality in South Asia. In regard to population there should not be such difficulties. We should be able to deal with the factors of population in a relatively simple and straightforward manner. Size of population, its age and sex distribution, the number of births and deaths, are biological facts definable in a way that is both logically tenable and adequate to South Asian reality. These observations relate to formal demography, in particular the quantitative relationships among fertility, mortality, and age structure. When, however, we proceed beyond simple demographic analysis and inquire into causes and effects, we immediately run into complex social and economic conditions of a non-biological nature. We must then, even in the study of population changes, resist the temptation to simplify by applying concepts and approaches formulated in the developed countries.

But what obscures the operation of the mechanism of

population change in South Asia is the paucity and unreliability of vital statistics. Demographers have been trying to overcome this handicap, both by improving the data and by developing techniques for using poor data to achieve the maximum results possible. Nevertheless, the inadequacy of population statistics remains a major obstacle. Reliable figures on total population size in Burma and South Vietnam, for example, are not available, and in every country the registration of births and deaths is incomplete. In general, the data become less reliable as the degree of refinement progresses from a simple count of total population to a count of the number of males and females in particular age groups and occupations. But even the figures for total population vary in their range of error, depending on the country and the date of the most recent census.

Only a little more than ten years ago the question of whether, and in what sense, the countries of South Asia were faced with a problem of excessive population growth was still the subject of controversy. But today it is commonly recognized that all countries in the region have entered a critical phase of sharply accelerated population growth, and that the prospects for successful economic development are crucially related to population trends. Recent years have been witnessing a veritable demographic revolution, the pace and dimensions of which are without precedent.

This revolution was not foreseen by the experts. Until recently, they simply extrapolated from earlier trends. As a result, their calculations have proved to be consistently below what was actually happening. In sum, recent census data and other information indicate that dramatically large upward revisions in expected growth rates were necessary and that the rate of increase has been and is rising. The mechanism of this demographic trend is simple. Mortality rates have declined sharply, while fertility rates have remained at the very high levels that seem to have prevailed as far back as any reliable estimates exist, or have lately even reached higher. The rates of natural population increase—and of reproduction—have therefore gone up suddenly and rapidly, reflecting to the full the decline in mortality.

It is apparent that the high rates of fertility and the decline in mortality are occurring independent of any changes in the levels of living, of which there has been none for the masses of the people. If no forceful policy measures are taken to bring down fertility, South Asia will continue to experience a very high and even rising rate of population increase. As that occurs, we meet the demographers' dictum that, in the long run, deaths and births must again approach balance: if fertility cannot be adjusted downward to the new levels of mortality, then mortality must rise again at some future time. Applied to South Asia, the assumption must be, first, that under the conditions of life and work we have described in preceding chapters, the present population trend, if not reversed, is bound to thwart development efforts. This would lead in the end to a progressive deterioration of incomes and levels of living. This will happen sooner in the larger, more populous and poorer parts of the region, which weigh heaviest in the over-all analysis. Once incomes and living levels have begun to fall, mortality will at some point lose its autonomous character and be directly affected by this.

In regard to the anticipated increase in the size of labor force in relation to natural resources and land resources, the emerging population crises are more specifically an Asian phenomenon so far as poor countries are concerned. Outside South Asia, only China, North Africa (including Egypt), and the Caribbean part of Latin America are faced with a similar situation. Even parts of South Asia— such as the small Laos and Cambodia and individual areas in all countries—continue to be "underpopulated" rather than "overpopulated" in the abstract sense that there are plenty of untapped natural resources that could be used to absorb increases.

But even in these cases development must then occur, and this hinges on domestic institutional reforms, especially in land ownership and tenancy, improved education and training, and, prior to these, a political climate favorable to reform. It also requires, on the part of the rich countries, financial and trade policies that will aid the developing countries. If these conditions are not created by policies at home and abroad, people can continue to be crowded, and an area or a country can remain "overpopulated" even if there are abundant natural resources nearby.

The colonial era had established the foundation for South Asia's great growth in people. As we have discussed in other parts of this book, the colonial powers did little, for many generations, to improve the levels of living in their possessions. But toward the end of their reigns, some progress was made in providing health facilities. Also, the presence of the colonial powers in South Asia, as in Africa, greatly reduced the rate of death from wars among the indigenous people. The effects of all this was obviously cumulative. From 1800 to 1850 the rate of population growth in South Asia was 9 per thousand, compounded annually. By the beginning of the twentieth century, it had risen to 10 per thousand. By the beginning of the 1960's, it had skyrocketed to more than 20 per thousand.

Population forecasts are notorious for their subsequent repudiation by events, and the discrepancy between forecast and fact has often been extreme. At the International Population Conference in Paris in 1937, for example, a forecast was presented of the population of Java, one of the world's most crowded islands, through the end of this century. Already by 1955 the actual population of Java was estimated to be five million in excess of the figure forecast for the year 2000. Even comparatively recent forecasts failed to foresee the true proportions of the population growth that started in South Asia after the Second World War. Thus most of the public development plans have until fairly recently underestimated, often grossly, the rate of population growth.

With this warning, we venture the following conclusions about the prospects for fertility and mortality in the South Asian countries during the next couple of decades, assuming there is no deliberate government effort to spread birth control and no change in present population policies or their effectiveness:

(1) Mortality will continue to decline, though at varying rates in the several countries. Thus by 1975–80 life expectancy at birth may be expected to be: (a) around 65 years or slightly higher in Malaya and Ceylon; (b) around 60 years in Thailand and the Philippines; (c) 50 to 52 years in India, Indonesia, South Vietnam, Burma, and Pakistan.

(2) Fertility will remain constant throughout this period or rise slightly, in all countries of the region.

(3) International migration will not have any significant influence on population trends anywhere in South Asia.

It is a fact that the populations of South Asia are at present growing very fast—faster than the growth rate in Europe at any time during its recorded demographic history—and that among several of them the rate of increase is showing signs of accelerating still further. The most important feature of this momentous growth process is that within the next decades, government action, no matter how vigorous, determined, and concerted, could do very little, if anything, to hold in check the powerful social forces propelling it. Even if fertility were to decline substantially during the next decades—which our analysis indicates could not happen spontaneously—this would not change the trend in population size very much within the span of even three decades after the decline began.

The present age distribution in these countries with their relatively large numbers of young people—itself due to the high and rising fertility rates in recent decades— implies a high growth potential that will be operative for a generation. The number of people of procreative age could only begin to decline one generation after fertility itself began to decline.

The important point to note is that for a couple of decades the inertia of population growth guarantees the continuance of a high rate of increase in total population, even on rather extreme assumptions regarding the decline in fertility brought about by population policy. The effect on the growth of the labor force is delayed even more. The implication for population policy is obvious and important. The high inertia of population growth makes it all the more urgent to put the brake on as rapidly as possible, through an active policy of population control. But this urgency will be apparent only if those responsible for policy are prepared to take an unusually long view of the national interest. In a shorter perspective— even one of fifteen to thirty years—the change that can be brought about even by a very successful population policy must appear to be quite limited.

Emigration and immigration will not significantly influence the future size of population in any of the South Asian countries. After the First World War, most developed countries in the world established national policies restricting immigration from abroad. There is no sign that in developed countries such restrictions, particularly against the entry of poor, unskilled, and often illiterate non-white peoples, will be relaxed in the foreseeable future. We must assume that there will be no emigration to speak of from any South Asian country. Even if some of these barriers were lowered, the leaders of South Asia are unsympathetic toward emigration. Again, even if they weren't, the people in many parts of South Asia are not eager to uproot themselves and face the stringencies of a new life in a foreign country. But if the South Asian population problem cannot be alleviated through emigration from the region, neither can it be eased by migratory movements within the region. There are today no prospects of a revival of the movements from India (and from China) into Ceylon and Malaya that continued until the Second World War.

Demographically, we have come to the end of an era. Peaceful migration of poor people will play an ever smaller role in adjusting economic conditions. The borders of the rich countries began to close with the First World War; the poor countries themselves followed; and the newly independent underdeveloped nations in South Asia have aligned their policies with this world-wide trend.

It is clear that the rate of population growth in the South Asian countries is now largely independent of their rate of economic development. Development could affect the speed and extent of decline in mortality rates, since it determines the level of living and may influence the amount of public expenditure devoted to improving health conditions. But fertility, if left to spontaneous forces, will remain at traditionally high levels, or may even increase slightly, whether or not there is economic development. Generally speaking, the rapid and accelerating population increase in South Asia is retarding economic advance and holds the threat of economic stagnation if not deterioration—sooner or later, depending on the conditions in each country. As emigration is not a feasible policy, and as no government can but choose to decrease mortality, the practical problem facing the governments in the region is whether they should attempt to induce a fall in the fertility rate that will not come spontaneously.

Basic to our analysis of the economic consequences of population trends is the fact, demonstrated by Coale and Hoover, that a decline in fertility rates would have no substantial influence on the size of the labor force in underdeveloped countries, for as long as twenty or even thirty years. For fifteen years ahead this is self-evident; but even for some fifteen years beyond that calculations indicate the effect to be gradual and slow. Thus the impact of a decline in fertility on the number of producers is delayed for almost a generation. Its impact on the number of consumers, however, is immediate. The relative number *outside* the labor force begins to fall as soon as the fertility rate declines.

The positive effects of a decline in the rate at which children are born in South Asia are not hard to discern. The decrease in the proportion of children in the total population would be progressive—the fewer young people who reach child-bearing age, the comparably fewer children will be born. Still further ahead, if fertility should be stabilized at a lower level than now, the age distribution would tend to become "normal" instead of having an abnormally high proportion of younger people and children.

With fewer children to care for, income per parent, however we calculate it, would rise. If all of the rise in average income were devoted to increased consumption and if the average child and adult maintained the same relative shares of consumption, there would be a general rise in levels of living corresponding to the increase in income per head. Everyone would eat better and be better housed; all would have a larger share in the educational and health facilities and other benefits provided for in the public budget.

A secondary effect of higher consumption levels would be to raise productivity by increasing both labor input and labor efficiency. With higher levels of income, more could also be saved and perhaps invested and government income from taxes might be raised. In addition, there could be more subtle effects from rising levels of living. The great poverty in some sections of South Asia must account, at least in part, for the apathy of the masses and their unresponsiveness to efforts to change attitudes and institutions, spread modern technology, improve hygiene, and so on.

It seems apparent then, that *the effects of a decline in fertility would be immediate and favorable in both economic and more broadly human terms and that these effects are very considerable and cumulative, gaining momentum over the years.* They would also be *independent of the man/land ratio:* the same causal mechanism must operate in sparsely as in densely populated countries.

A second line of effects accompanies the increase in the labor force. In all the South Asian countries the labor force is now increasing much more rapidly than it ever did previously in these countries, and two or three times as fast as it ever did in Western Europe, even before the effects of birth control began to materialize. This increase will continue. Most of those who will be of working age fifteen or twenty years from now are already born. Whatever efforts to reduce birth rates are made, they will have no effect on these age groups.

We have contended in a previous chapter that the only hope *in the long run* that these rising numbers can be productively utilized lies in expanding industrialization. But *in the short run*—meaning the next few decades—a major premise of planning in the South Asian countries must be that agriculture will have to absorb by far the larger part of the expected rapid increase in the labor force. *The aim of agricultural planning must be to raise labor utilization, and to do so while the labor force is increasing rapidly.*

But this at best can be no more than a respite. If industrialization does not eventually expand to a point where its net effect on employment of the expanding labor force is positive and substantial, there will be greater misery for the masses in agriculture and stagnation or even retardation of economic development generally. It is entirely unrealistic to assume that a growth in the labor force, corresponding to present and prospective rates of births and deaths, can be absorbed indefinitely in any South Asian country without causing calamity.

Population policy, by its very nature, needs to be viewed in the very long time perspective, and the need is the greater in South Asia because of the youthfulness of the population. As some 40 percent of the South Asian population is below 15 years of age contrasted with 20–25 percent in Western countries, and as the age distribution even in the procreative age group is correspondingly skewed, the braking distance is extremely long before population growth and, especially, labor force growth can be significantly slowed down. Even if to one or another of the South Asian countries the projected growth of the labor force would not seem dangerous for some period ahead, this could not be an argument for postponing efforts to reduce the birth rate. And it must not be forgotten that a period of mass education will be needed before a policy of spreading birth control can have significant effects on fertility rates.

Although our treatment of the problem has been in general terms, and although we have consistently avoided making it more specific than our knowledge of the facts permits, we believe we can conclude that *a consideration of the economic effects of population trends should give the governments of the South Asian countries strong reasons for instituting as soon and as vigorously as possible policy measures to get birth control practiced among the masses of the people.*

All of these governments, with the qualified exception of the Roman Catholic Philippines, at least until recently, have been groping toward public policies on birth control. But no country in South Asia has yet been able to effect any measurable reduction in fertility rates. Even in India, where a population policy was begun early, birth rates are not yet decreasing. As of the mid-1960's any gains there may have been from birth control policies have in any case been offset by lessened morbidity and mortality rates and perhaps a relaxation of fertility-depressing customs; the rate of population is still increasing.

Yet the fact that the governments in the region have made or are making a deliberate choice of a restrictive population policy based on contraception has been unique in modern world history. Japan is the only country outside South Asia that has made such a choice, but it did so after India had taken the step and in the beginning was not as explicit. The dramatic decline in fertility in the Western countries since the last quarter of the nineteenth century, and the earlier manifestations of this trend in France and elsewhere, were not the result of a restrictive population policy. On the contrary, all the forces of organized society —the law, officialdom, the clergy, educators, the press, the medical profession—were mobilized to prevent birth control from spreading. Birth control practices spread in spite of these forces because the people themselves wanted them and made themselves familiar with them.

Today the Roman Catholic Church remains the largest and best organized force against birth control. But even here the solidity of the opposition is cracking. The Communist countries once actively opposed birth control, repeating the "Marxist" position that a socialist state had no need for it. At the 1954 World Population Conference in Rome, delegates from the Soviet bloc and Catholic scholars engaged in a curious competition, each group vying with the other in arguing that there was no real population problem anywhere in the world but only a need for huge social and economic reform. We are now witnessing a softening of the "Marxist" doctrine on population in the European Communist countries. This may in part be an incidental effect of de-Stalinization. But more fundamentally, it is a reflection of a need to bring public policy into closer conformity with private morals, an issue that is bound to come to the fore in any country and which now seems to be exerting pressures on the Catholic Church.

In the latter days of the colonial era in India the intellectual elite and the leaders of the nationalists began to believe the Indian subcontinent "overpopulated." Their fears were repeated in the West, and the contentions of Malthus that the world was outbreeding its resources were embraced by many Western intellectuals. Malthus had been a stubborn opponent of birth control as a means of checking population growth. Thus "neo-Malthusians" is a misnomer for those radicals in the Western countries who carried on their fight for birth control and, in the end, won the day.

In India conditions were very different. There the spectre of "overpopulation" and pauperization was not vanishing; large-scale mass poverty was a stubborn reality. Only small Westernized groups in the cities practiced birth control, and its spontaneous adoption by the masses was not in sight. In India the population problem could not, in fact, be rationally discussed in other than neo-Malthusian terms, because the control of population had to be viewed in the context of raising the levels of living. The demand, spurred by radical English friends of Indian intellectuals, was raised not so much for breaking down public policies against the spread of birth control— which were insignificant—but for initiating a positive public policy promoting the popular spread of birth control in order to put a brake on fertility. The urge to do so became particularly strong once the vision of economic development toward higher levels of living had arisen. The intellectual groundwork had been laid when the colonial era came to an end. A rational policy could thus be pursued in the era of independence.

In the other South Asian countries, the neo-Malthusian movement was slower to take hold. For a long time there were only some statements by national leaders to the effect that the problem of population policy must be taken up for consideration, some private efforts to start clinics or propagandize family planning, and occasional reference to the population issue in documents on planning. But in none of these other countries had a national policy to promote birth control been established in the middle of the sixties.

Nevertheless, it was apparent that the idea of a population policy to spread birth control was already then gradually catching on in all the South Asian countries, including even the Catholic Philippines but excluding, of course, the most backward countries such as Laos and Cambodia. In Indonesia and Burma there have been, at best, only spurious and ambivalent expressions of interest in such a policy. But in Thailand the late prime minister, Field Marshal Sarit Thanarat, in his presentation of the 1962 state budget, already expressed anxiety about the high rate of population increase in his country—at that time calculated at not less than 3.6 percent per year.

Concurrently, a sometimes overbearing popular enthusiasm began to spring up in the Western world for birth control in the South Asian countries. The clamor for action was and still is restricted mainly to the Protestant countries, but these are the richest and the most powerful ones, and they set the tone.

However, this sudden interest by the West had a reverse effect on many South Asian leaders. It came at the same time that the former colonies were emerging in a wave of nationalistic emotion. The urgings of the white man for a curtailment of their numerical growth looked too much like a Western effort to blunt Asian power. To some of the more fervent nationalists it even smacked of genocide through contraception. But whatever the darker thoughts of such leaders may have been a decade ago, they are now beginning to accept the obvious premise that they themselves must consider a slowing down of the population growth.

In facing up to their population problems and striving to formulate an appropriate policy, the South Asian countries are bound by one rigid value premise, which has important practical consequences: any attempt to depress population growth is restricted to work on the fertility factor. Complacency about or even tolerance of a high level of mortality because it slows population growth is simply not permissible. As a value premise, this is as indisputably the basis for public policy in South Asia as it is elsewhere throughout the civilized world. *All that can reasonably be done to combat disease and prevent premature death must be done, regardless of the effect on population growth.* This valuation, consistent with the long-established ethos of the medical profession, has in recent times become the keystone of population policy in both the Communist and non-Communist orbit. The value premise is here presented for what it is: a moral imperative.

As the major argument for population policy in South Asia is economic—to maintain and raise living levels and to create a broader scope for economic development—this policy is focussed on population size. Its main urge is that of decreasing fertility and, thereby, the growth of the population. It is in this sense that South Asian policy is truly neo-Malthusian. In the final analysis it became neo-Malthusian because birth control did not spread spontaneously, as it did in the West and in the Communist countries in Europe, and because there is little reason to expect that it will do so within the foreseeable future. On this point it may help put the complex requirements of the South Asian policy rationale into perspective if we compare the emerging population policy in South Asia with the policy emerging in the most advanced Western countries now that public and private morals are being reconciled and birth control is widespread.

The differences between the two are drastic. To begin with, in Northwestern Europe there was no reason to fear overpopulation and, indeed, no economic motive for desiring a lower aggregate number of births. On the contrary, there was a public awareness that fertility could easily fall to the point where the population stock would not reproduce itself. A decline in population was commonly deemed to be undesirable. Behind this value judgment, economic reasons played a minor role, but they certainly did not speak for an opposing valuation. Certainly nowhere in Northwestern Europe will there be, as there are in South Asia, grounds for attempting to depress fertility by means of public policy measures.

Instead, the measures to remove opposition to birth control and to promote "family planning" are taken not to reduce fertility but to create conditions that would encourage people in all social and economic classes to choose the size of the family that offers all of them the best conditions for family life. In promoting birth control, the interest in Northwestern Europe centered on the quality of the population, not its quantity, and on improving conditions under which children grow up. Broadly speaking, the policy trend in the Communist countries of Europe is similar. In some respects the consequences of the new situation have been accepted even more rapidly and fully in these countries. This again testifies to certain important elements of ideals and policies that rise above the cold war issue.

In contrast, the South Asian countries are compelled to lay the main stress on the quantitative aspect of population development. Paramount economic interests force them to strive to depress fertility by spreading birth control; it does not spread spontaneously, least of all with the required speed. Their population policy is forced to be neo-Malthusian, whereas that of the Western and European countries is not.

Nevertheless, the outcome is very similar. As the South Asian countries try to give reality to their neo-Malthusian population policies, they can, to begin with, have no other principle than that of voluntary parenthood, which is at the basis also of the emerging population policy in the West and is becoming so in the advanced Communist countries. It is within the framework of that principle, and by its ever fuller realization, that the South Asian countries will have to recondition people's motives in various ways—in their case, primarily to induce them to have fewer children. State direction by compulsion in these personal matters is not effective. It has not been so even in the Communist countries where it was once tried. Birth control information must then be disseminated and the most effective means of achieving birth control must be made available to the masses.

It is true that the South Asian countries must be wary of policies that would favor families with many children, who will tend to be poorest and most in need of aid, lest they thereby encourage childbearing. But the conflict here is only present as long as the aid to large families is in the form of cash payments to parents. There is undoubtedly a form of aid in everything that is done for children, from expanding health, educational, and training facilities to providing school meals. But if the advantages are directly steered toward the welfare of the children and if they are awarded to the children in kind and not to the parents in cash, the risk of encouraging childbearing is minimized. Often such measures will have the opposite effect of decreasing the economic advantages parents gain from having children. Child welfare in South Asia, even more than in the West, will usually have to operate by means of *socialized consumption, awarding the children more and more of what they need directly and in kind by building up community facilities.*

In South Asia, too, the natural goal to be realized, if and when fertility levels have been pressed down, must be an improvement in population quality. Once birth control is commonly practiced, population policy will naturally become increasingly directed toward the welfare of the families and the quality of the nation. And even while pursuing their primary interest in depressing fertility, the South Asian countries will in many ways be improving the welfare of the children and the quality of the population. The population issue is fundamentally a moral issue, and it will be increasingly recognized as such as humanitarian principles come to the fore. With regard to the manifold social and economic problems related to it, something like a common ethos is beginning to develop throughout the world.

Up to now, numerous ideological, political, economic, and social factors have prevented some South Asian countries from officially declaring a policy of birth control and until very recently have prevented any of them from adopting a policy that would have the scope and impact necessary to bring about any measurable slowing down of population growth. But inhibitions and obstacles originating in religious systems, which have played such a major role in the rest of the world, are much weaker in South Asia. In fact, there are no explicit and clear-cut strictures against birth control in the scriptures of the major South Asian religions—Hinduism, Buddhism, and Islam. While the leaders of these religions could not at this juncture be expected to emerge in the intellectual vanguard supporting birth control, some have explicitly condoned at least some forms of and motives for it. The Catholic Philippines is, of course, atypical. Any official move in favor of birth control was until recently prevented or made difficult, even though the Catholic position is no longer solid.

But in the other countries, where Buddhism, Hinduism, and Islam still fill such a major role in the daily lives and social patterns of the people, it is not enough to have an absence of objection. All established religions, however, share an instinct for conservatism which fears and dislikes changes coming from deliberate rational reflection and using technical means; it is the same instinctive apprehension that, in all countries at an early stage of their development, was manifested toward machines and new means of transportation. But the important point is that once the need for a population policy is recognized at the political level, there will be no tenacious and strongly organized opposition from a church in South Asia—except to an extent, at least for a while, in the Philippines—as there was in the Western world.

A political source of inhibitions to population policy exists in countries that have a serious minority problem, such as, for instance, Ceylon. On the side of the majority there will be a desire to remain as large a majority as possible, while the minority will often want to increase itself. It is reported that a Swedish family planning project in Ceylon ran into difficulties because it was begun in districts with a Singhalese population. It was feared that it might decrease the fertility within that group without the Tamils following along. Where there is real ethnic dualism, this in itself will almost of necessity provide a formidable inhibition to an agreed policy of limiting births. In Malaya, the attitude of Malays and Chinese alike is apt to be influenced by fear that births might decline in their own community without the other following suit. Nevertheless the government, which is dominated by the Malays, has been supporting family planning clinics.

A different example of misinterpretation of the real

situation was the belief of the Sukarno government in Indonesia that population problems could be solved by transplanting settlers from Java and Bali to the outer islands and Sumatra. Their mistake was not their interest in migration out of Java, which was a most sensible and worthwhile policy, but their tendency to exaggerate its potential influence on the rate of Java's population growth. President Sukarno, whose blindness toward the economic facts of life contributed greatly to his downfall, did succeed in instilling a sense of nationhood in the scattered Indonesians. He had a fierce pride in the potential of his country, and the thought that Indonesians could not provide for their own expanding population was repugnant to him.

The underlying attitude of Indonesia's leaders toward birth control was clearly expressed by Sukarno in an interview with Bernhard Krisher of *Newsweek:* "I still believe we ought not to have birth control here. My solution is exploit more land—because if you exploit all the land in Indonesia you can feed 250 million people, and I now only have 103 million. It was President Mohammad Ayub Kahn [of Pakistan], who seeing so many children in Indonesia, said: 'Sukarno, I tremble when I see children. Children create problems.' 'Yes, your country is poor,' I said, 'In my country, the more the better.'" Sukarno refused to believe that his migration program was failing badly and the number of people going from Java and Bali to Sumatra was far less than the number of children being born in Java alone. Since the removal of Sukarno the military junta that rules Indonesia has at least allowed the Ford Foundation to establish some birth control clinics on Java.

Everywhere, India included, a systematic bias has operated to understate the urgency of the population problem. The future economic difficulties of creating work opportunities for the growing labor force are pushed to the forefront, diverting interest from the possibilities of immediate economic relief inherent in a reduction in the number of children per household.

Then there is what we may call the "number illusion." The distinction between "large" and "great" is never kept clear in common language and thought, and few intellectuals can entirely free themselves from the confusion. Size is consciously and unconsciously related to power; its relation to prestige is obvious. It is hard for anyone to accept that this nation may be too big and that it should not grow—a difficulty apt to be reinforced by Western alarm over the population explosion in Asia.

In assessing these attitudes, we must remember that we cannot compare them directly with the European attitudes that fostered birth control there. With these reservations expressed, it would seem that conditions in South Asian villages are vastly less favorable for awakening a desire to limit the number of children, a desire strong enough to lead to effective and sustained birth control. Up to a point, bearing and rearing children can even be looked on as an investment; they offer a measure of security in illness and old age, and all too frequently begin to lighten their parents' work load while still in early childhood. Comparatively speaking, the setting of South Asian life is such that children are expected to fulfill obligations to parents more than parents to children. In addition, most South Asians live closer together, both physically and as a family, than do Westerners. There are more women, mothers, grandmothers, and older sisters nearby to share in the burden of tending children.

Another major attitudinal factor among all South Asian societies, and among the Hindus especially, is the craving for male offspring. A young man does not acquire the status of full manhood in these societies before a son is born to him, and the Hindus believe it essential that a man's skull, after his death, be opened by a son. There is thus an urge to have a son and, in view of high mortality, preferably two or three. This stands in the way of birth control, especially in the early period of married life. Hopefully, this should decrease once mortality rates among infants and children begin to show a pronounced decline.

It must be remembered that these opinions have been developed not in isolation, but in the context of daily political reality. And from a short-run perspective, it is easy to grasp the reluctance of any government to give due attention to the population issue. The governments of South Asian countries are burdened by all sorts of pressing political worries and they are valiantly trying to plan for economic development. The population problem tends, therefore, to loom on the far horizon as a dim cloud over the national destiny. This is a particularly natural outlook of planners who are preoccupied with economic matters, and they usually set the framework for all thinking about planning. The South Asian governments are forever in a situation of grave crisis. To look very far ahead and shoulder a huge task, in addition to coping with all the immediate problems, must be the more uninviting as the population issue is undoubtedly controversial. In India and Pakistan the trend has nevertheless been toward increasing the emphasis on birth control policies, and some other South Asian countries are, as we have pointed out, moving in the same direction.

But it is not enough to have decided on a policy. In implementing a program to spread birth control among the masses, large cadres of workers at different levels have to be trained, organized, and put into efficient action; the whole effort has to be integrated into the general framework of administration. As in all other fields, what the governments are up against are the difficulties we have summed up in this study under the heading "the soft state," which in general tend to keep effectiveness and implementation of policies at a low level. If the new birth control plans should fail to attain their goals, any shortcomings of plan implementation will more likely be due to this set of impediments at the administrative level than to obstacles posed by the attitudes among the masses of people.

We have emphasized that there has been almost no historical experience of a spread of birth control among largely illiterate populations, subsisting for the most part in a rural economy that is stagnant and provides very low levels of living. There are, however, two important differences in initial conditions that are potentially of great advantage to the South Asian countries. For one, in the South Asian countries population control can be deliberately brought about by measures of public policy. For another, there is the opportunity to rely on technical means of contraception. The spread of birth control in the West—and, in all likelihood, in the European Communist countries as well—resulted directly from changes in attitudes, before such means were readily available. For a long time, conception was prevented mainly by *coitus interruptus;* it still remains a major means of contraception in Western countries where the people are otherwise sophisticated and incomes are very high. Public campaigns initiated in the South Asian countries will be able to make use of technical contraceptives from the beginning to a far greater extent than would have been possible in Western countries. The availability of the intra-uterine contraceptive device completely changed the prospects for a rapid spread of birth control, and the active assistance of such non-profit organizations as the Ford Foundation in making it available in South Asia is another favorable factor. Now the widespread acceptance of the effectiveness of oral contraceptives, "the pill," has led to the availability of another and even easier method of birth control.

In conclusion, we are certain that the South Asian countries not only will experience a slower economic development if they do not institute effective policies to bring down fertility rates, but will be in danger of sooner or later having levels of living deteriorate. It cannot be excluded that Pakistan, India, and Java have already entered the period in their history when this has begun to happen. Population policy must be regarded as an integral part of economic policy. Especially in the larger and poorer countries, there is a desperate need for strong and coordinated efforts in population planning, and all other planning, if disaster is to be avoided.

The economic effects of levels of fertility are not only very considerable, but cumulative and progressive. Particularly as policy measures can only gradually affect fertility rates, it is imperative that they be initiated as soon as possible. The inarticulate masses of people must be induced to change their behavior, and the articulate upper strata must overcome their inhibitions and end their resistance to taking vigorous measures for spreading birth control.

There is a latent readiness among these masses to take a positive attitude toward birth control. Educational propaganda should be a prime force in stimulating this readiness. Such propaganda should have greater prospects of success with higher educational levels among the people.

The Indian government, in its Third Plan, set a main goal of accelerating family planning to the degree that it could reduce the birth rate to 25 births per 1000 population by 1973. Taking into account the experience until now, it is difficult to believe that anything even close to this target could be a realistic forecast.

As has been emphasized in this study, the population explosion is the most important social change that has taken place in South Asia in the post-war era. It has been far more important than any reform or development efforts and it has done a great deal to thwart these efforts. The possibility now exists that the spread of birth control will be the greatest change in the next few decades, gradually making reforms and development easier to accomplish. But whether the birth rates will decrease, and decrease rapidly, within the next decade must seem uncertain.

Part Five

POPULATION
QUALITY

Chapter 22

"INVESTMENT
IN MAN"

No inquiry into the poverty of nations could hope to be complete without a study of the quality of men's lives. And the two basic elements in this are health and education. In our premise of the interlocking circles of development, we hold that to improve his economic and social life a man must also improve his health and his education. We hold this belief knowing that it is impossible to define rigidly or to measure precisely these qualities.

When we turn to a study of South Asia, we do so with two assumptions: one is that there is no convincing evidence that the people of South Asia have inherited any biological qualities that make them more susceptible to disease than the other peoples of the world; the differences in health conditions are explained by environmental factors. The other assumption is that the average levels of apparent intelligence and mental aptitudes important to the effectiveness of learning differ only because of these environmental factors.

Given the best statistical data in the world, it is still not possible to state precisely what the "levels" of health and education are, nor can we even be dogmatic about what the "levels" of these two qualities should be. Added to the difficulties of establishing a quantity on health is the fact that information about health conditions in South Asia is deficient and often totally lacking. Even when there are estimates of the prevalence of specific diseases with known symptoms, only the crudest guesses can be made about the prevalence of so-called incipient diseases and general psychic or physical weaknesses due to malnutrition and the diffusion among the population of pathogenic agencies. In South Asia these hard-to-diagnose health deficiencies may be more important for national development than the more obvious ones. The quantity of the various types of medical facilities available bears no definite relation to health conditions or their improvement, and this is even more true of expenditures allotted to health work.

In the discussion of health conditions, reference is frequently made to mortality. We define this term rather formally as the total absence of health. In this manner it is a much simpler concept than health conditions, and it is easier to quantify or measure. The information on mortality is, therefore, vastly superior to that available on the much more complex set of conditions that we denote by the term morbidity, or the presence of ill health. Using mortality rates—general or age-specific rates or life expectancy tables—to indicate general health conditions is not permissible, however. They merely give an indication of the resultant of two component factors: the prevalence of diseases that can be fatal and the extent to which these diseases are not prevented from becoming fatal. They are, in effect, a deficient measure of morbidity. Alone they do not tell about the frequency or duration of diseases nor the degree of health deficiencies, such as blindness or debilitating intestinal diseases.

It is, indeed, conceivable that a large part of a population may be diseased, or at least lacking in normal vigor, all or most of the time, even though rates of mortality are decreasing and life expectancy is increasing. It is even conceivable that people live longer only to suffer debilitating conditions of ill health to a greater extent than before. These precautionary reflections are especially pertinent in the present changing health situation in South Asia. A powerful new medical technology is being used to prevent and cure potentially fatal diseases, but the living levels of the masses are not rising appreciably, and in some areas may be falling. If medical technology and its application continue to improve, mortality may decline for some time to come, even though levels of living should deteriorate, and people become less resistant to diseases, progressively weaker, and less able to work effectively. It is not impossible that, unless a rapid decline of the birth rate occurs, or radical social and economic reforms are made, or much larger and more effective assistance from abroad should intervene, some of the poorest countries in South Asia may shortly find themselves in such a situation—or even that they have already entered it.

It is equally, if not more, difficult to define relative levels of education. Education may take many forms, and again there is no common denominator. Important efforts may be made, for example, in agricultural extension work among people who are illiterate and will remain so. In all forms of education, improving attitudes is at least as important as imparting skills.

There is a great dearth of factual information in regard to all aspects of education in South Asia—even the estimates of such simple items as literacy and school attendance are very deficient. But even if reliable data were available they would not afford a basis for calculating a "level" of education or a change in such a level.

Any attempt to measure educational levels in terms of the financial resources devoted to education—or the facilities provided, such as teachers employed—is bound to fail. For one thing, the "output" of education, both in imparting of abilities and the improvement of attitudes, would bear no definite relation to the "inputs" of resources. There is a great wastage in all forms of education in South Asia, and much of it is plain miseducation. Given modernization and development as goals, the wrong types of abilities and the wrong attitudes are imparted or preserved. This implies that improvement of education requires a better use of resources, not simply an increase in the volume of resources used for that purpose.

Moreover, neither health nor education can be dealt with in isolation. To begin with, conditions of health and education are closely interdependent. On the one hand, a child's ability to take full advantage of the schooling provided him depends on his health. An adult's ability to use the knowledge and skills he has acquired depends on his mental and physical fitness. On the other hand, the extent to which health conditions can be improved depends on people's knowledge of and attitude toward hygiene. Standards of both health and education depend, in turn, on the whole societal milieu, especially the prevailing attitudes and institutions. Reforms in the fields of health and education are of necessity social—or even communal and familial—reforms. For technical reasons, they are usually wasteful unless undertaken on a large scale and integrated into a planned development.

In this connection it should be noted that attitudes, in particular, can be improved through legislative and administrative measures that make certain behavior patterns subject to rewards or penalties. The effectiveness of such policies can be increased by directing educational efforts toward the same goal. Thus a propaganda campaign, directed toward a specific purpose—for instance, the spread of birth control—may be launched. If the purpose is achieved, this is, of course, an educational improvement, even though brought about by means not usually thought of as educational efforts.

Since health and education are such unruly subjects, our treatment of them will encompass a very wide variety of phenomena and stress interrelationships in the entire social system, including the legacy from the past. It will not yield a clear-cut summary statement about the relative levels of health and education in the South Asian countries and rates of change in those levels. Moreover, because of the lack of reliable statistics, even on specific elements in the situation, our analysis will have to be based largely on estimates, the opinions of experts with first-hand experience, and our own impressions and conjectures.

Our value premises in approaching the questions of health and education are epitomized by their part in the desirability of development.

To every individual health is an important element of his well-being and the well-being of those close to him. The health facilities made available to him are an item in his level of living. Indeed, the enjoyment of health has come to take a place among the "human rights," a position in accord with the modernization ideal of equality. But besides having an independent value, health advances have an instrumental value in the development process in that they affect other social and economic conditions. The other side of this circular causation is that health itself is affected by socio-economic factors, notably income, levels of living, and, in particular, nutrition.

At first glance an upward movement of health would appear to be wholly favorable, since the efficiency of labor depends in part on the state of a nation's health. However, improved health conditions are likely to be accompanied by a decline in mortality rates and even some rise in fertility rates, and hence by a population increase with detrimental effects on development. A conflict thus exists, but the improvement of health conditions is a moral imperative, as we hinted in the previous chapter.

Education also has an independent value. Certainly an individual benefits from the development of his faculties, and anything that enlarges his opportunities to participate in the life and culture of his country and the world enriches him personally. On a more practical plane, education is important to individuals because it gives them a chance to increase their incomes and raise their levels of living; educational facilities, like health facilities, are an item in those levels. And like the enjoyment of health, access to education has gradually acquired recognition as a "human right."

In the nature of the case, educational improvements should lead to an improvement in social and economic conditions. But education in South Asia does not always have these beneficial results. Sometimes education is valued by students (and their families) for reasons that are inimical to development. For instance, there is throughout the region a dislike for manual work, and this affects the way people approach education and the use they make of it. But if, as a result of educational efforts, attitudes can be changed so that individuals can identify their own ambitions with the nation's striving for development, the conflict of valuations will have been resolved and the independent value of education would even justify extending efforts in this field further than its instrumental value for development alone would indicate.

In recent times there have been a number of achievements that have heightened the interest in health and education among the leaders of South Asia. The examples of Western welfare states, the emphasis the Communist countries have placed on these two qualities, the help of the United Nations agencies, have all combined to strengthen the zeal for improvement. So far, the impact of these influences has been felt the most among the educated and advantaged strata in South Asia. The broad masses of people in these countries have been touched only slightly as yet.

An indication of this is the fact that the authorities encounter difficulties when they attempt to induce people to behave more rationally in regard to sanitation and hygiene. The masses are perhaps somewhat more interested in better schooling, even though they often resist the changes in attitudes that are intended to be among its effects. Governments have shown an increased readiness to take action in both fields, but on a limited scale. Except for a few measures, such as anti-malaria campaigns, health policies have not been given a high priority. Measures to raise educational standards have been more prominent in the plans. That they have not had a greater effect on development is due partly to the explosive rise in the school-age population and partly to faults and weaknesses in the direction of the educational effort.

The relatively low priority given to genuine and radical reforms in the fields of health and education is also traceable to the prevailing philosophy of development. As we have noted throughout this study, the economic literature and the plans have been dominated by theories based on an uncritical application of concepts and analytical models from developed countries to the South Asian situation. Models centered on the concept of a capital/output ratio have dictated the direction of economic planning in underdeveloped countries. One implication of this postwar approach is the assumption that "non-economic" factors—not only institutions and attitudes but also levels of living, including health and educational facilities—can be disregarded. The primary and often exclusive importance given to investment in physical capital for economic development requires this assumption.

In even more recent times, however, some economists have rediscovered that the economic growth of the highly developed Western European countries has to be explained in some other terms besides the amount of investment in physical plant. But these economists were not willing to abandon the traditional capital/output ratio.

Instead, they widened the concept of capital investment to include, besides physical investment, "investment in man," sometimes labelled "investment in human capability" or "investment in human resources." In doing this, they still needed to reduce the wide variety of specific factors to one, or perhaps a few, categories for which definite amounts of expenditure could be calculated. From the beginning, interest focussed on education, though health has occasionally shared the spotlight. But the more elaborate models all reduce investment in man to the single factor of education.

The finding that in developed countries there was a "residual" in the capital/output model that could not be fully explained by physical investment, which was then imputed to education, was based on statistics such as no underdeveloped country keeps. Nevertheless, economists have not hesitated to apply this theory to the underdeveloped countries. Some economists point to the fact that since the underdeveloped countries must use modern techniques as worked out in the advanced countries, investment in education is even more important to them than it was to the Western countries when they were in early stages of development. Except for such general considerations, there has been little interest in research determining the effect of education under the very different conditions that prevail in the underdeveloped countries. The new theory has simply been applied by analogy. The situation is, indeed, somewhat paradoxical. While most of the planning in South Asia and the other underdeveloped regions, and most of the economic literature on development, continues to be based on the notion that physical investment is the engine of development, there are today an increasing number of economists who denounce that view and who regard development, particularly in underdeveloped countries, as primarily an educational process.

Leaving aside for the moment the question whether it is

possible and correct to treat education in financial terms simply as an investment, educators in South Asia and elsewhere certainly agree with this new school of economic thought. It is, indeed, a remarkable fact, testifying to the damaging compartmentalization of the social sciences and the insularity of traditional economics, that after the Second World War economists could build up a theory of development based solely on physical investment—a theory so incapable of explaining the process of economic growth that a group of them later "discovered" investment in man.

This is so surprising in view of all the thinking and writing in the past by students and practitioners who have specialized in the educational field. Nowhere before has there been any discussion of economic development that did not give educational improvement a predominant role. The major exception has been the post-war economic theorizing and planning for development in underdeveloped countries. For well over a century education for development has been a central theme of pedagogical literature. Economic historians have regularly paid a great deal of attention to education and educational reform when seeking to explain why the rate of economic development has varied in different epochs in different countries. Yet none of these scholars has tried, as many of the post-war economists have, to put educational reform into the conceptual straitjacket of a quantity of financial investment, accounted for in a capital/output ratio. This is the only innovation in the newest economic approach.

Certainly the fact that there is a new approach, stressing the importance of education, should be welcomed. But we criticize it because it has not been carrying its rebellion against the post-war approach far enough. Economists of this "newest school" restrict themselves to including education as an additional item of investment. But the model they so present is based on a number of unwarranted assumptions. In this instance it requires the assumption that education is a homogeneous magnitude, measurable in terms of financial expenditures. The model also implies that prevailing attitudes, institutions, and levels of living other than educational facilities are of no consequence for the problem, and that the effect of all other policy measures applied at the same time can be completely disregarded. As these assumptions are logically inconsistent and inadequate to reality, use of the capital/output model can only block the way to realistic and relevant research.

Our studies clearly indicated that productivity-raising effects of education, and even people's interest in acquiring education, will depend on the extent to which institutional reforms take place. Such reforms can come about only through legislative and administrative means, and they require many additional policy measures to make them effective. The treatment of education only in terms of investment also implies a bypassing of the equality issue. Yet social and economic inequality decisively determines the effects of attempts to improve education, and educational advance now often serves to stratify inequality. This newest theory of investment in man is, consequently, heavily biased, and in a way that conflicts with our value premises.

We do not mean to deprecate the efforts in the educational field or to deny the importance of physical investment. The point is that an analysis which does not fully take into account the institutional framework within which the economic variables operate, and which aggregates disparate activities while isolating them from other, complementary activities, is bound to be not only superficial but misleading. Abstraction from the institutional framework, and from the attitudes that are molded in that framework and in turn support it, is opportunistic both in South Asia and in the West. It is a biased approach.

This tendency to restrict the category of investment in

man to expenditures on education immediately raises the question of why the economists have ignored the other major population quality, health. The answer cannot be the difficulty of defining health or health objectives, as it is at least equally difficult to define educational "levels." Measuring efforts put forth and their effectiveness in financial terms is no more feasible in the case of education than in the case of health. Factual information is about equally lacking in both instances. In any event, neither definitional difficulties nor a lack of empirical data has ever deterred economists, and least of all the model-builders among them, from tackling problems and presenting solutions that pretend knowledge. The fact that improved health is regularly accompanied by demographic changes (a fall in the death rate and perhaps a rise in the fertility rate) which exert a downward pressure on incomes and living levels, does not justify leaving the health factor out, especially since allowance could be made for these secondary changes by slightly complicating the models.

Thus there can be no warrant for leaving health out of the development picture. Ill health is a very serious deterrent to a rise in labor input and efficiency in the underdeveloped countries in South Asia. But if we do add investment in health to investment in education and define human resources in terms of the two dimensions of population quality, we must include all costs involved in improving conditions of health, not just expenditures on health facilities. In all South Asian countries, and particularly in the biggest and poorest of them, India and Pakistan, a major cause of ill health is serious undernutrition and malnutrition among the masses of the people. The majority of South Asians spend much more than half their income on food, and still they are undernourished. Nor do they have access to the clothing, housing, and sanitary facilities they need to keep them reasonably fit. On the margin, then, increases in the consumption of essentials, food especially, or the expenditures that make such increases possible, are bound to be productive of better health, which is not the case in the highly developed countries.

The implication is that the new term "investment in man" should include not only the consumption of educational and health facilities, *but practically all essential consumption*, if the underlying reasoning is to be logically consistent. *The productivity effect on the margin of the various items of consumption differs, however.* Some consumption is relatively unproductive, and some even has a negative value for health. The *real planning problem* is how to squeeze and twist consumption in such a way as to speed up development. This problem would not be clarified to any degree by the statement that much of the consumption in these poor countries constitutes investment in man. What the planners need to know is the effect on productivity of increases in the consumption of various items, and here the model offers no guidance at all.

To sum up, the most recent opposition of some economists to the post-war approach is certainly wholesome, insofar as it challenges the exclusive role given in this period to physical investment. The general policy judgment of the rebel school that greater efforts to improve education, if wisely planned and directed, can be more conducive to development than are some physical investments, is probably correct—though it does not follow as a conclusion from use of the conventional model with only a broadened definition of capital investment. The same probably holds true of greater efforts to improve health, though these efforts would have to have as a major objective the increasing of essential consumption and, in particular, food intake. Again, this would not follow from the use of a capital/output model, even if the model took health measures into account. The investment approach entirely ignores the fact that institutional and attitudinal reforms, which depend on political decisions rather than budgetary considerations, are needed to make investments in education "pay off," and the broader consideration that the success of educational programs depends on the policies pursued in all other fields as well as the direction of the educational programs themselves.

It is possible that some members of the school of economics whose views have been discussed here would agree generally with our evaluation. But *if the concept "investment in man" is revised to take account of these criticisms, it becomes virtually empty of theoretical content; it becomes merely a vague propaganda term for a more rational and circumspect development planning that takes into account not only physical investments but all other induced changes.*

To avoid any misunderstanding it should again be stressed that we are not adverse to the use of models. Still less are we opposed to efforts to make quantitative judgments. We are not in sympathy with the view that some factors are "qualitative"; in principle social scientists must strive constantly to translate all of their knowledge into measurable quantities. However, *both models and quantitative pronouncements must be logically consistent and thoroughly grounded in facts.* There is a great need to know more about how different development efforts affect one another and how they are affected by institutional settings. When more data becomes available, there will be room for models that are clear, logically consistent, and adequate to reality.

The judgment that the South Asian countries should devote more resources to improving health and education is probably correct as far as it goes, but it is vague and does not clarify the really important issues, namely: where should health and educational programs be directed, how far should they be pushed, what means should they employ, and what other policy measures are needed?

The criticism of the conventional post-war approach to

planning, which relates development to physical investment alone, is valid—but for reasons more fundamental
than those advanced by the newest school of economists.
It is not in the slightest degree strengthened or rendered
more precise by a general "theory" of investment in man
as the engine of economic growth. The quantitative inferences frequently arrived at by the use of the new, extended capital/output models are as fictitious as, for
instance, the calculations of the percentage of the labor
force that is "underemployed." By presenting an elegant
appearance of knowledge where none exists, they make it
easy to avoid the laborious task of studying reality in all
its complexity. The abstract criticism in this chapter is
intended to help clear the deck of useless theories, based
on preconceptions that obstruct and misdirect scientific
advance.

Chapter 23

HEALTH

Poor health conditions are intimately linked with almost every aspect of life in South Asia. The fact that improved health has an independent value for individuals implies that the health facilities available are an important item in a country's level of living; at the same time, the availability of almost every other item of consumption, including foodstuffs, housing, clothing, sanitation, and educational facilities, is relevant to health conditions. Improved health conditions should increase labor input and efficiency; they can also increase the acreage of cultivable land, as when malarial areas are drained and sprayed. The influence of the climate on labor utilization is closely related to the influence of the climate on health conditions. Health conditions are obviously a determinant of fertility and mortality, and, consequently, of quantitative population trends. A policy that succeeded in spreading birth control among the masses of people should have the effect of improving health conditions for mothers and children. Insofar as a decrease in the number of children raises levels of living—directly because of a lower dependency burden and indirectly because of its effect on labor utilization—such a quantitative population development affects conditions of health generally.

During the long centuries when South Asia passed from independence to colonial domination, the progress of medical care and health facilities, in the modern sense, was minimal at best and in some instances almost nil. Nevertheless, after the Europeans arrived to establish their colonies, the beginnings of Western medical practices were introduced. But for the most part the little aid that did arrive was concentrated on the European colonials and on the indigenous aristocracy they wished to favor.

There was, during the colonial era, a marked decline in mortality. Part of this was ascribed to the absence of wars (the colonial powers did little fighting between colonies). But part was due to gradual increases in colonial health services and the efforts to prevent starvation when crops failed. For a long time, however, there were few notable efforts by the colonial governments either to train indigenous persons in medicine, sanitation, and health care, or to provide these for the natives as well as themselves.

The indigenous people continued to rely on their own traditional medicine with its combination of native herb remedies and spiritual cures. Actually, when the first European doctors arrived, there was no vacuum to be filled in the field of native healing. The proficiency of this healing, which deteriorated during the colonial era, was another matter. By the end of the colonial period, the masses of people in the rural districts and in the urban slums were hardly touched by the preventive medical work undertaken in the colonial era, except insofar as they were affected by edicts decreeing compulsory vaccination against smallpox.

In the independence era that started after the Second World War, the population of South Asia suddenly and unexpectedly began to grow at an explosive rate. Ominously, this development has been the only really significant social change in South Asia in this most recent period. As we explained in Chapter 21, it stems from a decline in mortality so rapid as to have no historical precedent. The explanation cannot be sought in any improvement in the levels of living, as these have not changed appreciably for the broad masses of people. Nor have there been advances in education or attitudes toward hygiene great enough to have had much influence on morbidity and mortality.

The rapid decline in mortality—starting from different levels and at different times in the several countries—is ascribable instead to the application of a new medical technology, based on recent scientific discoveries, which makes it possible to prevent and cure some diseases at small cost and almost regardless of living levels, attitudes, and habits of the people concerned. Powerful chemotherapeutic drugs and antibiotics have revolutionized the treatment of a number of infectious diseases, and DDT and other insecticides have been of particular import. These products were developed in the advanced countries over a couple of decades. With mass production they became available in quantity at a low price. They had the added merit of being so simple that they could be dispensed by people with rudimentary training.

Collectively such products changed the conditions for preventing and curing disease in somewhat the same way that the discovery of atomic energy changed the nature of military warfare. Malaria, once the most common single cause of illness in South Asia, has been reduced throughout the area, and India in particular has made commendable headway against it. All the South Asian countries have programs for control of tuberculosis, which became quite widespread after the beginning of this century. But only Malaya, Singapore, and Ceylon have pursued these programs with much vigor. Outside the Indian subcontinent and Burma the ravages of smallpox have been checked fairly successfully. Looking toward the future, there are good prospects that malaria will soon be almost eradicated everywhere in South Asia. The same should hold true of smallpox, although since millions of persons will have to be vaccinated and re-vaccinated, more scarce resources of personnel and equipment will have to be devoted to this task.

The new medical discoveries and the technique of mass campaigns enabled the South Asian governments to vastly improve morbidity and mortality rates with only a relatively minor expenditure of resources. Presumably medical scientists will develop still more potent drugs, pesticides, and vaccines in the years ahead. *But efforts to prevent and cure disease will increasingly require reforms in the fields of nutrition, sanitation, and hygiene and an increase in the supply of properly trained medical personnel, equipment, clinics, and hospitals.* Medical technology will be helpful, but mainly in conjunction with larger efforts in these other fields. Further advance will thus be more expensive and slower in coming.

The launching of mass campaigns indicated that the South Asian governments accepted the idea that preventive measures were of vital importance in the war against disease. This, in turn, implied that they subscribed to the precepts of modern medicine, since indigenous medicine is in principle merely curative. A factor strengthening the hold of modern medicine in the South Asian countries was their participation in the newly created World Health Organization and the help this agency and other public and private health groups have given since the war.

Against this background it is rather surprising that health programs have not so far been given a higher priority in the development plans of the South Asian countries. Improved hygiene is rarely mentioned among the principal objectives of such plans. Although each country has a separate ministry of health, the ministers usually do not have cabinet rank in countries where such distinction is observed. Another means of assessing the value placed on health by the South Asian governments is to relate public expenditures for health to national income or gross national product. Generally, public expenditures for health in all the South Asian countries were not only much lower in absolute terms but also formed a lesser proportion of their gross national product than in the developed countries. Ceylon and Malaya, even taking into account that they are relatively well off by South Asian standards, give a higher priority to public health policies than the other countries in the region. Yet in terms of public expenditures per capita, Ceylon and Malaya spend only about 10 percent of what the rich Western countries spend.

All countries in South Asia began their independence with seriously deteriorated health facilities and a reduced number of doctors. India and Ceylon were in relatively a better position than the others, but Indonesia, Pakistan, and Burma were left virtually without qualified medical personnel. While all have made considerable progress, compared with their starting point, even the best endowed countries in South Asia had less than one-fifth as many physicians as the Western European countries had, even by 1960. They are even less well off when their higher rates of diseases are considered. Moreover, medical practitioners are not as well trained and those who are studying medicine do so under much more difficult circumstances than in the West. There is, in particular, a great paucity of specialists throughout the region.

Despite the generally low level of competence among South Asian physicians, it is sometimes suggested that they are being over-educated in view of the poverty of the countries and the tremendous unmet need for medical care. Thus John Kenneth Galbraith reflects: "As a layman I have sometimes wondered if medical education has been really adapted to the situation of the poor country. . . . The provision of . . . total training is the sine qua non of modern medical education [in the United States, Europe, and also in New Delhi]. But in the developing country, with scarce resources, if we insist on . . . high standards for the few, may we not deny medical assistance to the many? Do we not get good doctors in the capitals at the price of having no one to set a broken leg or prescribe some morphine in the village?"

Yet in every South Asian country, the policy has been to raise the standards of qualification for medical practice as far as possible, even though this means there will be a severe shortage of physicians for a long time to come. The shortage of nurses in South Asia is even more acute than that of physicians. This stems from other factors besides the expected shortage of training facilities and basic education. In India, in particular, higher-caste Hindus have an abhorrence for bodily contacts, particularly those of the type involved in nursing and midwifery. This prejudice has been taken over by the Moslems in Pakistan and Malaya.

In most of the region, except in parts of India, Ceylon, Malaya, and Singapore, there is also an acute shortage of qualified pharmacists. In rural areas particularly, well-run dispensing establishments are practically unknown. In every section the rural populations are almost entirely out of reach of what trained medical and nursing personnel there are, and must go into distant cities if they are to find any hospital facilities at all. However, some governments in South Asia, with the help of outside agencies, have begun moving toward helping the rural populations by establishing country-wide networks of health centers where some treatment may be had.

Although indigenous medicine has deteriorated and receives little official support, it has not lost its grip on the rural populations or on the lower classes in the cities. The reasons are not entirely economic or due to a shortage of modern medical facilities. In the eyes of the villagers, a practitioner of native medicine has qualities transcending those of a Western-trained doctor. The native practitioner does not isolate his patients in hospitals, away from their families, nor does he laugh at them when they ascribe their diseases to vengeful gods. He never says he does not know what ails them, and he does not ask payment in advance of results. These attitudes and the vested interests of native practitioners might impede the growth of modern medical services in rural areas, were it not that the supply of such services falls far short of meeting the demand that does exist.

The climates of South Asia, which are such a powerful factor in so many elements in the conditions of the region's society, provide the ideal environment for the growth and spread of parasitic and infectious diseases. The new medical technology has provided the countries of the region with effective weapons with which to fight some of these diseases. More could be accomplished with improved medical facilities, better sanitation and hygiene, and higher living levels, particularly in regard to nutrition. But the supply of these factors is dependent on economic levels, and here, too, the climates exert an adverse influence through their effect on labor efficiency, soil, vegetation, and physical capital. All these chains of circular causation of ill health can also be the more difficult to break up because of the poverty of the South Asian countries, which itself, however, is partly caused by the detrimental effects of the climates on health.

The main cause of undernourishment and malnutrition in South Asia is, of course, poverty and, in particular, the low productivity of man and land in agriculture. The remedy is generally development, but the way will not be easy, partly because the dietary deficiencies themselves have reduced people's ability to work.

Another major contributor to the debilitating state of general health in South Asia is the lack of advance in environmental sanitation. One reason, of course, is the costliness of requisite materials and the scarcity of supervisory personnel. Again we find poverty to be a primary cause of the stubborn survival of conditions that gravely menace health, though at the same time inferior health conditions help to preserve poverty by lowering labor input and efficiency. Another reason why progress is slow is a lack of responsiveness among the people.

The improvement of public hygiene is thus not merely a problem of acquiring the necessary financial, material, and human resources. It is also a problem of educating the masses. People must be taught to be more rational and more concerned about their health. If they could be persuaded that the effect was worthwhile, they could take advantage of the long slack periods in agriculture and of suitable local materials to improve their houses. In particular, if they could be prevailed upon to regard cleaning chores with less distaste, they could keep their homes and their surroundings in a more healthful condition.

Attitudes toward public and personal hygiene are woven into the very fabric of society and are reflected in the religions, superstitions, sexual mores, and rites of the region. But this does not imply that campaigns to improve habits of hygiene are hopeless. A study of health conditions in South Asia leaves one with the impression that there is an immense need for such campaigns and that, in particular, teachers and schools should be systematically involved to a greater extent than has usually been the case.

In assessing actual health conditions in the region, what we know about the timing and effectiveness of the mass campaigns, which have decreased not only mortality but also morbidity, and about the improvement of health facilities, suggests that the rank order of the countries in terms of health conditions would be somewhat similar to their rank order in terms of mortality. The latter, in turn, corresponds fairly well with their rank order in terms of economic levels and levels of living, particularly standards of nutrition. It is natural to assume this, because the more prosperous people are, the better able they are to avoid deficiency diseases and to obtain adequate medical treatment. Nevertheless, in South Asia even the higher income strata must often fall prey to the ubiquitous transmissible diseases. Measures designed to prevent disease may have benefitted all classes of people in roughly equal manner, but measures designed to increase the supply of medical personnel and hospital facilities have favored those in the higher income strata.

In relating health to labor efficiency, we must concede that there is a complicated causal relationship between them. But practically no efforts have been made to measure this relationship. Some research has been made into the connection between poor nutrition and labor efficiency. These studies corroborate in a general way the conclusion that sub-optimal food intake has a very marked direct effect on people's ability to work.

Health deficiencies might have less influence on labor input and efficiency were there not a widespread belief among South Asians that hard manual labor or the lifting of heavy weights causes illness. Such notions are understandable, since work is often performed where grave health risks do exist. But it can itself deter people from working long and hard. Misconceptions of this type are to an extent rationalizations of attitudes, which themselves are not independent of health conditions. Some of the characteristics of South Asians, often idealized there, as in the West, as "Asian values"—their bent to contemplation, other-worldliness, leisureliness, and spirituality—may be due in part to deficiencies in health and nutrition.

We have stressed that all the factors involved in the health problem are inter-related. From the planning point of view, the effect of any particular policy measure in the health field depends on all other policy measures, and is, by itself, indeterminate. This means that it is impossible to impute to any single measure a definite return in terms of improved health conditions. More than any other type of planning, planning for better health conditions must proceed by an intuitive process wherein segmented information is complemented by informed estimates and made to yield the outline of a strategy. The matter must be attacked on the broadest possible front, combining a number of mutually supporting policy measures. Education and the spread of more rational attitudes have a general bearing on health conditions which adds weight to all other reasons for adopting policies to improve education. The task of instructing people about specific health hazards belongs, however, more specifically to the health authorities, as does the task of improving sanitation.

It is our impression that generally too little is done in regard to health education. As in the field of birth control, large-scale intensive propaganda campaigns are needed. There is also need for improved health legislation and more adequate law enforcement. Ideally such policy measures in the legal and administrative fields should be integrated with the health campaigns, supporting them by providing inducements and punishments.

The new medical technology has been used to good advantage in recent decades to fight certain diseases that have been ravaging South Asia. These campaigns have been largely responsible for the improvement in morbidity and mortality that has taken place. Further progress will increasingly depend on public expenditure and advances in popular cooperation on hygiene and sanitation, and on more and better medical facilities.

From the scattered and inadequate information available, we conclude that the South Asian countries would be wise to pursue more vigorous health policies and to find a firmer basis for their direction by collecting fuller health statistics and undertaking more intensive research.

Chapter 24

EDUCATION:
THE LEGACY

Whenever education is considered from the point of view of development, its purpose must be to rationalize, or modernize, attitudes as well as to impart knowledge and skills. This challenge is far greater in the underdeveloped countries of South Asia, where attitudes and institutions that hinder development have become so firmly rooted. This is one of the pressing reasons why the educators of South Asia cannot adopt uncritically the educational practices and policies of the Western developed countries. Nor can they afford to develop their educational programs during the coming years at the same slow pace.

The South Asian countries must strive for a much speedier dissemination of the attitudes, knowledge, and skills favorable to development, inasmuch as they have handicaps to overcome in their planning for development, including an unprecedentedly high rate of population increase. Since their "initial conditions" are less favorable in numerous respects, they cannot rely on the slow process of exposing successive generations of school children to new ideas and attitudes, but must make a determined effort to educate adults. And since irrational attitudes, as well as ignorance and lack of skills, among the adult population tend to thwart efforts to teach young people, adult education also has an additional instrumental value, as a means of increasing the effectiveness of child education. In regard to the rationalizing of attitudes, it should be recognized that whatever attitudinal changes a government attempts to accomplish by means of legislative and administrative policy measures implying punishments and inducements should come under the heading of educational policy in its broader sense.

For both children and adults, literacy and general knowledge facilitate the acquisition of specific skills, and may help to bring about a rationalization of attitudes. In turn, more rational attitudes provide a motivational preparedness that can facilitate the acquisition of literacy, knowledge, and skills. In general, educational policy must have the central purpose of directing and apportioning educational efforts so as to give a maximum impetus to national development.

The problem of reforming education in South Asia is far from being merely a quantitative one of providing more schooling. It is as much or more a problem of eliminating miseducation and large-scale waste of educational resources. And while in the field of health policies there is a medical technology that is applicable to all human beings, and largely also to animals, there is no such "objective" educational technology available.

The educational problem in South Asia has to be thought out anew, taking into account social conditions in the countries concerned and their quest for development. And to do so the planners cannot simply discard all the old traditions for an ideal simple educational technology, as in health. We cannot delineate the problem of reform in this field without devoting attention to what those traditions are and what impact they still have at the present time.

Generally speaking, that impact is detrimental, but not wholly so.

The platform of past educational traditions, on which the South Asian nations are now attempting to build their modern educational systems, is a complex structure. Its outline began in the dimly perceived dawn of South Asian history. In that time education in the region was a primary concern of the religious functionaries. South Asia was the birthplace or proving ground of three great world religions: Hinduism, Buddhism, and Islam. Each gave rise to mighty educational efforts of a distinctive type. But the activating force was not the religion as embraced by the masses.

Then, as now, popular religion had little dynamism. It served mainly to give the sanction of sacredness to inherited attitudes and institutions. The people were not inspired to demand instruction for themselves. The educational impulses came instead from the higher level of the priesthood in the religious "organizations." The priests in all three religions were teachers more often than not, and this is to an extent true even today. Most were able to use script as a vehicle of education, since their sacred texts were early made up into written form.

According to Hindu tradition, education was exclusively or mainly the prerogative of one social group, the Brahmans. But there were early important deviations from this main line of Hindu tradition. As the noblemen and merchants who were not Brahmans acquired wealth and power, they began to demand, and to get, a more pragmatic education for themselves, their children, and their subordinates.

Buddhism and Jainism, the extraordinary reform movements that challenged Hinduism, reached a high level of influence and began their systems of religious teachings. Later, among the Buddhists, it became the practice for their monasteries to take in boys, not all of whom were expected to become monks, for periods of instruction in the scriptures and, in addition, for rudimentary training not only in reading and writing but also in more worldly subjects. Sometimes the monastery schools came to function more like ordinary schools, with the boys attending while they continued to live at home with their families. But the Buddhist religion is not any longer, and has not been for centuries, an active force for modernization and development.

Islam came to South Asia from the outside, in the wake of conquest. As a result not only of religious conviction but also of pressure or appeals to opportunistic interests whole communities or castes were converted, often without much spiritual preparation. According to the Koran it was, however, a religious duty to educate the young. Like many other excellent prescripts of that sacred book, that duty was never carried out on a large scale. It is unlikely that many of the Moslem children attended the schools at the mosques regularly, and most probably did not attend at all. And as these schools concentrated then, as they largely do now, on teaching pupils to recite the Koran in Arabic, they cannot have been very effective institutions of secular learning. Even today, among the Malays and among some of the Indonesians, elementary schools are taught by Moslem instructors and are based to a large extent on the recitation of the Koran.

The earliest colonial intruders from Europe in South Asia were the two Catholic imperialist powers, Spain and Portugal. Unlike the Protestant powers, the Netherlands and Britain, who arrived later, they had a planned educational policy from the beginning. One of their missions, in addition to economic exploitation, was to convert the pagans to the Christian faith. What is important is that this duty was interpreted as requiring the education of the people to read and write—a policy that would hardly have appeared warranted had political power or commercial and fiscal exploitation been the chief and only purpose.

This had the most far-reaching effect in the Philippines, which was under Spanish rule continuously for more than three and a half centuries. By the early part of the seventeenth century, the ground had been laid for a system of even secondary and tertiary education that was not directed merely toward religious teaching. And the priests and monks, who worked closely with the civil authorities, began creating a network of elementary schools, in which both religious and secular subjects were taught. By 1863 the Spanish colonial government had adopted a program of compulsory elementary education that was to be free to all children between the ages of seven and thirteen. When the Spanish left a generation later, this ambitious program was far from being fulfilled. Nevertheless, the Philippines was already ahead of most other South Asian colonies in popular education. From the beginning the American colonial authorities in the Philippines placed a major emphasis on education and gave it their own impress. They also gave education there a new impetus, since they aimed at an Americanization of attitudes. All in all, so far as education is concerned, the short reign of the United States over the Philippines must be judged a remarkable success. It left a literacy rate among the highest in South Asia and a budding system of secondary and higher education.

The Dutch, who soon followed the Portuguese into what is now Indonesia, had little of the proselytizing zeal. Their policies on colonial education varied with economic circumstances. At times more ambitious programs were announced, but little was actually accomplished, and when Dutch rule was ended by the Japanese in the Second World War the literacy rate was among the lowest in the region. The Dutch record on secondary and higher education was even poorer. Only a handful of Indonesian youths ever got through a university and less than a thousand had professional educations at the beginning of independence. Ironically, they formed the cadre for the independence struggle.

Ceylon, which now shares with the Philippines the honor of having the highest literacy rates in the region, profited by the influence of Portuguese, Dutch, and finally English rule, plus the important educational efforts of the Buddhists. While Ceylon never gained a university in colonial times, it was more common in Ceylon than in the other South Asian colonies for students to continue their education abroad, usually in India or England. Ceylon was early granted increasing installments of self-government, beginning in 1924, which the Ceylonese politicians used to press advances in education as well as health.

It was also the missionaries, both Catholic and Protestant, who at first brought the Western educational impact to India. They did this most often with little help from the colonial officials and more often in the face of their opposition. It is interesting to speculate on how the history of Indian education might have turned out differently if India had been colonized and ruled by a Catholic country —or, in more recent times, if the British had been a nation early committed to the ideals of popular government and popular education at home, as were the Americans.

The British colonial authorities eventually did come to take an interest in secondary and higher education. In the 1760's and 1770's, they gave financial support, on a small scale, to Hindu and Moslem institutions of higher learning, and this practice was further encouraged by the East India Company Charter Act in 1813. In a dramatic policy shift it was decided in 1835 that all funds appropriated for education should be employed to provide an English education, with classes conducted in the English language.

The British authorities of the period pressed the new policy both because they needed to employ indigenous persons in the administration and because they wanted to spread Western or, more particularly, English civilization among the upper strata of the Indian people. This decision would hardly have been taken, however, had not the articulate Indian upper class felt strongly that a Westernization of Indian culture was in their own interest. This attitude paid off, and increasingly so when the British began to follow a much more liberal policy than the Dutch and the French in their colonies, of giving properly qualified Indians access to responsible posts in the administration.

But there was no thought to making English the language of the people. Furthermore, the new policy line, adhered to almost until the end of the colonial era, implied that there would be no support for popular education in the vernacular languages. This was more easily accepted in part because at that time the articulate among the Indians themselves did not demand that anything be done to educate the masses. When such demands were later revised, they were rather platonic in ideology and ineffective in practice, until Gandhi forcefully introduced egalitarian ideals into Indian discussion and lined up the nationalist movement in support of the interests of India's "dumb millions."

In the field of secondary education the policy decision of 1835 opened up an era of rapid expansion of school facilities for the Indian upper strata that continued to the end of the colonial period and beyond, on the whole with accelerating speed. But the structure of this whole system was determined by the fact that the degrees given were the primary objective and that these degrees served as passports to government service. In all Indian schools whose courses aimed at entrance to higher-level education, the emphasis was on "academic" subjects. Little, if any, attention was paid to scientific or technical subjects. Everything was geared to train individuals for subordinate positions in the colonial administration.

In Burma, which did not come completely under

PART FIVE: POPULATION QUALITY

British rule until the 1850's, the Indian pattern was repeated, but to an even lesser degree. In Malaya the ethnic diversity of the population gave a different character to educational developments. While the Chinese built up their own schools and often sent their young people to China for further education, the Malays, except for a tiny upper stratum of courtiers and landlords around the Sultans, were less enterprising. This being the case, the British proceeded quite slowly in opening up positions in the administration to indigenous persons, lest this should unduly favor the Chinese.

In French Indo-China education did not profit so much from early missionary activities as in the older colonies. The French were less liberal than the British in offering natives positions in the administration. The relatively limited number of schools they supported were stamped by the French educational system. Most of this effort went to the more advanced Vietnamese. Education in Laos and Cambodia continued mainly in the old Buddhist tradition, with the monks in the monasteries teaching the boys. The Indo-Chinese University in Hanoi was not founded until 1917.

The most severe handicap of the new nations as they emerged from colonial rule was the ignorance of their populations. One major element of this was a low rate of literacy and an even lower rate of functional literacy. This holds true as a general statement, despite considerable differences in this respect between the Philippines and Ceylon at the higher point and India, Pakistan, and Indonesia at the lower.

One element in the colonial legacy that constitutes a stubborn difficulty for the independent regimes to overcome is that, insofar as there were schools for the people, the training of teachers was neglected, particularly at the primary level. In India and Pakistan particularly, the traditionally low social status of teachers and their low salary scales impeded recruitment and stifled interest in raising the qualifications of teachers by giving them training.

The methods of teaching in the pre-colonial era were, as we mentioned, all heavily weighted in the direction of making pupils memorize texts, whether they understood them or not. This method was, of course, necessary in the Moslem schools at the mosques, where the important part of the curriculum was reading the Koran in the Arabic language. But learning by rote was the common method in all other indigenous schools in the whole region. Teaching still tends to be dogmatic and authoritarian; it does little to encourage a questioning, critical attitude or an interest in self-education outside and beyond the school.

This legacy of authoritarianism has carried over into university teaching to a marked extent. Every Western visitor to South Asian universities is even today struck by the uncritical attitude of the average student. He expects the professor and the textbooks—or selected pages in the textbooks—to impart to him the knowledge he needs, and accepts what is offered to him without contributing much intellectual effort of his own other than in listening, reading, and memorizing. His submissiveness in this respect stands in curious contrast to his readiness to protest if he feels that requirements in examinations are unduly taxing. He is also aggressively conscious that as a university student he belongs, or will soon belong, to an elite group.

The difference in motivation between an average student in the Western or the Communist countries and an average student in South Asia is, of course, only relative. But it is of supreme importance from the standpoint of national development. Teaching in South Asian schools at all levels tends to discourage independent thinking and the growth of that inquisitive and experimental bent of mind that is so essential for development. It is directed toward enabling students to pass examinations and obtain degrees. A degree, rather than the knowledge or skills to which the degree should testify, is the object pursued.

This is a legacy from colonial times and, more specifically, a holdover from the efforts of governing authorities to build up an indigenous educated elite that could serve in administrative posts and provide professional services. But the fact should not be overlooked that this type of education met with a good reception in South Asian countries because of the deeply imbedded status-consciousness of people in these stagnant old societies.

The educated throughout South Asia tend to regard their education as the badge that relieves them of any obligation to soil their hands through manual labor. Without doubt the downgrading of manual work is a very serious obstacle to development, as Mohandas Gandhi continually stressed. There is a broad inverse correlation throughout the region between the prevalence and severity of this prejudice and the level of popular education and literacy: the prejudice tends to be strongest in those countries where popular education is least advanced. An important corollary to these observations is that one reason for pressing on with literacy campaigns and making schooling of children universal is to eradicate this prejudice against manual work.

The colonial powers usually contributed to the strengthening of this prejudice by their educational policies, or lack of them. Their objective was not to change the people's basic attitudes and help prepare them for development, but to train docile clerks and minor officials. All this must be taken into account when noting that it has proved difficult to reform secondary and higher education by expanding vocational and technical courses of study at the expense of literary and academic courses. The educated elite in South Asia must, however, share with the colonial governments responsibility for the extreme conservatism of the school system, which undoubtedly supported their prejudicial approach to manual work and thereby their social and economic pretensions and what they saw as their interests.

In almost all the South Asian countries the educational system, even at the primary level, is heavily biased against girls, and throughout the region the literacy rate is lower among women than among men. This is partly because governmental efforts in the educational field were so modest. Facilities for popular education were woefully inadequate and secondary schools were "job-oriented" toward service in the administration. But mainly the explanation lies in the popular attitudes dating back to pre-colonial times. The three Asian religions cared little for the education of girls and generally placed women in an inferior position, though Buddhism was more egalitarian in this as in other respects.

These traits inherited from colonial and pre-colonial times constitute formidable inhibitions and obstacles to development, and we should not be surprised if educational reforms in the now independent countries of South Asia proceed more slowly and less effectively in raising their development potential than could be hoped. *The winning of independence has not worked any miraculous change in the people and their society.* The existing educational establishments are part of a larger institutional system, which includes social stratification; and this system is supported by people's attitudes, which themselves have been molded by the institutions. The South Asian peoples are not merely being insufficiently educated; they are being miseducated on a huge scale. And there are important vested interests embedded in the whole attitudinal and institutional system that resist and warp policies intended to overcome both deficiencies.

In all South Asian countries the task of bringing about educational reform is made much more difficult by the population explosion. The number of children is increasing so rapidly that the responsible authorities must exert themselves merely to maintain the *status quo* in schooling and literacy. This obstacle to educational reform was not among those inherited from the colonial era. Its effects were added after the Second World War to the set of inhibitions and obstacles noted above.

Chapter 25

LITERACY AND
ADULT EDUCATION

The new governments of independent South Asia have, from their beginnings in the post-war era, placed educational reform high on their lists of policy priorities. But it has been the tendency of the planners in all of them to think primarily in terms of "how many"—how many students enrolled, in how many courses, in how many schools —and not in terms of how well they learned, what they were taught, or how to improve the educational system they inherited from their colonial masters to speed up development.

All the countries in the region have attached great importance to raising the literacy rate of their populations. To achieve this objective, they have relied almost exclusively on an increase in primary school enrollment. Adult education, certainly one of the most vital elements in development, has been given a relatively low priority.

Many people, including ourselves, feel that it is of paramount importance for development that the under-developed countries in South Asia raise the level of functional literacy as rapidly as possible. Such a view is often supported by pointing to the Scandinavian countries, Germany, and the United States. All of these had a remarkably high rate of literacy early in the nineteenth century, and this is credited with making possible their rapid development. But initial conditions, as we have stressed, are so different in South Asia that one cannot automatically draw an analogy with Western countries.

Still less reliable information about the role of literacy in development can be derived from studies of present levels of literacy and development in different countries. The correlation appears high, but that fact does not tell us what is cause and what is effect. Yet obviously advances in literacy and advances in economic development are interconnected. In general terms it may be safe to assume that certain common factors are at work that lead the two types of advancement forward hand in hand; their influence on each other must be mutual and cumulative. International comparisons in terms of the correlation between levels of literacy and economic development do not even state the problem of that causal relationship. In the total absence of any intensive research on the value of literacy for development, the argument must be cast for the time being in general and common sense terms.

In the post-war era there has often been a downgrading in the importance of literacy. The argument, based on romantic and traditionalist ideas, plays up the wisdom of the illiterate peasant or worker. It assumes that these people can acquire useful skills without first learning to read. While this belief has not substantially diminished the desire to broaden elementary education for children, in most of the South Asian countries it has dampened the zest for literacy campaigns as a part of adult education.

We hold that those who would give priority to practical training overestimate the effectiveness of an education that is not supported by literacy and, even more important, underestimate what literacy can mean to elementary vocational education in South Asia. Persons who can read and understand drafts and written directives make better industrial workers than those who cannot. Farmers who can perform simply computations and can read pamphlets are more progressive cultivators than those not so equipped. The various efforts to organize local government, create cooperatives, and generally achieve the modern technological and industrial development South Asia is striving for all have need for a high degree of literacy among the people.

Generally speaking, literacy opens avenues of communication that otherwise remain closed. It is a prerequisite for the acquisition of other skills and the development of more rational attitudes. It is true that literacy cannot be the entire purpose of education even at the elementary level. But all the other elements in the complex of changes to be accomplished by education are related to literacy, though not in a simple and clearcut way.

Another school of thought holds that what South Asia most needs is an increase in secondary education. We think this approach is wrong. To stimulate economic development it is urgent that education early become as broad-based as possible, in order to increase the number of candidates for secondary and tertiary schooling and thus raise the caliber of those selected. Such a goal is also important in order to bring about a development of the whole national community, rather than merely enclaves in a stagnant economy. In the particularly precarious situation of the larger and poorer countries of South Asia, there is, in our opinion, need for a massive effort to make the whole population literate as rapidly as possible. A marginal advance will not suffice.

Once again, when attempting to measure South Asian educational factors, we are hindered by the extremely poor quality of the statistics. The data on literacy in the region are completely unsatisfactory. To begin with, there is a good deal of uncertainty concerning the definition of literacy and its application. Ordinarily, literacy is understood to indicate an elementary ability to read and write. According to UNESCO's definition, "a person is literate who can with understanding both read and write a short simple statement on his everyday life." Although in a general way this definition is accepted, it is not very specific and there are variations in the several countries.

Even when a criterion of literacy has been spelled out, there is no assurance that the census enumerators have understood it correctly, applied it uniformly throughout the country, or are told the truth when they ask general and vague questions about a person's literacy. In general, we assume that all the literacy figures in South Asia, as in underdeveloped countries everywhere else, are inflated, some of them grossly so.

As far as the current situation is concerned, nine countries constitute three distinct groups. In the first group, Ceylon, the Philippines, and Thailand, the general level of literacy seems to be high—over 70 percent for males and over 50 percent for females. In the middle group, Burma, Malaya, and Indonesia, the sex differential is wide. Over 50 percent of males are literate, but only 25 to 40 percent of the females are. In the bottom group of Pakistan, India, and South Vietnam, the male literacy rate is only around 40 percent or less and the female rate ranges between 8 and 13 percent. The rank order of the countries by literacy again corresponds roughly with their rank by economic level. These figures should, however, be taken with great reserve. They may, even if inflated, nevertheless give a broad idea of the relative differences within the region.

In Indonesia, the steep rise in the literacy curves tends to confirm that this country, unlike the other countries of South Asia, has had some success with adult education programs, since persons in the higher age range had already passed the school age when Indonesia started developing its educational system in the 1950's. But here again, caution is needed to separate fact from hopeful thinking and national pride.

Except in Indonesia, progress in literacy has almost entirely taken place within the framework of the school system. Most of the gains in literacy have occurred in that portion of the population under 30 years of age. Again, there is the familiar difference between urban and rural populations. The countries with the lowest literacy rates have the largest rural populations. Urban males are a select group. Even in India, over 60 percent of them are counted as literate. Rural females are at the other end of the scale; even in Ceylon, the literacy rate of rural females barely exceeds 50 percent.

The achievement of literacy in one language is in many South Asian countries qualified by the need to be literate in at least one other language or local dialect. There is also the question of how many persons have mastered one or more of the Western languages. This form of literacy is vital for those who want higher education or who prepare for government service. Often the Western language of the former colonial power has become the *lingua franca*, the only language understood in all sections of a country, though only in the tiny upper and middle class.

A person may have a little ability to read and write but not enough to enable him to put his skills to practical use. In the literature, therefore, we meet with the term "functional literacy." It is extremely difficult to give this a definite meaning. Defining it as the ability to read, write, and reckon intelligently for one's own practical needs fits with common sense, but this definition is not specific enough. "Arithmetical literacy" is a vital aspect of functional literacy. From the standpoint of economic development it is at least as important as "verbal literacy." Obviously, the ability not only to read and write figures with understanding, but to use them mathematically in simple addition, subtraction and multiplication, is of importance in agriculture as well as in all industrial work. *It is a serious deficiency in the discussion of literacy that the ability to use numbers meaningfully is ignored in the literature.* No information has been collected on arithmetic skills.

It has been so difficult to measure functional literacy directly that the analysts have assumed that a specified minimum of formal education produces this literacy. UNESCO has assumed a period of four years of schooling as a minimum norm. But we question whether this period could be long enough in South Asia, where the quality of education is often very low, the attendance rate very poor, and the family home and the village milieu illiterate.

Considering the large proportion of illiterates in the region, it might have been expected that when Asian countries became independent they would have been eager to embark on vigorous literacy campaigns for adults. UNESCO has estimated that only if each year at least 10 percent of the illiterate adults were given an opportunity to take a literacy course would there be good prospects that illiteracy would be eradicated within a reasonably short time. Not only is adult education so important to furthering development, but it should also help make the education of children more effective. All the information we have suggests that children of illiterate parents tend to fall behind scholastically and in turn lapse more easily into illiteracy. The detrimental effects of an illiterate home are felt most strongly in pre-school years, when attitudes are shaped that will tend to persist.

Despite such considerations, adult education has not been given a prominent place in the plans for educational reform in South Asian countries. Indonesia may be an exception to an extent. Organizations for adult education exist also in all other countries, but they have fared poorly in competition with the established school bureaucracies for budgetary allotments. This seems to have been inadvertently aided by the international and inter-governmental agencies that have tried to help with education in South Asia since the Second World War. These organizations soon turned to the idea of "fundamental education" or "social education" which became merged with what in India and in most of the literature is called "community development."

Literacy for its own sake was said to be not enough, and education should be directed toward imparting knowledge, skills, and attitudes of practical importance. This is naturally equally relevant to teaching at all levels and in all forms. The disquieting fact is, however, that comparatively little was done to reform the schools and make them more responsive to practical needs, while adult education was either neglected altogether or turned into something so "practical" that it no longer encompassed any serious attempt to make people literate. Literacy cannot, however, be put on par with the other good purposes enumerated, as it is primarily an instrument whereby the other goals can be attained. It is, indeed, a pre-condition for more considerable success in all practical strivings.

Behind this development was the romantic and traditionalist vision of the simple but astute peasant who does not need literacy to be wise in the conduct of his own affairs. In this context the intense interest usually expressed in making the next generation literate by expanding primary education appears somewhat paradoxical. The fact that agricultural yields stubbornly refused to rise led reformers to demand more recently that community development programs place greater stress on agricultural extension work aimed at raising production, even if this would entail cutting back on "social education." The latter was actually directed mainly toward preserving or reintroducing elements of the inherited culture and providing entertainment, recreation, and general moral uplift.

There are signs, fortunately, that the post-war ideological development we refer to may have reached a turning point. The instrumental importance of literacy for education in general, and thus for economic development, was rediscovered by educational planners at the top level about a decade ago. The determination to promote more adult education, expressed in governmental pronouncements and the agreements reached in international educational conferences, constitutes a recognition of the fact that South Asia cannot afford to wait for today's school children to grow up. Practically, however, not much has resulted from this ideological change.

A great number of closely inter-related problems have to be tackled in order to make adult education an effective part of the educational system in South Asia. In both the villages and the cities, the emphasis should be on modernization, that is, on change and mobility. Literacy campaigns must aim to instill a useful degree of literacy, and efforts must be made to see that people exercise their newfound skills. Literacy should not be ruled out of the job-oriented vocational training programs for adults. In any event, those programs, on which the Food and Agriculture Organization and the International Labor Organization have been doing pioneering work, need to be integrated into general adult education programs.

Above all, adult education should not be separated from the teaching of children in the primary schools. The primary school teachers should regularly devote a portion of their time to instructing adults. Indeed, they should be encouraged to serve as local leaders in the adult education movement. However, the value of their participation depends on the extent to which they are respected as "intellectuals" in their communities, which in turn depends on their training, salaries, and social status.

We have emphasized that in the South Asian countries adult education is needed much more than in the developed countries, and that it must have a different direction and content. Consequently, it is unwise simply to take over methods from the Western countries. There is need for experimentation. The whole pattern of segregating children in the schools and then perhaps organizing "classes" for adults should be questioned. It is quite possible that a program of teaching families or communities as units would be more effective.

In any case, the schools should become civic centers and take a more active part in inducing social change. So should the colleges and universities. Their cadres of students could assume part of the burden for adult education with great benefit to their home institutions and society. A lively university extension activity would also serve to allay the aimless restlessness of so many students and guide more of them into the teaching profession.

There is need for professionalism in the organization and conduct of adult education courses, but there is also need for enthusiasm. The literacy drive must have the character of a "movement" and a "campaign." The reputed "hunger for knowledge" in the villages—like the Marxist-influenced thesis of a "revolution of rising expectations"—is largely an upper-class myth, particularly when applied to the rural districts with a traditional self-sufficiency in agriculture. Education, even when directed toward practical problems of development, does not provoke an immediate response among the people, least of all in the villages. The beginning of any educational activity must be in the creation of this response, by propaganda and by local example. People have to be conditioned to welcome educational opportunities.

A serious hindrance to the creation of more modern attitudes toward education is the great paucity of communications media and the fact that such media as do exist influence mainly the minds of those who are already functionally literate and more up to date in their thinking. As might be expected, the rank order of the South Asian countries according to communications media corresponds rather closely to their rank order based on economic levels.

Audio-visual media, where available, could be used to instruct even the illiterates. They are now used more for entertainment than for information, but even so they could often help turn attitudes in the direction of modernization. The cheapness and accessability of the transistor radio should make it an instrument in the educational campaign. Even the native art forms, such as the molam players in Laos and Thailand, could be utilized in the promotion of education.

But the most serious deficiency hampering educational efforts is the scarcity of paper for writing and for printing books and other educational material. One of the main reasons why minimum literacy is often not transformed into functional literacy and why the barely literate lapse into illiteracy is that people have nothing to read and no paper on which to write. Despite a considerable increase from the 1950's in the amount of paper for cultural use consumed per head of population in all the South Asian countries, it is still merely a tiny fraction of that in advanced countries like the United States and Sweden.

For all the South Asian countries it is a serious and flagrant deficiency in their educational programs that they have not been in a position to ensure that a substantially increased supply of paper for reading and writing will be available to support their efforts. The Conference on Pulp and Paper Development in Asia and the Far East held in Tokyo in 1960 concluded in its report that unless positive action is undertaken to encourage development of paper industries in the region, "there is a serious danger that current educational programmes will be jeopardized, the creation of an informed citizenry retarded, antiquated distribution systems retained, and industrial progress hampered."

Chapter 26

THE SCHOOL SYSTEM

The nations of South Asia, all but one of them a former colony of a Western power, started their independent lives with a school system, copied in diluted form from the metropolitan countries. The character of that system, and how it corresponded with the interests of both the colonial power and the indigenous upper strata, was briefly hinted at in Chapter 24 when we discussed the legacy from colonial times.

When independence was won the leaders in several of the South Asian countries, and in particular Jawaharlal Nehru, insisted that the entire system of education must be "revolutionized." In India Mohandas Gandhi had raised that demand for a radical change of the educational system decades prior to independence.

But this is exactly what did not happen in India or in the other South Asian countries, except to an extent in Ceylon. The principal reforms of the system as it was inherited remain largely unaccomplished even today. As one of India's distinguished educationists, J. P. Naik, expressed it in 1965: "What has happened in the last sixteen years is merely an expansion of the earlier system with a few marginal changes in content and techniques."

Without any serious attempts at reform, the inherited school system has in the main been allowed to follow a conservative *laissez-faire* line, letting a swelling stream of pupils through the established channels without interfering other than by trying to enlarge those channels where the pressure was greatest. Meanwhile, adult education, that very important complement to giving children schooling, has been largely neglected, as was pointed out in Chapter 25.

Those who can exert pressure are students and parents in the "educated" and articulate upper strata. The teachers and the school bureaucracies are also important, and on the whole conservative, forces. The inertia toward reforms is rooted in the inegalitarian economic and social stratification and the unequal distribution of power. The revolution of the school system of which Gandhi and Nehru dreamed would assume as a precondition the "social and economic revolution" of which they also spoke but which was delayed and put off for an uncertain future, while the actual development went toward increasing inequality. On the other hand, that latter revolution would assume the former one.

Indeed, even the outer structure of the school systems has been preserved. The continued domination of education at all levels through the examination system of the colleges, which prepare students for entrance into public services, has already been noted in Chapter 24. The "examination craze" reflects not only the undue influence of the tertiary institutions on the lower schools but, more primarily, the abnormal concern over status in an unegalitarian and still largely stagnant society.

As part of their colonial legacy, India and Pakistan have a large number of private schools, even at the primary level. There are no statistics as to their standards, but we know that they are more heterogeneous than public schools. Some, including those established to serve European children and those of the indigeneous top upper class—called, according to a strange English custom, "public schools"—are among the very best. Other private schools, because of the laxity of inspection, are very inferior.

The main problem created by the prevalence of private schools is a weakening of the educational authorities' direction, inspection, and control over the development of the school system. It must, for instance, be more difficult to redirect secondary education into technical and vocational lines, which is the announced policy of all South Asian countries, if the private schools continue to offer only the traditional courses. It may seem surprising, under the circumstances, that the nationalization of school systems has aroused so little interest in South Asia—the more so when we recall that many of these countries profess a socialist orientation. From a modern Western point of view the strengthening of the public school system and the discontinuance of state subsidies to private schools— particularly the denominational ones—unless they are firmly incorporated in the public school system, would seem a logical decision. Ceylon is the only country in South Asia that has taken action in this direction.

In most South Asian countries tuition fees are charged at all levels in the school system, both in private and in public schools. Many of these fees are low, partly because so many of the private schools are subsidized by the government. But it is strange to find that there has been so little constructive discussion of the fees systems. Such as they are, these discussions have most often focussed either on the desirability of an indiscriminate lowering of the fees, particularly in primary schools, or on the necessity of retaining the fees for financial reasons. Regulation of fees as a means of guiding students in a planned direction—for instance, away from general secondary schools to vocational ones—has not been raised as an issue. With all the emphasis on planning in the South Asian countries, this again illustrates how in the educational field there has, in fact, been a *laissez-faire* attitude.

Here again Ceylon is different. It has adopted the principle of free education in all schools, including those on the tertiary level, except for a very few private schools that have chosen to be unaided. More generally, education in all other South Asian countries is also gradually becoming free in those primary schools that are public.

One crucial demand for reform was from the beginning of their independence raised in all South Asian countries—namely, that the illiteracy of the masses be overcome. As, on the whole, efforts for teaching adults were pushed aside—which also, of course, was in line with the vested interests of the school bureaucracies—the literacy goal was translated into a program for rapidly enlarging the intake of children into the primary schools.

The Indian Constitution of 1950 bravely stipulated that within ten years' time compulsory, free education should be the rule for children up to fourteen years of age. In 1951 the Indonesian Government put as its goal universal elementary schooling by 1961. The other countries in South Asia were somewhat more cautious, in spite of their already having higher literacy levels, except for Pakistan, and more primary schools. But in the Karachi Plan of 1959 the ministers of education of all the Asian member states of UNESCO agreed to the provision of not less than seven years of compulsory, universal, and free primary schooling as a target for 1980.

There is no point in criticizing most of these countries for falling far behind their unrealistic targets. Their difficulties in enlarging the intakes of the primary schools are simply tremendous, particularly in the poorer countries. Generally, to provide elementary schooling for all children in South Asia is a much more burdensome project than in the developed countries. For one thing, children of school age form a much larger percentage of the population, which itself is increasing much more rapidly. For another, the South Asian countries, and particularly the poorest among them, do not have much of a foundation on which to build. They start out with a considerably smaller proportion of their children in school. And there is at the start less of everything needed to run schools: school buildings, teachers, textbooks, writing papers, etc.

But there is another and more valid criticism to make. Although the declared purpose was to give priority to the increase of elementary schooling in order to raise the rate of literacy in the population, what has actually happened is that secondary schooling has been rising much faster and tertiary schooling has increased still more rapidly. There is a fairly general tendency for planned targets of increased primary schooling not to be reached, whereas targets are over-reached, sometimes substantially, as regards increases in secondary and, particularly, tertiary schooling. This has all happened in spite of the fact that secondary schooling seems to be three to five times more expensive than primary schooling, and schooling at the tertiary level five to seven times more expensive than at the secondary level.

What we see functioning here is the distortion of development from planned targets under the influence of the pressure from parents and pupils in the upper strata who everywhere are politically powerful. Even more remarkable is the fact that this tendency to distortion from the point of view of the planning objectives is more accentuated in the poorest countries, Pakistan, India, Burma, and Indonesia, which started out with far fewer children in primary schools and which should therefore have the strongest reasons to carry out the program of giving primary schooling the highest priority. It is generally the poorest countries that are spending least, even relatively, on primary education, and that are permitting the largest distortions from the planned targets in favor of secondary and tertiary education.

. . .

The above comparisons are made on the basis of the published statistics on school enrollment. Throughout this study we complain frequently about the poor quality of the statistics on education and the questionable way in which they have been compiled and used. In Chapter 25 we pointed to the unreliability of the statistics on literacy and expressed the view that they grossly underestimated the existing illiteracy, particularly functional illiteracy.

The second main concept employed in the discussion of education in underdeveloped countries is enrollment of children in schools. It is quite commonly, innocently, and uncritically assumed in most of the literature, particularly that part of it produced by economists who have lately become interested in education as a factor in development, that the published figures for enrollment are fairly accurate and record the extent to which children attend school. Often very over-optimistic judgments about the educational situation and the recent improvement of it are based on the enrollment statistics.

The unreliability of enrollment figures may be illustrated by an example: according to the 1961 census of Pakistan less than 15 percent of the children aged five to nine attended school, while according to the enrollment statistics almost 30 percent were enrolled in the slightly different age group of six to ten years. It must also be remembered that in Pakistan pupils in primary classes attached to private secondary schools—perhaps more than 20 percent of all pupils—are not in the enrollment statistics for primary schools.

That type of statistical discrepancy is probably particularly prevalent in Pakistan, which in the South Asian region is in the bottom rank in regard to both economic levels and educational achievements. But a scrutiny reveals that very generally the enrollment statistics give an inflated account of school performances, or the extent to which children actually attend school, which is, of course, the important question.

The bias in the enrollment statistics works most strongly for primary schools and less for secondary and tertiary schools. Moreover, this bias toward inflation of the statistics on enrollment is most accentuated in the very poor countries with the least satisfactory educational situation, such as Pakistan, India, and Indonesia—which also are by far the biggest and account for the great majority of people in South Asia. Thus the published statistics tend to underestimate the existing differences between very poor and less poor countries in the region. The distinction of this actual development away from targets in disfavor of primary education becomes also in reality correspondingly greater in the very poor countries than is shown by the comparison of their enrollment figures.

Something similar is true of differentials within the individual countries. In other words, the rate of school attendance for girls, children in rural areas, and, generally, children in poorer districts becomes more inflated when measured by the enrollment statistics. If we had information on class differentials, we would undoubtedly find not only that the enrollment figures are lower for the children of the poorer families but also that their lower figures are more inflated.

The major fault of enrollment statistics is that a child who is counted as enrolled does not necessarily go to school for the whole year, or regularly, or at all. This bias is strong because both teachers and administrators want to meet targets and show results. Thus the crucial magnitudes are actual school attendance and retention rates at the end of a stage of schooling. Besides noting enrollment figures, we have based our evaluation of these on all scattered information we could find in official and unofficial literature in these countries. These estimates are, of course, extremely uncertain. But they are probably better than the figures based on the uncorrected enrollment figures. They also call attention to the really relevant problems and thus constitute a challenge to improve the official statistics.

While in India probably not many more than one child in three ever begins and completes a course of primary education, in Pakistan only one in six does. Only in Ceylon and Malaysia do the majority of children complete the primary course. Burma falls somewhere between. In the Philippines and Thailand, where relatively more children start in the first grade, the wastage percentage continues to be very high. Indonesia stands in this respect somewhat better, though not much.

Irregular attendance, repeating, and dropping out represent a huge waste of resources. If the total expenditure for primary schools were expressed in terms of cost per child who successfully completes primary school and acquires some degree of functional literacy, the cost per pupil would be much greater than is commonly accounted for. Unfortunately the cost per pupil so calculated would be particularly high in the poorer countries and the rural districts. The wastage is greater where it can be least afforded.

The laws about compulsory school enrollment and school attendance which have frequently been passed cannot remedy this situation. To begin with they cannot be applied where adequate school facilities are not made available. But apart from this they will not be obeyed and enforced where regular school attendance has not become a firm part of the mores. Parents, especially in the poorer countries and the rural areas, can find justification for keeping their children out of school in many of the long-established traditions and circumstances of living. A major justification is economic. Children have traditionally participated in work at even a tender age; they are regarded as a reserve pool of cheap manpower.

Little attention has been given to counteracting these customs. The timing of vacations is usually about the same for schools in all areas in a country, urban and rural, and at all levels. Few serious efforts seem to have been made to have vacations coincide with periods of the year when the children are most needed as helpers in the fields or as substitutes for adults in shepherding or caring for younger children. Particularly in the poorer countries and the poorer districts, a general lack of efficiency and discipline permeates the school system. When pupils have been kept out of school for a while, they become repeaters, which is often preparation for a situation in which it seems a natural thing to allow them to drop out altogether. The conditions under which they attend are poor and there is little there to encourage them to stay on.

There has been little research on the problem of irregular attendance, repetition, and dropping out. It would seem to be a most urgent task for the educational authorities in the South Asian countries to acquire comprehensive, detailed data on these problems. This is a primary requirement in any policy planning that looks toward the elimination of inefficiency and waste of resources at the very base of the school system.

Unlike many parts of the Western world, South Asia need not have a serious problem with school buildings. With the warm climate in so much of the region, it is often sufficient to set off the school premises and provide a simple shelter from sun and rain. If vacation periods were better scheduled, the difficulties would be further reduced. Where school buildings are necessary, they can be constructed from local materials and should not cost very much. This is particularly true at the primary level, where equipment needs are not so great. But if school buildings are not a problem here, the shortage of teaching supplies, of textbooks, writing paper, and all sorts of teaching aids certainly is, particularly in the poorer countries and especially in their rural districts.

The availability of adequately trained and motivated teachers is an even more crucial precondition for effective primary education. All the countries in South Asia operate with a large number of teachers classified as "untrained." Taking into account the facilities now available or planned, only the Philippines—where teacher training is given on the tertiary level—and perhaps Ceylon and Malaysia may be able, within the next decade or so, to substitute trained for untrained teachers. The teacher shortage is further complicated by the reluctance of young people to enter the teaching profession, except in Ceylon and the Philippines. In the other South Asian countries the problem is heightened by traditional attitudes toward women working outside the family household, and single women find it particularly difficult to live and work in villages.

The classification of teachers as "trained," moreover, has to be viewed with the greatest suspicion. Most of them, particularly in the poorer countries, are not well trained in any sense of the word. The trained teachers also tend to be concentrated in the cities and, more generally, in areas with high literacy. In India and still more in Pakistan, differing in varying degrees from Ceylon, the Philippines, Thailand, and even Indonesia, the salaries of teachers in primary schools are exceedingly low and their social status depressed. In turn, this has negative effects on professional recruitment and on teachers' acceptance, particularly in rural areas.

In the poorer countries in particular there is an urgent need for improvement of the teacher-training schools and, at the same time, for a rise in economic and social status of teachers in primary schools, which would encourage

talented young people to enter the profession and increase
the possibility of the teachers' influencing the children
and the community. Improving teacher training would
assume a number of things difficult to accomplish rapidly
in a poor country: better school preparation before entering the training schools, often a longer period of training,
and above all a radical reform of the curriculum and,
indeed, the whole spirit in which teachers operate. Raising the salaries meets particular difficulties in the poorer
countries, as the teachers' salaries, though so extremely
low, represent a very large percentage of total school
costs—mainly because so little is spent for equipment and
other teaching facilities.

Already at the primary level, the complex linguistic
situation in South Asian countries has serious implications
for teaching. It so happens that the two very poorest
countries, India and Pakistan, meet the greatest difficulties because of the need to teach several languages—
and scripts—in the primary schools, often by teachers
who are not very proficient in any of them. However good
the broader cultural and political reasons might be for
this multi- or bi-lingualism of the schools in these very
large countries, where the hope for national consolidation
and popular participation in government must assume it,
it has rightly been called a "roadblock to educational
progress." As Edmund J. King puts it, "the curriculum of
any child is bound to be congested on the linguistic side
before anything else is learned."

The schools are for this reason becoming much too
"bookish," even though very few books and little writing
paper are available to the pupils. This tends to strengthen
an evil tradition from colonial and pre-colonial time that
we noted in Chapter 24. In India, Gandhi's intention to
make the curriculum more oriented to the life in the
community and to incorporate elements of manual work
has not been successful. And the "basic schools," representing a diluted form of Gandhi's proposals, that have

been kept going as part of the primary school system are mostly shunned by the upper class families.

Putting together all that has been mentioned, in the poorer countries and the poorer districts, where by far the greatest number of children in South Asia grow up, the situation in regard to primary education must be described as almost desperate. Even when the schools are attended by the children until the end of the primary course, they do not prepare for development but continue to educate for stagnation and poverty.

As we have already noted, the number of pupils in secondary schools has been rising faster than that in primary schools. With the exception of Malaya and Indonesia, at least half of the primary school graduates are entering secondary schools. These have almost entirely remained "general" schools of the colonial type.

The situation in secondary schools begins with the serious handicap that the pupils have generally not been given satisfactory preparation. This handicap is greater in the countries where the extent of primary schooling is five years or less—that is, in Pakistan, most of India, and Burma.

The barrier to effective teaching created by the linguistic complexities becomes even more serious in secondary schools. In addition to indigenous languages, at least one Western language is often required. Even today it would be almost impossible to administer any of the South Asian countries except Thailand, Burma, and perhaps Indonesia without recourse to a foreign language. The official indigenous languages are linguistically underdeveloped; complex concepts, especially in the technical and scientific fields, cannot be expressed in these languages. As in the primary schools, language study crowds other subjects out of the curriculum and proficiency in languages becomes the yardstick of educational achievement. This is one reason why it has proved so difficult to transform the "general," "academic" schools, inherited from the colonial era, into schools of a more practical type.

No statistics are available on the physical equipment of secondary schools—buildings, libraries, science laboratories, and teaching aids, especially textbooks and writing paper. Judging from general impressions and scattered information in the literature, such equipment is, if not sufficient, at least superior in both quantity and quality to that of primary schools. Secondary schools are more often to be found in urban areas, and their pupils come mostly from the upper class in a somewhat broad sense of the term. Still another impression is that the standards for physical equipment, as well as for the qualifications of teachers, though generally low, are considerably higher in the countries that are on a higher economic level—especially Ceylon and Malaya—and, even in the poorer countries, in those private schools that cater mainly to the children of the top upper class.

Considering also the damaging traditions inherited from colonial times, the poorly prepared pupils entering secondary schools, the largely unqualified and frustrated teaching staffs, and often the extraordinary burdens of teaching several languages and scripts, it should not be surprising that the teaching in most secondary schools in South Asia, particularly in the larger and poorer countries, does not measure up to high standards. One dynamic factor holding back efforts to improve teaching in the secondary schools is the unprecedented and unplanned rapid increase of students in secondary schools. Particularly in the poorer countries and the poorer districts, this expansion has tended to imply the lowering of already low standards in teaching.

One specific problem that demands attention is the character—and the bias—of the textbooks; this problem is of particular importance in the secondary schools. After seeing some hundreds of textbooks in various South Asian countries and making a cursory study of the fairly extensive collection of school manuals at the International Bureau of Education in Geneva, we judge that only very slowly are their books being adapted to present-day needs. The "foreignness" of the books stems in part from the syllabuses, which to a surprising extent are survivals from colonial times. In part it also reflects the scarcity of writers who can compose textbooks without relying heavily on the foreign tradition. Not only do the textbooks have a strong flavor of "foreignness"; they are also out of touch with the modern world.

It is, of course, risky to draw conclusions based on impressions from a random and cursory sampling. But the evidence available seems to indicate that there is little purposeful orientation of the secondary schools toward building a modern and national, but also rational, culture, with potentials for further development. Changing to an indigenous language as the medium of instruction has scarcely improved matters.

Considering all this, it should not be surprising that the teaching in most secondary schools in South Asia does not measure up to high standards. In its outspoken 1958 report, the Indian Secondary Education Committee offered a good general summary of criticism of secondary schooling in the region. Since then little has been done to meet these criticisms. The rapid expansion of secondary schooling has tended to lower the quality level still more. The Committee found as follows:

　(i) the present curriculum is narrowly conceived,
　(ii) it is bookish and theoretical,
　(iii) it is overcrowded, without providing rich and significant contents,
　(iv) it makes inadequate provision for practical and other kinds of activities which should reasonably find room in it, if it is to educate the whole of the personality,

(v) it does not cater to the various needs and capacities of the adolescents,

(vi) it is dominated too much by examinations, and

(vii) it does not include technical and vocational subjects which are so necessary for training the students to take part in the industrial and economic development of the country.

One important aspect of this situation is the fact that in spite of all efforts in the post-war period to orient teaching to practical life, to impart useful skills, and in particular to give more emphasis to practical, vocational, and technical training, the great majority of secondary schools have retained, as we already noted, the "general," "academic," and "literary" character established in the elite type of upper-class education in colonial times. This has happened to the extent that in accounting for the statistics on secondary education we could mostly disregard other types of schools.

In no country of the region are there signs that a radical change is under way. The increase in vocational and technical school enrollment—though generally somewhat larger in percentage terms—has been small in terms of absolute numbers. And almost nowhere has the curriculum of the general secondary schools, where the larger part of the expansion has continually taken place, been modernized in any appreciable manner. This may seem astonishing as in this respect there has been unanimous agreement among political leaders as well as experts that a radical change was needed; even before independence in British India such a demand had been raised in official reports for almost a century. The explanation of this conservatism has a number of elements.

Some of them we have already noted: the influences in this direction of the colleges and the examinative system; the actual need for further preparatory general education of the pupils entering secondary schools, particularly in the poorer countries with the shorter duration and often lower effectiveness of their primary schools; the tendency of language study to crowd other subjects out of the curriculum, again particularly in the poorer countries. An important additional difficulty is the scarcity of persons who can teach technical subjects, particularly as they are also needed in government and industry, where they can expect higher salaries and social status than as school teachers. Moreover, instruction in science and technical and vocational subjects mostly requires costly laboratories and other special teaching aids.

Added to all this is the heavy weight of tradition. It is strengthened by the vested interests of all those employed in the school system, most of whom have good reasons of their own to resist change in the light of which their training and methods would seem less desirable. More fundamentally, the dominating upper class, who are the "educated," feel a vested interest in maintaining the cleft between them and the masses. The fact that a more practical and vocational orientation of the secondary schools would often require participation in manual work, which is despised, and that the schools would presumably prepare students for jobs where manual work is part of the regular routine, helps make such schools less popular than the traditional general ones.

The result is a persistent lack at the middle level of industrial management of trained personnel who do not insist upon being merely desk men. Those graduates from the general secondary schools who do not continue to study at the tertiary level, but who in the colonial tradition seek work as "clerks," are usually not even trained to meet modern requirements for that type of employment, as they have no knowledge of shorthand, typing, filing, etc.

The situation is almost nowhere improving. As a recent Indian report notes: "The maladjustment between the education system and the socio-economic needs of our developing economy has further increased. A result of this has been the increase in the number of educated unemployed side by side with the shortage of trained personnel."

The expansion of tertiary education has generally been even more accentuated, not least in the poorer countries. Again, tertiary education is suffering from insufficient preparation in the secondary schools, particularly in the poorer countries where the secondary schools are handicapped by the shorter duration of primary schools and generally lower levels of efficiency of both primary and secondary schools. The linguistic difficulties are still more compounded on the tertiary level, where functional ability to read a foreign language is needed, though this need is seldom met in a satisfactory way.

In spite of huge investments in buildings, libraries, laboratories, equipment, and teaching aids, the extraordinarily rapid increase of students in these countries tends to perpetuate low standards and, indeed, often reduces them further. The quality of academic teachers is low and has often tended to deteriorate. More than the secondary schools, the tertiary schools have a very high wastage percentage of students who never graduate.

At the tertiary level even more than at the secondary, the schools should, of course, be job oriented and directed toward preparing the students for particular professions. Practically all experts, South Asian and foreign alike, are unanimous in complaining, however, that the tertiary schools continue to produce an oversupply of "generalists," who have been trained in the humanities, law, the social sciences, and "academic" natural science, and who swell the ranks of underqualified administrators, clerks, and "educated unemployed," supported by their families while pressing for enlargement of the publicly employed. At the same time, more engineers, agricultural technicians, doctors, dentists, pharmacologists, and, not least, teachers on all levels are needed. This holds true in all South Asian countries.

The difficulties in changing the structure of higher education to meet development needs more adequately are similar to those already mentioned that hinder the efforts to make secondary schools vocational or at least more practical and less "academic": the higher costs of all technical education in terms of equipment, and the difficulty of recruiting the teachers in competition with government and industry. The tertiary schools, which usually charge high fees, have additionally a financial interest in increasing their enrollments in arts and law, where the marginal costs per student are low. Underlying all these causal factors, and inherited from colonial times, are the traditional ideas of what upper-class elite education should amount to.

One theme that has been recurring through the preceding account of the educational situation in South Asia is the rather close correlation between the economic level of a country and its achievements in regard to its schools.

The two small and less poor countries, Ceylon and Malaya, are now well on the way to giving the whole child population a primary education of six years. Ceylon in particular is increasing the number of pupils who also receive a secondary education. Starting out with relatively higher literacy rates, they are now approaching general literacy in the younger generations. This should make it more possible to eradicate that serious obstacle to equality and development which has as its basis the disdain for manual work on the part of the "educated." Where being educated is no longer a monopoly of a small upper class it should be easier to dissolve that class barrier based on who performs manual work and who does not soil his hands.

After the war Ceylon and Malaya started out with a

quantitatively less developed system of tertiary education and a smaller percentage of high-school graduates continuing in tertiary schools, which, however, were generally on a high level. They also relied relatively more on sending students abroad for tertiary education. Both these countries are now rapidly building up their tertiary schools and keeping them at a rather high standard. As relatively more children receive secondary education, they are thus on the way to breaking through the wall of the upper-class monopoly of higher education. Ceylon in particular has taken a very important step toward democratizing education by making it free on all levels.

On the whole, however, they have as yet not been much more successful than the poorer countries in changing the tertiary, and still less the secondary, education from the "general" to the practical and job-oriented type. Even their primary education has a curriculum that is unduly "academic." Undoubtedly a change away from the traditional general orientation of instruction in schools on all three levels, if it were courageously followed, would speed up the eradication of the prejudice against manual work.

Except for these two small and less poor countries, the vast majority of children in South Asia either receive no schooling at all or terminate their schooling before they have established a lasting functional literacy. The Philippines and Thailand should, however, be able to emulate Ceylon and Malaya if they succeed in decreasing the rapid and continuous wastage of dropouts. Indonesia, though relatively poorer, is somewhat better placed in regard to primary schooling, being the one country where, in spite of exceedingly inferior levels of planning and policy generally, there has been relatively more popular enthusiasm for educational improvement.

The Philippines in particular excels in being able to give a very large part of its youth secondary and tertiary education. Though not always of high quality, this greater supply in the labor market of the relatively better "educated" should, in turn, counteract their unwillingness to do manual work. Dating back to the colonial era under the United States, the Philippines has also striven to give teachers and schools a higher economic and social status and a more central position in the life of the local communities, has shown more intent in attempts to improve and modernize teaching, particularly on the primary level, and has even made a little more advance in adult education than all other countries in the region except Indonesia.

Though all these countries mentioned have policy problems in education not yet solved, the problems are compounded and magnified in the poorest countries of the region, Pakistan, India, and Burma. Together they contain by far the largest part of the population in the region. In considering hereafter the policy conclusions we shall have this larger and poorer part of the region in mind primarily, but in various particular questions many of the conclusions will have bearing also on the other countries mentioned.

Part of the basic explanation of the less fortunate educational situation of the poorer countries is simply and directly their poverty. There are fewer resources to place at the disposal of educational advance. But the problem is more complicated. These countries—with the exception of Burma—are also more inegalitarian, with wider chasms between an educated upper class and the masses.

There is a causal interrelation between poverty and inequality. Monopoly of education is—together with monopoly of ownership of land—the most fundamental basis of inequality, and it retains its hold more strongly in the poorer countries. It does so even when attempts are made to widen the availability of popular education. The mechanism is the class bias that operates in wastage, which in the poorer countries is also greater: dropping out, repetition, failure to retain children to the end of primary courses, and, at higher levels, failures in examinations.

Among the fewer children in the poor countries who begin in the first grade of primary school, girls, children from rural areas, and generally children from the more disadvantaged families are less well represented. Irregular attendance, repeating, and dropping out then occur most frequently in these categories. Only a small percentage of all children complete primary school, which is, as we have seen, ordinarily of shorter duration and lower quality in these poorer countries and particularly so in the poorer districts.

Thus, even at this early stage of education, a severe process of selection is at work which, on the whole, tends to exclude in particular children from the less privileged groups. This helps to explain why in these countries such a high proportion of those children who finish primary school can go on to secondary school. The dropouts in secondary schools and later the failures in graduation examinations imply a further selection along the same line. Of the still smaller proportion of an age group who graduate, again the majority enter tertiary schools. Once more the pattern is repeated: the relatively fewer students from families in the lower social and economic strata are more often dropouts or fail more often in the examinations for graduation from the tertiary schools.

In this mechanism of selection there are several economic and social operative factors at work. One major set of factors is economic. Although primary education is supposedly becoming free, there are often incidental costs of various sorts. The need to use the children for work is, of course, more strongly felt in poor families. At the secondary and still more at the tertiary levels the system of tuition fees continues to be of importance.

The economic deterrents to the schooling of poor children operate in a social setting that in many other ways tends to perpetuate the upper-class monopoly of education. Since lower-class parents usually have had little or no education and are illiterate, they tend to have less interest in seeking education for their children. The talk of the "hunger for education" in the villages is largely a romantic illusion, most of all in the poorest countries of the region—though undoubtedly there are exceptions.

For the vast majority of lower-class children who do attend school, the home environment is not conducive to educational progress. The family lives crowded in a shack, usually without a table or a chair; reading and writing rarely have a place in family life and the materials are not available; when the sun sets there is no light, especially in the poorer rural districts. As a factor in school success, the difference in the home environment of the very few well-to-do and "educated" families and that of the enormous number of lower-class families is tremendous. It is far greater than in the advanced countries. Even if the schools were excellent, there would still be serious problems of inducing the children to enter school, to remain in school, and to succeed.

The result is an inbuilt bias strongly favoring the upper class and fortifying its monopoly of education. Professor P. C. Mahalanobis states: ". . . the power and privileges of a small group of people at the top tend to be not only preserved but strengthened. . . . This has created an influential group of people who naturally desire to maintain their privileged position and power."

J. P. Naik concludes: "Educational development . . . is benefitting the 'haves' more than the 'have-nots.' This is a negation of social justice."

The excellent Indian *Report of the Education Commission* (*1964–66*) stressed: "The social distance between the rich and the poor, the educated and the uneducated, is large and is tending to widen . . . education itself is tending to increase social segregation and widen class distinctions. . . . What is worse, this segregation is . . .

tending to widen the gulf between the classes and the masses."

The situation is not different, but worse, in Pakistan, though there is less sophisticated discussion of it. Both these countries have a small highly-educated upper-class elite; at the same time the masses in these countries have had little or no education and do not get much now. The ignorance of the masses stands as a complex of serious inhibitions and obstacles for economic development holding these countries down in poverty. At the same time, the harsh inequality in these countries—stratified and strengthened through the continuing virtual monopoly of the upper class on education—tends to emasculate reforms meant to democratize education.

In this and the foregoing chapter we have seen this mechanism of upper-class power over educational policy and development in operation: in contradiction to the announced aims, adult education has been played down; the more expensive secondary and, in particular, tertiary education has been permitted to expand at the expense of primary education; the reform efforts to make schools on all levels less "general," and, on the two higher levels, more practical, technical, and job-oriented, have been frustrated. Before going on to enumerate the main policy conclusions, which have already been anticipated in the statements on deficiencies, we have needed to stress the operation of the mechanism of upper-class power over education in a very inegalitarian society where the masses are very poor.

Educational reforms are most needed there, but there they also meet the greatest inhibitions and obstacles. So little power belongs to the poverty-stricken masses, and these masses remain inarticulate and passive. Neither individually or collectively are they alert to the need for educational reform. Like the idea of "the revolution of rising expectations," their "hunger for education" is largely a rationalization—a reflection of how well-to-do

Westerners or South Asians would react if they had to live in such miserable conditions.

One major conclusion is the need for radical change in the entire educational system. As the comprehensive and penetrating Indian *Report of the Education Commission* (*1964–66*) stresses: "Indian education needs a drastic reconstruction, almost a revolution. . . . This calls for a determined and large-scale action. Tinkering with the existing situation, and moving forward with faltering steps and lack of faith can make things worse than before." This holds true for Pakistan and Burma as well as India, and also, though less emphatically, for the middle group—Thailand, Indonesia, and the Philippines.

Much of the current efforts to integrate educational policy in the plans by stressing the need for graduates in various occupations has been rather pointless. It has even tended to draw attention away from the major development interest in raising rapidly the level of functional literacy of the whole population. What is now most urgently needed is planning of education itself as an integrated whole.

Effective reform of the educational system must assume a firm government control of educational institutions. There is no point in devising any over-all plan for the development of the educational system unless the government exerts its authority to ensure realization of the plan. In the region, only Ceylon is now on the way to solving this problem.

The first requirement is to maintain and raise the quality of education and, in any case, to prevent an expansion that is not real or that is detrimental to quality standards; such expansions have been the rule during the whole independence era. As *The Fourth Five Year Plan: A Draft Outline* (1966) points out: "The expansion of numbers . . . has been accompanied by a certain measure of deterioration in quality. . . . It is obvious that in the immediate future larger and more effective attention has to be paid to factors like consolidation, quality, diversification, terminalisation, and work orientation than has been the case so far."

The second requirement, which largely concurs with the first, is the need to keep a balance between the three stages of education and, in particular, to give reality to the priority that primary education has been awarded in the programmatic pronouncements. This requirement should imply calling a halt to the more rapid increase in enrollment in secondary and tertiary schools or even decreasing it.

Inasmuch as the secondary and tertiary schools produce an over-supply of "generalists," there is no reason why technical, vocational, and professional training should not be increased substantially within the present or even a somewhat smaller secondary and tertiary school system—thereby providing more teachers, agricultural extension workers, and medical personnel, to point to only a few of the fields where more trained young people are urgently needed. Fewer admissions to the secondary and tertiary schools should also make it possible to maintain higher entrance requirements and thereby decrease the wastage of repetition, dropouts, and failures on that level. It should generally permit the attainment of higher-quality standards by these schools.

More resources should then become available for primary education. But even so, and considering in particular the present scarcity of well-trained teachers, serious consideration should be given to reducing for a time even the pressure to increase the number of children who enter the first grade of primary schools. Two interrelated purposes should then be easier to attain: the raising of the miserably low quality and quantity of all physical educational facilities in primary schools, and the intensification of exertions to decrease the tremendous wastage of dropouts and repetitions. Both these deficiencies are greatest in rural areas. As the Indian *Report of the Education Commission (1964–66)* stresses: ". . . the most important programme to be implemented at the primary stage during the next ten years is to improve the quality of education and to reduce stagnation and wastage to the minimum."

This reduction of the increase in the intake in primary schools should, however, only be temporary. It should turn into a new vigorous expansion as soon as the contraction and changing direction of secondary and tertiary schools has resulted in increased resources for primary schools, especially in an increased number of better-prepared teachers, and as soon as real advances have been made in reducing that enormous leakage in the primary school system that is caused by repetitions and dropouts. If it were prolonged, it would increase the time many poorer districts would have to wait for opportunities to send children to primary schools.

Lower tuition fees and increased financial aid to poor students must be part of the educational reform. This would intensify pressure for admission to the secondary and tertiary schools. As a result—and particularly if, at the same time, attempts were made to slow down the very rapid rise in total enrollment in such schools—the selection of students would have to be based on stricter criteria. The problem thus facing educational reformers is how to develop more exacting examinations and yet liberate the schools from the deadening influence of the inherited examination system. It will be a formidable task to enforce rational directives to accomplish this in countries where the articulate strata attach extraordinary importance to the symbols of status acquired by taking examinations—diplomas, degrees, honors, and passing grades. Such a task assumes a radical change in the spirit of all educational institutions and a changed outlook on life and work in the entire society. However, a change in the examination system is of paramount importance, not only for the functioning of a more democratic selection process, but for reforms in the orientation and content of education at all levels.

Throughout South Asia, and not only in that larger part of the region which is very poor and is least advanced in primary education, there is in addition a need for vigorous efforts in adult education, in order both to speed the rise in functional literacy and to support the exertion to keep children in primary schools and prevent their relapse into illiteracy. These efforts should be closely related to and, indeed, be an extension of the activity in the schools.

A crucial task in the reform of the school system must be to increase the number and qualifications of trained teachers. The Indian Education Commission's report of 1966 continually stresses that a supreme aim of education should be to change the attitudes of the children and, ultimately, of the whole people—"the values of the people as a whole." This would be a hopeless task without teachers who are not only satisfied with their economic and social conditions and are accepted as intellectual and moral leaders in their communities, but who are also dedicated, enthusiastic, and imbued with the zeal to disseminate useful and practical knowledge and with the will to advance.

From this point of view the institutions for teacher training are strategically important in educational reform. They should be the "power plants" that generate moral and intellectual energy among the students to prepare the people for development. Popular enthusiasm will have to be built up into a "movement" if the forces to accomplish these improvements are to gather. The lead should come from persons in the articulate, educated higher strata who have been the harbingers of the modernization ideals.

Enough such leaders must come forward to break the short-sighted selfish interests of the upper class. Ultimately the educational reforms must be pressed for by the masses of the people. Is such a break possible in these inegalitarian poor countries? Even though it would be possible to reach broad agreement in general terms on every point in the reform program sketched above, there is in the power structure of these countries a built-in resistance to reforms.

The already quoted Indian Education Commission of 1966 asked for "determined and large-scale action" along basically the lines presented above. It stressed that its report was "not a substitute for action," and concluded: ". . . the future of the country depends largely upon what is done about education during the next ten years or so." Since the Commission's report was published, the trend in Indian planning and policies has not gone in the direction it recommended. This report, like so many other reports that in the great tradition from the British time have been worked out and published in this and many other fields, has been applauded but then laid aside. The trend in Indian planning and policy has not gone in the direction of meeting the needs for radical reform of its educational system. Nothing very different has happened in the other extremely poor countries in South Asia.

Chapter 27

PREMISES

Throughout the preceding chapters of this book we have presented the social and economic factors and conditions that affect South Asia's attempt to move from underdevelopment to development by means of planning for that development. "Development" means the process of moving away from "underdevelopment," of rising out of poverty; it is sought and perhaps actually attained by means of "planning for development." What is actually meant in characterizing a country as "underdeveloped" is that there is in that country a constellation of numerous undesirable conditions for work and life: outputs, incomes, and levels of living are low; many modes of production, as well as attitudes and behavioral patterns, are disadvantageous; and there are unfavorable institutions ranging from those at the state level to those governing social and economic relations in the family and the neighborhood. They are evaluated as undesirable or unfavorable from the standpoint of the desirability of "development"—a characterization afflicted with vagueness but definite enough to permit its use. There is a general causal relationship among all these conditions, so that they form a social system. "Development" means the movement upwards of that whole system.

It is the task of a study of underdevelopment and development to determine the relationship between conditions within the social system. The social systems consist of a great number of conditions that are causally interrelated, in that a change in one will cause changes in the others. We have broadly categorized these conditions as output and incomes, conditions of production, levels of living, attitudes toward life and work, institutions, and policies. The first two are certainly "economic factors," while attitudes toward life and work and institutions are "non-economic"; levels of living are ordinarily excluded from the "economic" plans, except as a general goal for planning. Policies are a mixture, though when policies are aimed at inducing changes in the economic conditions, they belong to the economic factors. However, in a social system there is no up and down, no primary and secondary. Economic conditions do not have precedence over the others. The demonstration and analysis of the interdependence that pervades the system could just as well have been made from another angle; and the conditions could have been classified in different categories and in a different order. Such a classification would have covered the same social reality and would have had the same analytical content.

These various conditions are characterized as *undesirable or unfavorable* in South Asia, because a one-way change in them is deemed desirable for engendering and sustaining development, the movement of the whole social system upward. By "upward" is meant in the direction of greater desirability from the development point of view; by "downward" is meant a movement that is undesirable for development. We have further assumed that a change of direction in one condition will tend to change the others in the same direction, upward or downward.

In the preceding chapters we have shown that one of

the most important general characteristics of underdevelopment in South Asian countries is the low average labor productivity. Consequently, there is a low national product per member of the labor force. And on the other side of this situation is a low national income per worker or per head of the population. With a number of qualifications, this can be taken as an imperfect indication of the level of underdevelopment in a country. It is not, however, a definition of "underdevelopment," nor can its upward change be used as a definition of "development."

Conditions of production are another factor that affect the structure of an economy and the direction and intensity of change. The industrial sector, as we have shown, is small, particularly in organized large-scale industry. In all other sectors, but especially in agriculture, crafts, and traditional industry, techniques of production are primitive and capital intensity is low. The ratio of savings to income is also low. Savings per head is lower still. There is little enterprise, particularly in long-term productive investments. The overhead capital in the form of roads, railways, ports, power plants, and so forth is inadequate. Labor utilization is low in regard to worker participation and duration of work and also in labor efficiency.

These conditions are directly related to each other in the one-directional way mentioned above. Thus the low savings ratio tends to keep down the formation of capital. Crude production techniques are partly the result of low capital per man. The distribution of labor is faulty, in that too many are occupied in relatively unproductive activities. In turn, low labor input and efficiency are in part a result of primitive techniques and lack of capital.

We have catalogued the low levels of living for most people in the countries of South Asia. These low levels manifest specific deficiencies: insufficient food, bad housing, poor public and private hygiene and medical care, insufficient facilities for vocational and professional instruction, and education in general. These low levels of living are caused mostly by low levels of productivity and income, and low levels of living cause low efficiency of labor.

In another section of this causal circle, South Asian attitudes toward life and work are deficient from the development point of view. Levels of work dicipline are low. So are punctuality and orderliness. There are many irrational outlooks and superstitious beliefs, as well as a lack of alertness, adaptability, and ambition. There is a low readiness for experiment and change. There is contempt for manual work in certain classes and a submissiveness to authority and exploitation in others. Added to these is an unreadiness for deliberate and sustained birth control. The steep and accelerating rise in population in most South Asian countries is a principal cause of poverty, and birth control is the only means of checking this trend.

In the opposite direction, these undesirable attitudes and patterns of performance in life and at work are all, to some extent, a function of the low levels of living and thus, indirectly, of output and income, at the same time they are a cause. Here is another causal relationship crucial for the explanation of underdevelopment.

It has been our premise that there must be an institutional approach to the problems of moving from underdevelopment to development through planning for development. But there are a number of institutional conditions in South Asian states that are unfavorable for economic development. The system of land tenure is detrimental to agricultural improvement. Agencies to promote enterprise, employment, trade, and credit are underdeveloped. Some nations have not yet consolidated their diverse elements into a unified state. Some have government agencies that lack the needed authority. And there are low standards of efficiency and integrity in public administration, all of which combine to constitute a "soft state." At the root of these institutional debilities is a low degree of popular participation and a rigid, inegalitarian social stratification.

All these institutional deficiencies are closely inter-related with deficiencies in public attitudes. These attitudes generally support institutions and at the same time are supported by them. Both share responsibility for low levels of productivity and low incomes. These latter two in turn perpetuate low levels of literacy and education, and these perpetuate deficiencies in communal institutions.

In the absence of policies, a social system would, as a result of primary changes and the interaction of all the conditions we have discussed above, either stagnate, develop to a higher level, or regress to a lower level. But if there is planning, there is a coordination of policies in order to attain or speed up development.

Allowing for the differences between and within the various communities, which we have laid out earlier in this book, all the South Asian countries regard themselves as "underdeveloped." This is important, because the people's desire for development, or at least the desire of their leaders, implies an interest in changing the conditions that affect their development. Unlike climate and natural resources, these conditions are not fixed. They can be changed by policies—by governmental and institutional action.

These conditions are, in this sense, all "social." And the social sciences today do not reckon with inborn differences in capacities or aptitudes between the people of South Asia and those in the rich Western or Communist countries. Hereditary differences in physical and mental makeup that would contribute to a low level of development cannot be excluded. But these have not, so far, been demonstrated. Our analysis assumes that the people in these countries are not, by nature, different from those who have had a more fortunate economic fate. Their circumstances are simply the result of different conditions of living and working, both now and in the past.

When we have characterized these conditions as undesirable for an underdeveloped country, we have done so simply from the point of view of the concrete development goals of that country—or, more precisely, the goals of those in that country who decide policy. In particular, a moralistic attitude toward a country's conceptions of life and work and community institutions has had no place in our analysis.

Although our interest has been focussed on the underdeveloped countries in the South Asian region, the interdependence of various conditions of life and work is, of course, a general characteristic of organized society and thus present in every national community, however highly developed. But a low level of development has, as we have stressed, important consequences not only for the character but also for the strength of that interdependence. Our assumption of an entire social system of interdependent conditions has, for this reason, much greater relevance in South Asia.

Primary changes in a social system can be caused from the outside—by a good or a bad monsoon that affects crops, or by economic measures applied by a foreign country. Or they can be internally induced by policy measures taken within the country in an effort to improve one or several unfavorable conditions. We have defined development as the upward movement of the whole social system. But for the purposes of planning, we need an immediate *indication* of development that is easier to ascertain and measure than this ideal index. The natural choice for such an indicator is to measure the growth of national product or income per head of population. There is a basic interdependence of all conditions in the social system and a dominant importance of personal incomes in setting levels of living. We have assumed that these levels of living are important, affecting attitudes, patterns of behavior, and institutions. We in turn know that if these latter conditions do not change, or if they lag very much, this will show up by preventing productivity and incomes from rising. Yet a change in the national income per head can never be used as more than a rough and ready indicator of that more complex change in the entire social system that we really want to record. Nor should the use of a magnitude such as income per head as an indicator be permitted to cause undue concentration on the more easily accessible economic conditions, which could bias the choice of changes to be induced in the system. In the final analysis, we have insisted that development is always a human problem.

A major part of the work on planning for development in South Asia has been hindered by the assumption that beginning analysis can be concentrated on the economic conditions—output and incomes, conditions of production, and levels of living—plus those policies that affect only these conditions. Frequently, even levels of living are ignored. There is also the assumption that the chain of causes linking these economic conditions is not affected by attitudes and institutions. Instead, it is often assumed that the latter will automatically be highly responsive to changes in the economic conditions.

In reality, attitudes and institutions are stubborn and not easily changed, least of all indirectly. Policies, on the other hand, represent induced changes in the causal circle, applied to one or several of the economic and social categories; planning means coordination of policies to attain or speed up development.

Prima facie the causal interdependence would seem to indicate a highly unstable social system where the force of change in one direction would move other conditions in the same direction. But in sharp contrast to this expectation are not only the common experience of low-level equilibrium in underdeveloped countries and the serious obstacles to development policies, but more generally the astonishing stability of most social systems in history. Balance, instead of being the fortuitous result of an obviously unstable combination of forces, seems to be the rule, not the rare exception. All our evidence suggests that social stability and equilibrium is the norm and all societies, particularly underdeveloped societies, possess institutions of a strongly stabilizing character. In view of these findings the real mystery is how they can escape from equilibrium and can develop.

In the case of many underdeveloped countries the reactions of other conditions to a change in any one of them are seldom instantaneous. Usually they are delayed, often for a considerable period. Sometimes there is no reaction at all in some of the conditions, and this becomes more important if it happens at an early stage so that circular causation is stopped. Thus a peasant who has the opportunity to cultivate more land or raise yields through technology may not grasp these opportunities if he has no ambition to raise his level of living. Certain other institutional conditions, such as unfavorable land tenure laws, may be such that there is no inducement to this peasant to exert himself.

The existence in South Asia of genuine "back-slopers" of this type has been questioned. But there can be no doubt that in the traditional setting of South Asian societies (except to an extent that of the ethnic Chinese) many people are only survival minded. They strive for nothing other than to preserve their customary low levels of living. As always, attitudes and institutions support each other. Even apart from this, there can be other delays in the effects of changes in conditions. Improved nutrition, for example, should improve labor efficiency. But its major effects may not be felt for years, until a new generation that enjoyed this improved nutrition from childhood enters the labor force. Even if education levels are raised, attitudes and community institutions may remained unchanged if inequality prevails and the nation remains a "soft state." These factors of inertia prevent or delay development because the circle of causes moves upward only when there is interaction by all elements of the social system—when a change in one condition is ultimately followed by a feedback of secondary impulses which in the end cause a further change in the original condition great enough to move it even further.

Planning must not only start and sustain impulses, but also speed up the responses if stability or stagnation is to be transformed into a cumulative upward movement. But the chances of this happening are also reduced if there are other changes working simultaneously in the opposite direction.

All South Asian countries are pursuing development policies, with varying effectiveness. Most are receiving grants or loans from Western or Communist countries or both. When this aid is large enough, and other policy-induced changes are great enough, there should be an upward movement of the circle. But this would be more likely to happen if the governments of South Asia were wise enough and had enough courage to act against the rigid and unequal social structures and attitudes. Because if these are not changed, they may nullify all the other efforts, including the aid.

Other forces, besides these forces of inertia, are also occurring, independently and at the same time as the development policies. Some of these tend to drag the social system downward. The most important of these is the population explosion. If it continues in South Asia, it may in time become the dominant influence in the social system. It could make futile all the powerful intensification of development policies and foreign aid that may be attempted. Another counteracting force, as we have noted, is the deteriorating trade position of most South Asian countries because of the slackening demand for their exports while their import needs are rising.

The opportunity for movement in an interlocking social

system offers the basis for what hope there now is that the underdeveloped countries of South Asia may lift themselves up. But there are exceptions to the general rules when the secondary changes actually move the system in a direction opposite that expected from the primary change. It is not difficult to imagine numerous counteracting changes resulting from development. The provision of irrigation works, for example, may lead to a destruction of soils if adequate attention is not given to drainage. Schooling may actually have a negative economic result if educational policy does not prevent the newly educated from believing they are too good to soil their hands. Government controls may foster increased corruption if vigilance is not applied. New legislation that is not enforced may breed cynicism.

In most cases where a change upward produces instead a downward change in other conditions, however, more purposeful planning could have prevented this regression. Rarely are such secondary effects likely if the planners are circumspect and the government is prepared to act with determination.

Behind any general discussion of planning there is the concept of an ideal, or optimal, plan. In theory we should be able to construct the ideal plan by choosing the policies that would produce the maximum upward change in the social system. To determine this, we would have to have a full knowledge of all conditions in that system, including attitudes and government policies. We would also need full knowledge of their interdependence, as well as a sound valuation of what conditions were good. We would have to attach definite independent valuations to the changes in conditions that, directly and/or indirectly, are the result of the execution of the plan. Although this ideal situation is virtually impossible to obtain, this should not rule out the notion of an ideal plan. To approximate and simplify is legitimate in all scientific endeavor and it is equally so in planning for development.

One difficulty is that the broad value premises we hold—the post-war ideals—can only be presented with considerable vagueness. Nevertheless, they do permit us without much ambiguity to classify conditions and their changes as broadly "desirable" or "undesirable" from a development point of view.

Another difficulty is that a plan is fundamentally a political program. It has to be produced in terms of the government's valuations. These valuations, on some points, may be different from those of this study. The government itself is a part of the social system from which a plan cannot be separated. Moreover, a social system, including the attitudes of the government and the people, can change in the midst of a plan as a result of following the plan itself. The attitudes of the people and their institutions can represent obstacles to a plan. No government is entirely free to follow its own subjective valuations.

But obstacles raised by the population should not pose a logical difficulty. In principle they are no different from the climate or the other obstacles that planning must take into account. Planning must, however, also consider the inhibitions of the government and its leaders. Those responsible for directing planning and the implementing of planning are never wholly disinterested or socially detached. They themselves are part of the social system that is to be reformed. This tends to influence and sometimes to limit their vision. But the remarkable thing about the spread of the desire for planning and development among the articulate members of the South Asian national communities is not that they are unable to free themselves entirely from these attitudes and inhibitions, but that they can detach themselves at all from the prevailing attitudes in their societies and that they show any desire to change them.

Again, the planning process itself will help to rationalize the valuations in the direction of greater conformity with the ideals, the first of which is rationality itself. The attention drawn to development as the desired objective will tend to influence people to attach a positive, independent value not only to a rise in levels of living—itself a novel valuation to many people in a backward, stagnating country—but to a change upwards in all other conditions in the social system, including attitudes and institutions. In the course of planning, upward changes in conditions acquire instrumental value because people realize that such changes will push up other conditions too. From one point of view, development from a traditional to a modern economy is largely the creation and expansion of a sphere of instrumental valuations where previously only independent valuations reigned. Development thus leads to a widening of choice. This is not directly the result of greater opportunities but of changing valuations, although the opportunities may induce a change in the valuation. It stems, rather, from an increasing understanding of circular causation and greater readiness to regard change as a means to further ends. This would occur, for example, if certain trades or economic activities were detached from caste and evaluated according to their financial rewards—if, for instance, the taboos on work by upper-strata Moslem and Hindu women were replaced by an evaluation of the advantages of leisure compared with work, or if sacred cows, literal and figurative, were made into veal and beef.

Indeed, unless an area of independent and instrumental valuations can be mapped out, the whole discussion of the optimal plan is pointless. Considered, calculated, rational choice assumes either that some events have no value in themselves or that whatever independent value they have is not absolute but can be compensated for by the achievement of rival objectives. In a world where nothing has a price, there can be no optimal plan and, indeed, no planning whatever. Planning must assume that the people in power—the government—have already gone some way toward overcoming inhibitions and freeing choices and that the people will be induced to follow them. It also assumes that planning and development, once started, will by themselves tend to change valuations by further breaking down both inhibitions and obstacles created by traditional attitudes and institutions.

The optimal plan, then, should rather be regarded as a steadily forward-moving pattern of policies that has to be modified continually in the light of newly emerging events, changing causal connections, and changing valuations among the rulers as well as the ruled. But planning, in the final instance, can never be a substitute for policy-making. On the contrary, its value premises must come from and by the political process. These value premises cannot be simple and general; they must be as specific and complex as the valuations that determine, and become determined by, the political process. It would be impossible, for example, to work out a plan for animal husbandry in India that did not take into account the common aversion to slaughtering cows. An agricultural policy dealing with land ownership and tenancy must be framed so that the government will find them both feasible and desirable in view of the actual power situation in a country.

All planning thus implies political choices. These choices do not concern only broad and abstract goals. They relate to all stages in the process of planning and to each specific step implied in planning. Means have to be evaluated as well as the goals they may achieve. A plan for development is thus essentially a political program, and plan-making is, in itself, a part of the political process. It follows that the planning organs, if they are to cope successfully with their task, must become largely negotiating and almost diplomatic agencies of the government. Only a relatively small part of their activity is devoted to scientific study.

In those countries of South Asia where planning has

become only loosely connected with the government, it has not gone far or deep, even as a technical exercise. When there is no government willing or able to integrate planning in its functions, the temptation is strong to over-stress the technical, or "objective," character of planning itself. Many plans broadly state objectives or main goals that are in line with the post-war ideals. But little effort is made to clarify their relationship to the actual policy prescriptions in the plan. They appear as conventional rationalizations that have no relation to the valuations on which the government is prepared to act. Often they serve only as tranquillizers offered to the intellectuals and radicals. They belong to the dream world of ideals that have little relation to the immediate and practical work of constructing the plan.

At an early stage in any plan a choice has to be made of certain main features. This choice must be guided by a broad conception of the current attributes of the country, its natural resources and its people, its trading position in the world, and so on. It must conform to the major ambitions and valuations of the government, including the inhibitions of the governors. Further, it must permit a working compromise between the various social and political forces—pressures, vested interests, ideals, and the heavy obstacles presented by prevailing attitudes and institutions. The procedure in planning has perhaps its closest analogy in an architect's preparation of a sketch of a public building for the city council. The architect takes into account the purpose of the building, the money available, the ground at his disposal, and the inclinations of the people he serves, which, like this own, are influenced by the fashions of the day. In some instances he knows his ideas are ahead of theirs, and therefore he must sell his to them. He will present both his sketch and his later drafts as rational responses to the given requirements. Similarly, once the crucial choice of the main features in a plan is made and this choice presented to the government, the planners can go on to elaborate it in greater detail. This elaboration will always be in the direction indicated by the main features. As it takes shape, the plan will differ from the original sketch, but the main features will have conditioned and given direction to the later work. In a plan, as in the architect's work, there must be scope and ideals, desires and imaginative thinking. At the same time, the actual material conditions in a country must be faced and the plan must seek political moorings.

Once a plan is established, it is vital that it be given a big push; and unless that push is hard enough, no development will occur. This concept of a "critical minimum effort," as Harvey Leibenstein calls it in his *Economic Backwardness and Economic Growth,* is now widely embraced by economists. But too often the discussions of the "big push" are confined to economic factors. Instead, this idea must be extended to all parts of the social system. The big push must jerk the whole system out of the grip of the forces of stagnation. Unless conditions are changed by specific, powerful, and coordinated efforts, they will not change at all or perhaps change in the wrong direction. This would halt development or even reverse it. The effort must be great enough to produce a positive feedback of effects, even from those conditions that were not initially lifted by these efforts to those that were. As the upward movement gains momentum, the continuing changes can be greater with less effort. But the mass must be started moving first. It is for this reason that underdeveloped countries cannot rely on a gradualist approach. Backwardness and poverty naturally make it difficult for a country to mobilize enough resources for a big plan, but they are precisely the reasons why the plan has to be big in order to be effective.

The principle of the big push is accepted by many planners. However, they insist that the effort should be concentrated, either in a limited number of areas or on a limited number of conditions. They hold that the results of this concentration will be passed through the whole system by spread effects. But spread effects themselves are a function of the development plan, and in South Asia these are generally weak. Actually, there is economy in a big, widespread push. Smaller efforts only mean waste. Not only do these efforts have to be larger than a critical minimum level, but from our general knowledge of South Asia we know that they must be directed simultaneously at a great number of conditions and that this direction must be concentrated within a short period of time and applied in a rationally coordinated way. The need for a set of policies on a broad front, in which all state intervention is coordinated, is very much greater in underdeveloped than in developed countries.

In writings on development problems of underdeveloped countries, it is commonplace to acknowledge that a close relationship exists between the effectiveness of development policies in the economic field and the prevailing attitudes and institutions. But it is fair to say that almost all economic studies of these problems, whether by South Asian or foreign economists, neglect almost completely this relationship and its consequences. Even when plans do express a wider conception of the problems of planning and devote much of their space to changing non-economic factors, they still have at their core an investment program in which output is treated as a function of capital input, usually in terms of physical investment. They have clung to the belief that development efforts aimed at increasing output through investment will induce favorable changes in all other conditions. They have also assumed that efforts to change non-economic conditions by direct action are difficult or impossible. As we have pointed out in preceding sections of this book, "economic" policies are undoubtedly easier to carry out than are social policies that challenge vested interests, violate deep-seated inhibitions, offend cherished traditions and beliefs, and work against the heavy weight of social inertia. Yet if development policies are mainly directed at economic development in the narrow sense, they will prove less than effective.

The majority of Western economists are planners, but they are influenced by Marx to a degree of which they are rarely aware. They usually assume that economic advances will have strong and rapid repercussions on attitudes and institutions. But the Communists themselves have obviously not relied on Marx's optimistic hypotheses of the rapid and effective spread of impulses from the economic sphere to the "superstructure." Instead, they have directly intervened to change social conditions, while, as always, preserving Marx's doctrine in reinterpreted form. They have used the government to reshape society, instead of letting society, changed by the modes of production, determine the government.

As we have stressed earlier, though, the South Asian countries do not want to follow the Communist line of development. They aim at "democratic planning." Unfortunately, as we have argued, the term "democratic planning" has been used to justify a very serious lack of determination to enforce existing laws and to enact and enforce new ones. The dictum of the highly respected American jurist Learned Hand that "law is violence" would not appeal to, or be understood by, the greater part of the South Asian intellectual elite. Their governments have been much more reluctant to promulgate and enforce obligations than have the rich democratic welfare states of the West, which do not regard the use of force for social ends as a retreat from democracy. This reluctance not only helps explain the relative absence of successful development in South Asia, but can itself be explained by the status of underdevelopment. In the present era the soft state does little to remove, and in fact helps to create, almost insurmountable obstacles and inhibitions to planning.

The prospects for breaking down these barriers in the

South Asian countries would be quite different if in a country like India, for example, the government were really determined to change the prevailing attitudes and institutions and had the courage to take the necessary steps and accept the consequences. We have contended that, in many respects, a large and rapid change of attitudes and institutions is not any more difficult to achieve than a series of small and gradual changes, just as a plunge into cold water is less painful than slow submersion.

As we have suggested earlier, there may have been good reasons, when planning for development in Western countries, to neglect changes in attitudes and institutions. But we have also insisted that this premise cannot be applied in South Asia. The same principle applies to changing the levels of living. For example, in the rich countries, standards of nutrition for most people are generally so high that a rise in the quantity or quality of the food eaten has no effect on labor productivity. But this is not so in most South Asian countries. In India and Pakistan, and to a lesser degree in other South Asian countries, the total calorie intake for most of the people is too low to maintain optimum levels of health, energy, and labor efficiency. Similarly, the level of elementary education in Western countries is already so high that further advances would have no immediate effect on the ability to work. In South Asia, the low levels of labor efficiency are partly the result of poor elementary education. They are also caused by the dearth of usefully educated persons. Not only is more education needed, but a different kind must be offered. Too many South Asian schools turn out graduates who are neither fit nor willing to become semi-skilled and skilled artisans or craftsmen or even bookkeepers. Instead, they have been taught to shun manual work.

These differences between conditions in the West and those in South Asia have important implications for planning. Although it makes sense in the rich countries to think of economic development in terms of savings, investment, employment, and output, and to disregard levels of living, except insofar as consumption decreases that part of income which could be saved, the situation in the underdeveloped countries is quite different. For the broad masses in South Asia, an increase in consumption raises productivity, with variations according to the direction and composition of the increase. To this must be added a further complication. Whereas in the rich countries of the West the expansion of certain policy measures directed toward higher levels of living, such as improved health services, has become essentially a technical problem that can be treated in isolation, in the South Asian countries all policies affecting levels of living are interdependent. The reason, as we have emphasized earlier, is that these levels are so low. Thus Western thinking applied to South Asian problems is bound to yield false conclusions. In South Asia it is not possible to deal with specific components of the level of living as technical problems, isolated from other components. They are all closely inter-related. The health problem is, for instance, to a large extent an educational problem. Neither can measures that increase production and productivity be separated from measures that raise certain kinds of consumption. It follows that development policies, if they are to be effective, must be coordinated over a much wider range of activities, including some that are components of the level of living insofar as they raise production. We must also emphasize that saving in the sense of non-consumed income (which *ex post* is identical with investment) has a fairly clear meaning in the rich countries, and aggregate output can be viewed as a function of the increase in the stock of accumulated capital.

But in the underdeveloped countries, where "underconsumption" on a vast scale is normal, the basic distinction between investment and consumption does not hold, and reasoning based on it is irrelevant and invalid. Higher consumption forms "investment"—that is, raises production—and at the same time remains consumption.

It is interesting to note that the Soviet Union's planners have never restricted themselves to Marx's definition of investment merely in terms of industrial plant and the accumulation of capital as the only source of higher productivity. Their plans always contained sections devoted to huge expenditures on the creation of non-physical productive assets. It is now evident that the Soviet Union's high growth rates were largely due to this "investment in man."

It is true that the Soviets had a better food supply than most South Asian countries. It has been possible for them to maintain fairly adequate levels of nutrition. So their planners saved resources by squeezing consumption of housing and clothing while increasing efforts in education and health. The government was able to free resources for investment by this consumption squeeze, while at the same time twisting and redirecting consumption in such a way as to combine suppression in some directions with rapid and substantial increases in others, as dictated by the requirements of growth. Recognizing the differing effects on productivity of the various components of consumption, Soviet planners did not apply a simple formula of enforcing a savings ratio to secure expansion of planned physical investment. The savings *squeeze* was supported by a consumption *twist*.

The underdeveloped countries of South Asia should accord consumption policies an integral and important role in their economic planning. Their task should not be merely to compress consumption in order to achieve a certain savings ratio, as domestic and foreign experts usually assume. Since their levels of living are so low that reduced consumption in almost all directions lowers productivity and even prevention of an increase in consumption is detrimental, they must weigh carefully the effects on productivty of changing the components of consumption, and must then attempt to steer consumption in the most productive directions.

They must, in other words, break with the Western policy of allowing the free choice of consumers to be decisive. Otherwise they will not be able to provide the necessary conditions for raising production, including the provision of enough savings for desirable investment— and they will inflict undue suffering on their people. Those countries that, unlike the Communist countries, do not tightly control all production, prices, and consumption are obviously at a disadvantage not only in squeezing consumption in general but also, and more important, in steering it into productive channels. They must nevertheless face the problem. Their taxation policy, for example, can be conceived in broader terms that would help in accomplishing this. They have to accomplish what the Soviet Union has done, though their methods may be different. Failure to do so will frustrate their hopes of development.

A basic weakness of all South Asian development plans has been their concentration on the financial or, even more narrowly, on only the fiscal aspects of planning. Though a fiscal plan is necessary to insure administrative efficiency and a wider financial plan may also have limited usefulness, neither of them can be *the* plan. A plan that conveys what it purports to convey must be based on some kind of physical planning in terms of input requirements and output expectations of physical factors, goods, and services in the various sectors of the economy. It has been argued that the setting of targets for specific categories of final output from specific investments and their coordination in order to minimize the risk of bottlenecks and excess capacity, although desirable in principle, is often not feasible because adequate statistical information is lacking. If this is so, it is pertinent to ask how it is then possible to draw up a workable financial investment plan. One difference between financial and physical planning is simply that the latter cannot help revealing the weak factual information on which a plan is based, while the former often serves the function of concealing it. This is not to deny that every government must plan investments and their coordination as best it can, even though it cannot draw on adequate information and must rely largely on guesses. The point is that these guesses and estimates must, in the final analysis, relate to concrete physical items and their changes. The fiscal-financial plan can be at best only a superstructure, built on the basis of a physical plan. All effective planning must be physical planning. This is exceedingly difficult, and rough estimates and guesses are often necessary, particularly in countries with an extreme scarcity of relevant facts. If there is only fiscal-financial planning, there is the tacit assumption that finance is the only bottleneck and that physical resources flow smoothly, at constant unit costs, in the direction indicated by money expenditures. Further, even if the financial or fiscal plan is given the more modest role of merely reflecting an underlying plan that coordinates physical magnitudes, it is impossible to avoid the implicit assumption that all of the obstacles to development can be overcome by a sufficient expenditure of physical resources and that, even where non-physical obstacles exist, the effectiveness of policies to remove them is related to resources used up in the process. Neither assumption is justified in the countries of South Asia.

Another great difficulty in approaching the problems of South Asia through classical Western economic concepts is in the consideration of inflation and deflation in Western terms. The typical situation in the underdeveloped countries of South Asia is substantial underutilization of both capital and labor while, at the same time, there are shortages and bottlenecks. It is questionable whether the terms "inflation" and "deflation" can be applied to such a situation. If we mean by inflation a tendency for prices to rise and shortages and rationing to appear, then clearly there is inflation in South Asia. But if we mean by deflation that capacity and manpower are not fully used, then equally clearly there is deflation. The tendencies toward inflation in the underdeveloped countries are related to bottlenecks, both in the market and in the sector of utilities, transportation, distribution, and credit. The response to this cannot be a reduction in demand across the board. There must be, instead, an attempt to raise the supply of the bottleneck items. This could sometimes be done by permitting their price to rise and bigger profits to be made in their production. More likely, other measures will be needed in South Asia, because too often a price rise may reduce the supply, and it certainly may reduce the demand. A rise in the price of food will not necessarily spur a South Asian farmer who does not own his own land to produce more. But it might well cause a South Asian worker to buy less. Planners must strive to divert bottleneck demands to substitutes that are in surplus. They certainly must try to confine price rises to those sectors that actually promote growth, and they must attempt to anticipate future bottlenecks in their planning.

Finally, in planning for development in South Asian countries, the plans themselves can be set for a fixed period when they are started—three, four, five, or more years. This provides simplicity and encourages the government and the people to move along a chosen track. But once started, they should be highly flexible, particularly in providing opportunities to adapt to changes and responses. The purpose of planning is to facilitate rational adjustment of means to ends in the light of changing circumstances. These changes should include reaction to new experiences and new ideas from the planning process itself.

To gain the greatest advantages from this principle, South Asian countries would be well advised to adopt "rolling" plans. In these, three new plans should actually be made each year and acted upon. The first should be the plan for the current year, and should include an annual budget and a foreign exchange budget. The second should cover a number of years—three, four, or five—and it should be altered each year as changes occur. Finally, every year a perspective plan for ten, fifteen, or twenty years should be presented in which the broader outlines of future development are forecast. The annual one-year plan should be a part of the annually revised three-, four-, or five-year plan, and so on. To some extent, any plan, fixed or flexible, involves rolling planning, because changes in all of them must be made. But if a rolling plan is formally adopted, its rationality and effectiveness would be increased. Conversely, this would decrease the disappointment and public cynicism that arise when a fixed plan fails to meet its goals.

Index

adult education, 378, 389–98, 425

agriculture, 70–83; animals in, 260–1; commercialization, 77–8, 81–2, 239–40; controls, 188–90; cooperatives, 170–3, 270–3, 277; dry land farming, 72–3; fertilizers, 262–3; industrialization, 91–2; institutional reforms, 256–8; irrigation and, 261–3; labor in, 228, 235–7, 244–56, 264, 276, 334; labor in food production, 71–2, 75–7, 88–9; land redistribution, 275–8; land reform, 265–70; land resources, 61, 74; land tenure: *see* land tenure; land utilization, 258–60; man/land ratio, 70–2, 74–5; manufacturing and, 81; occupations in, 88–9; output per acre, 70–1, 74–5; output per person, 89; plantations, 72–3, 78–82, 91–2, 163, 164; policy, 254–84;

policy proposals, 279–84; population density and, 72–4; population growth and, 75–7, 254–5; production, increasing, 255–6; products exported, 91–2, 112; rice, wet paddy cultivation, 72–3, 81; seeds, improved, 263–4; sharecropping: *see* sharecropping; shifting cultivation, 72–3; in socialist economy, 163; technology in, 66–7, 256–8, 261, 264–5; traditional patterns, 235–6

animals, farm, 260–1

Asian Highway, 123

Australia, 22

authoritarian government, 153, 154

Ayub Khan, Mohammed, 156, 344

Bali, 344

banking, 163–4

Bendix, Richard, 178

451